Hakuin's Song of Zazen

Yamada Mumon Rōshi (1900–1988)

Hakuin's Song of Zazen

YAMADA MUMON RŌSHI
ON ZEN PRACTICE

Translated by

Norman Waddell

FOREWORD BY D. T. SUZUKI

SHAMBHALA

Shambhala Publications, Inc.
2129 13th Street
Boulder, Colorado 80302
www.shambhala.com

Cover art: *Shichiri beach in Sagami province*, c.1830 (woodblock print) by
Katsushika Hokusai / Bridgeman
Cover design: Jenny Carrow
Interior design: Daniel Urban-Brown

9 8 7 6 5 4 3 2 1
First Edition
Printed in the United States of America

Shambhala Publications makes every effort to print on acid-free, recycled paper.
Shambhala Publications is distributed worldwide by Penguin Random House, Inc.,
and its subsidiaries.

Library of Congress Cataloging-in-Publication Data
Names: Yamada, Mumon, 1900–1988, author. | Waddell, Norman, translator.
Title: Hakuin's song of Zazen : a classic of modern Zen / by Yamada Mumon Roshi;
translated by Norman Waddell.
Other titles: 880–01 Zazen wasan kōwa. English
Description: Boulder : Shambhala, 2024. | Translation of: Zazen wasan kōwa.
Identifiers: LCCN 2023005444 | ISBN 9781645471813 (trade paperback)
Subjects: LCSH: Hakuin, 1686–1769. Zazen wasan. | Meditation—Buddhism.
Classification: LCC BQ9399.E597 Y3513 2024
| DDC 294.3/443—dc23/eng/20230210
LC record available at https://lccn.loc.gov/2023005444

CONTENTS

CONTENTS

CONTENTS

CONTENTS

FOREWORD

FIFTEEN CENTURIES have passed since Zen first began to take root in China. Its fortunes waxed and waned over that time, reaching their height in the eighth century, the T'ang dynasty, and continuing to flourish until the eleventh or twelfth century. By the end of the Sung dynasty, signs of decline had become increasingly evident.

It was among the Chinese people that Zen developed and attained a kind of perfection. It became inseparably bound to Chinese ways of feeling and thinking and, as a consequence, to Chinese literature and ideographs as well. However, cultural developments have, for various reasons, led modern China to distance itself from its traditional writing and ideographs—a trend that by now would be exceedingly difficult to reverse.

But Zen has its own intrinsic characteristics. Even if traditional forms of Chinese literature continue their decline, that does not mean Zen itself will die out. It is, on the contrary, incumbent on Zen to take careful stock of those of its traits that are suited to the modern world. It must study and develop them and, what is more, be prepared to do what it can to rescue a world culture that is continuing down a path that, before long, will lead to a dead end where further progress becomes impossible.

There is little likelihood that Zen can be revived in the land where it originally appeared. I firmly believe the task of revitalizing Zen, turning it around, and giving it a new start so that it plays a significant role in the coming world culture is one that the Japanese must take upon themselves.

In undertaking this revival, those in the Japanese Zen school must first of all ascertain the place Zen occupies in modern world thought. They must also discern and clearly be aware that this impasse is coming—indeed, that is already taking place. They must extract what is vitally alive from within the Zen tradition, grasp it experientially and digest it, and then transmit it to men and women who for the most part have never seen or heard of Zen.

When Zen people in Japan realize this, I am sure it will also become clear to them how future Zen teachers will have to prepare to carry out such a transmission. Does not such a program represent the very foundation of the Buddhist ideal—the salvation of sentient beings?

I have not the slightest doubt that great Zen masters such as Mazu in the T'ang dynasty, Yuan-wu and Da-hui in the Sung, and Dōgen and Hakuin in Japan would all have agreed unconditionally with what I have just written.

Yamada Mumon Rōshi wrote this book for his fellow Japanese; he was not addressing readers in other lands, so these comments I have made may not apply directly to them. What becomes clear on reading it, however, is that Mumon views Zen with a different eye than teachers of the previous generation—priests whose books were written largely in the form of traditional Zen-style lectures.

When a writer's audience is young people who have received a modern postwar education, the various examples he uses to illustrate his ideas should have a close relation to their manner of thinking and way of life. Perhaps this is another example of the Confucian ideal of learning from the past in order to discover the new. In any case, I believe this is how such a book should be written.

There is a strong tendency in East Asian countries to value tradition, however, this has a shortcoming—the absence of initiative and creativity. These values are linked to a certain extent, perhaps tediously so, to an inherent lack of development. It should not be forgotten, of course, that it is because of their undeveloped nature that these countries have retained their meritorious Asian qualities. Nonetheless, for them to persist unduly in a state of stagnation will be a hindrance to human progress as a whole. What is important is to maintain a good balance.

Zen, at any rate, will under no circumstances tolerate stagnation. Confucians say, "All things are like a river in constant flux, never ceasing day or night." Zen, while letting time and life flow on like this, must not forget to welcome all those who come seeking help. For them, self-reflection and self-admonishment will be essential. One more step beyond that is also needed. There is no sense trying to know where you are going; and whatever happens, you must not just move idly round and round in one place like a wheel. Bankei has a verse:

> The old bucket's bottom has broken
> Through and through.
> The triple world has no ends,
> It is a perfect circle
> With no circumference anywhere.

A circle with no circumference, a rimless circle, is the "eternal present." It is what Master Lin-chi said is "being manifested vividly before your eyes." Not proceeding beyond this, not falling back from it, yet continuing to move ahead unceasingly—such is the stuff of human life.

Reading through Master Mumon's essays inadvertently and unknowingly brought forth facets of my own everyday thoughts on the subject. Stringing some of them together, I wrote this preface.

I would be obliged to Mumon Rōshi for his criticism of what I have written here. For myself, I believe that young people will find in this book something of genuine value to them.

SUZUKI DAISETZ
MARCH 1962

TRANSLATOR'S PREFACE

This translation was originally published in 2021, in a small edition by the Myōshin-ji headquarters temple of the Rinzai sect of Kyoto. It was commissioned by the Asia South Pacific Friendship Association, founded by Yamada Mumon Rōshi, in commemoration of the thirty-third anniversary of his death. I have made a number of revisions to the text, and have eliminated or consolidated several chapters that contained material of a similar nature.

IN 1962, Yamada Mumon Rōshi (1900–1988) published a series of loosely linked essays titled *Zazen Wasan Kōwa* (literally, *Talks on Hakuin's Song of Zazen*), which had appeared serially during the 1950s in the periodical *Hanazono*, issued by Myōshin-ji of Kyoto. *Zazen Wasan Kōwa* was the first of many writings on Zen Mumon Rōshi published during the final twenty-eight years of his life. It turned out to be one of his most popular works, issued many times and almost continually in print since its first appearance. *Zazen Wasan* (*Song of Zazen*), the subject of the essays, is a recitation text composed in forty-four lines of verse by the eighteenth-century Zen master Hakuin. It began being used around 1900 at religious services in Rinzai temples and has for over one hundred years now been one of the staples of the Rinzai liturgy, recited at daily temple ceremonies, zazen meetings, and other religious gatherings.

One of the most respected teachers of modern Rinzai Zen, Mumon Rōshi was also one of its most prolific authors, apparently regarding the printed word—which his Myōshin-ji predecessor Hakuin spoke of as "verbal prajna"—an essential weapon in his teaching arsenal. When Mumon Rōshi's complete works were published in 2004, they filled sixteen hefty volumes, embracing a wide variety of writings: religious discourses; homilies; essays for the general reader; and, aimed at a more advanced audience, a large body of learned commentaries on such classic texts as the *Blue Cliff Record*, the *Record of Lin-chi*, and *Hakuin's Poison Words for the Heart Sutra*.

This first book seems to have had special meaning for Mumon Rōshi. He is said to have singled out *Zazen Wasan Kōwa* unhesitatingly when he was asked in his later years which of his works he would most like to see translated into English. It was altogether fitting, then, that Kōno Taitsu Rōshi, a leading student of Mumon's, decided to commission a translation of the book as part of the celebratory events scheduled for 2020 by

Myōshin-ji to commemorate the thirty-third anniversary of Mumon's death.

One of Mumon's primary aims in the essays was to impart the true meaning and utility of the Zen teaching to contemporary readers, many of whom, including the first postwar generation to receive a modern Western-style education, had turned away from Japan's traditional culture and religion in the wake of its crushing wartime defeat. But as Daisetz Suzuki remarked in his preface to the original edition of *Zazen Wasan Kōwa* in 1962, what gave Mumon's book its unique flavor, making it different from previous works by Zen teachers, were the forays he made into matters of everyday life, his comments encompassing interests that would be closely associated with his lay audience. He responded to a news article that caught his eye in the morning paper; delivered appraisals of contemporary political and social trends; explored matters as diversified as the uses of atomic energy, the court culture of seventeenth-century France, a trip to Hokkaidō with a group of young mendicants, a leper hospital on an island in the Inland Sea, Albert Schweitzer and other noted Western figures—and more. In doing this, Mumon gave readers a map of his planet—open access to the opinions, judgments, and practical thinking of a leading Zen master. And this, as Daisetz Sensei points out, was also a feature that had been rarely seen before in writings by modern Zen teachers.

All footnotes and parenthetical information inserted into the text in brackets are mine. Japanese names are given in the Japanese style, family name first.

TRANSLATOR'S PREFACE

I must, first of all, thank Taitsu Rōshi, the former chief abbot of Myōshin-ji, for allowing me to undertake this work. I am also indebted to Nelson Foster, Tada Minoru, and Higuchi Shōshin for reading and offering suggestions on portions of the text; to Tom Kirchner, for general counsel and suggestions; to Bruce Bailey, for his continued generosity in helping make Hakuin better known in the West. A special debt is owed to Ian Hamilton, whose ungrudging efforts in editing the manuscript have helped smooth out many of the kinks and crumples in its borrowed plumage.

NORMAN WADDELL

SONG OF ZAZEN

For a little over a hundred years now, since the late Meiji period, Hakuin's *Zazen Wasan* (*Song of Zazen*) has been chanted at ceremonies in Rinzai temples and at other religious gatherings.

————

All beings are from the first buddhas,
Their kinship is like water and ice:
Apart from water there is no ice,
Apart from beings, no buddhas.
Unaware Buddha is right at hand,
Beings pursue him in far-off places.
Like someone surrounded by water
Continually complaining of thirst,
Like a person born to great wealth

xvii

Wandering out into a beggar's life.
The causes of rebirth in the six ways
Arise in the dark paths of ignorance:
Leaving one darkness, you enter the next,
Never breaking free of birth-and-death.
How great the *dhyana* of the Mahayana,*
No praise could ever exhaust its merits!
Charity, precepts, the other paramitas,
Nembutsu, repentance, ascetic practice,
And other good acts in countless number
Are all deep rooted in Zen meditation.
The merit you gain from just one sitting
Cancels vast stores of obstructive karma,
Keeps you from entering wrongful paths,
Keeps the Pure Land always close at hand.
If you can hear this Dharma even once
And hold it in mind in deep reverence,
Acclaiming it and embracing it with joy,
The blessings you receive will never end.
And how much more so if you turn within,
See beyond doubt your own self-nature,
Your own self-nature being no-nature,

*The unfamiliar term *zenjō* in the original text is translated using the Sanskrit word *dhyana* (which means "meditation" or "concentration"), although it is not an altogether satisfactory rendering. In Mumon Rōshi's comments on this line later in the book, I use the original word *zenjō*.

SONG OF ZAZEN

Has nothing to do with empty words!
The gates of nondual cause and effect open,
One way, not two or three, runs straight ahead;
Your form is now the form of no-form,
Coming or going, you never leave home;
Your every thought is a thought of no-thought,
Your singing and dancing the Dharma's voice.
How boundless the cloudless sky of samadhi!
How radiant and full the four wisdoms' moon!
Now that you have nothing further to seek
The peace of nirvana reigns far and wide,
Where you are is the Land of Lotus Flowers,
Your body is the same as Buddha himself.

Hakuin's Song of Zazen

1

FEAR OF HELL

I WILL BEGIN these essays by briefly introducing Zen Master Hakuin, the author of *Song of Zazen*. In Hakuin's native Suruga Province, people have been repeating a simple verse for more than a century now:

> There are two things
> > greater than Suruga—
> Venerable Mount Fuji
> > and Hakuin of Hara.

Hakuin truly does deserve comparison with this celebrated Japanese mountain. In fact, just as Mount Fuji is now known by people throughout the world, I have no doubt that in the not-too-distant future, Zen Master Hakuin will be recognized as a figure of worldwide importance as well.

While Hakuin himself would have been unconcerned with any such comparison, the peak's marvelous shape was nonetheless a presence, morning until night, from the time he was a small child. The name Hakuin (literally, "hidden white") itself seems to refer to the immaculate purity of the mountain's pristine whiteness soaring into the midwinter sky. Mount Fuji emanates an aura of stern and severe divinity, an ultimate sublimity, and into this the young Hakuin threw himself body and soul. As the Zen phrases put it, "Like a white horse entering the white rush flowers," "Like pure snow heaped in a silver bowl."

Hakuin was born at two in the morning on the twenty-fifth day of the twelfth month, the second year of the Jōkyō era (1685). The reigning emperor was Reigen; the shogun was Tokugawa Tsuneyoshi. The hour, day, month, and year of his birth are known; they all fall in the old zodiac calendar under the sign of the *ushi*, the cow or bull, one of twelve animals whose attributes are used to date the years. From the time of his birth, Hakuin thus had an unusually close association with the ushi, and this kinship continued later on in his life as well. His burly physique and his gait were both described as being bull-like, and legend has it that the first cries that issued from his mouth had a bovine resonance.

Hakuin was born in the village of Hara, a post station on the main Tōkaidō Road linking Edo and the capital of Kyoto. His father's name was Sugiyama; his mother's, Nagasawa. Hakuin's childhood name was Iwajirō, which was often shortened to Iwa.

He displayed an exceptionally good memory from the tender age of four, when he is said to have memorized a lullaby or folk song over three hundred words long about the "crying night stone" of Saya. A liking for Buddhist temples appeared at the age of seven or eight when his elders took him to sermons delivered by priests in neighboring villages. On returning home, he would repeat the sermons word for word for family members, whose eyes would glisten in thankful response.

Once, after listening to the Nichiren priest Nichigon Shōnin deliver a rousing sermon that described in vivid detail the terrors and torments awaiting sinners who fell into hell, Iwajirō was trembling with fear. The sermon made an exceptionally strong impression on his young mind and may even be said to have played a large role in deciding the future course of his life. The sermon made Iwajirō remember how he fought with neighborhood boys, told fibs, filched occasional coins from the family cupboard, and took the lives of fish and snakes and frogs, convincing him that he was a prime candidate for hell. "What would I do? How terrible it would be to fall into the hellfires!" he lamented, his young mind unable to come to grips with a matter of such gravity.

When his mother took him into the bathroom for his bath that night, the deep groans from the wood-burning stove that heated the water and the red sparks from the fire stoking the tub reminded him of the terrors of hell. Grabbing his mother tightly, he suddenly broke into wailing sobs. "What's wrong with you?" she asked. "Has something hurt you? You're a little boy, you shouldn't be crying like a little girl!" But the family's best attempts to humor Iwajirō, even intimidation and threats, were of no avail. He would not stop crying. After a while, when his bawling finally began to subside, he sobbed out, "Mother, I'm terrified of hell! I'm terrified of hell! I'm afraid even when I'm here together with you. What will it be like when I fall into hell all alone!" "If that's what's bothering you," his mother replied, "I can explain it all to you tomorrow. But tonight I want you to calm down and get some sleep."

Iwajirō trusted his mother's words and went to bed, but the next morning when he was out playing with the neighborhood children, he suddenly remembered them and immediately made a beeline for his house. His mother was busy with a guest, but he slipped into the room anyway. "Mother, Mother," he blurted out, "would you please comb out my hair?" "My goodness," she said, "you've never asked that before. Next thing we know, the sun will be rising up in the west." When she went behind him and began combing out his hair, he grabbed her arm. "You promised! You said you'd tell me how I can keep from falling into hell!" he demanded. Unsure what to tell him, she decided to answer as follows: "You, young man, were born on the day sacred to the deity of the Tenjin Shrine. You should place your trust in Tenjin. He will surely help you achieve your wishes."

Now began the young boy's first steps on his religious quest. With devotion earnest in the extreme, he made visits to worship at the local Tenjin Shrine. He faithfully engaged in recitations of the *Kannon Sutra* as well.

The next year, at the age of twelve, Iwajirō saw a puppet play entitled *Nisshin's Kettle Hat* (*Nabekaburi Nisshin*), based on the popular tale of Nisshin Shōnin. Nisshin was a Nichiren priest who was tortured for defying the government ban against spreading the teachings of the Lotus, or Nichiren, school in the capital. When asked by his tormentors, "Is it true as the sutra says that a person who practices the Lotus teachings can enter a blazing fire without being burned and plunge into the water without being drowned?" Nisshin replied, "It is true." They proceeded to clamp a red-hot iron kettle over his head, but Nisshin just sat there performing *gasshō* and quietly repeating the Daimoku, the sacred Nichiren formula: *Namu Myōhōrenge-kyō*. When the authorities, thinking he had succumbed to the ordeal, removed the kettle from Nisshin's head, they found him still calmly repeating the Daimoku, even more steadfastly than before. This deeply impressed all the officials who had come to witness the torture.

On returning home, Iwajirō thought to himself, "It must be true. A priest like Nisshin who has attained a stage of such absolute faith can undoubtedly overcome the terrible torments of hell." He increased his prayers to Tenjin and recited the *Kannon Sutra* hundreds of times daily for the next week. Singlemindedly chanting out the Tenjin formula, *Namu Tenman Daijizai Tenjin*, he awaited the moment his prayers would be answered. To test his progress, he heated an iron poker until it was red-hot and touched it against his thigh. All he got for his effort was a bad burn. "It's no good; I haven't gained enough spiritual power yet," Iwajirō said. "Unless I leave home, join the priesthood, and engage in authentic religious practice under a good teacher, I will never achieve the kind of power that Nisshin had. There is no other way. I must enter the priesthood."

2

YEN-T'OU IS SAFE AND SOUND!

WHEN IWAJIRŌ was fifteen, he received his parents' blessing and finally realized his desire to enter the Buddhist priesthood. He was accepted as an acolyte at Shōin-ji, a village temple next door to the family house. The head priest Tanrei ordained him, shaving his head and giving him the Buddhist name Ekaku, "Wise Crane." Feeling a throb of happiness and also as an encouragement to his young disciple, Tanrei tapped him on the shoulder and said, "Zen monk—give it your very best!" We can only imagine the joy the young boy, fired with passion to seek the Way, felt at this time.

At nineteen, Ekaku set out on a pilgrimage to visit Zen teachers in other parts of the country. His first stop was Zensō-ji in nearby Shimizu, where he set about studying Chinese and Buddhist texts, gaining the basic knowledge he would need in his future Zen practice. One day, he was brought up short by a story he read of a famous Chinese Zen priest named Yen-t'ou, whose head was cut off by bandits. It was said that his death cry was heard for miles around.

How could a priest of Yen-t'ou's caliber have been slain by bandits? Shouldn't he have acquired through his Buddhist practice the power to bring such evildoers to heel, and through his compassion turn them into right-minded men? To be attacked and killed by common bandits would seem to turn this noble idea on its head, making him no different from any ordinary person. The *Kannon Sutra* says, "Though you are surrounded by evil bandits with threatening blades, if you concentrate on the power of Kannon Bodhisattva, the bandits will at once give rise to compassion!" Could that just be tall talk? "No wonder that poker burned me," thought Ekaku. "Someone in later centuries must have made up that miraculous story about Nisshin Shōnin. I can only conclude that the Buddhist Dharma is not worth my time. But what can I do with the rest of my life?"

Ekaku's faith in Buddhism shattered, his pure young heart filled with disappointment that was as intense as his hopes had been large. He fell into the depths of despair, suffering miserably for months. He ceased practicing zazen and studying Buddhist texts.

The next year found him at Zuiun-ji, a Zen temple in Ōgaki in Mino Province, a nameless, callow young fellow trying to find himself through a diligent study of poetry and writing. But this sort of academic study was not something that could satisfy young Ekaku's deepest yearnings. Why had he left his home to join the Buddhist priesthood? How should he live the rest of his life? He was overcome with grief at having no answers for thoughts such as these.

On the occasion of the annual airing of the books in Zui-un-ji's library, Ekaku made the following appeal: "I pray to the buddhas of the three worlds and benevolent deities of every kind for their help and support. Which is the right path for me? Confucianism? Buddhism? Taoism? I pray that you reveal which path I should pursue." While focused silently on this prayer, he picked a volume at random from the books spread throughout the room.

It was a Chinese work titled *Spurring Students through the Zen Barriers* (*Zenkan Sakushin*). Opening it, he chanced upon a passage titled "Tz'u-ming Jabs a Gimlet into His Leg." It was the story of the eminent priest Tz'u-ming of the Sung dynasty, who, when he was traveling together with his fellow monks to pursue his Zen study, sought guidance during the winter from Master Fen-yang Shan-chao. Fen-yang's teaching style was rigorous in the extreme, and he accepted very few students. Acolytes were made to sit for days outside in the yard, and even if Fen-yang did relent and allow someone into the monk's quarters, if he detected the least sign of inappropriate behavior or caught him dozing off for even a second, he would immediately throw a bucket of freezing water over him and drive him off in the frigid cold.

Tz'u-ming alone sat steadily through the long winter nights. Whenever the sleep demon approached, he would urge himself on by taking a gimlet and sticking it into his thigh, rededicating himself to unrelenting practice in the thought, "The arduous striving of the ancient teachers endowed them with a radiance that could not help but grow and prosper. What benefit am I to the world—useless while I'm alive, completely unknown when I'm dead." Fen-yang finally accepted him as a disciple, and Tz'u-ming eventually became Fen-yang's Dharma heir. He greatly raised up the true Zen traditions, becoming known as the Lion of Hsi-ho.

"If the Buddha's Dharma is not to be trusted, if Zen practice is truly not worth one's effort, then why," Ekaku wondered, "did the worthy priests of the former times engage in such difficult practice, even at the risk of their lives?"

A second turning point in Hakuin's life arrived at the age of twenty. His pilgrimage had brought him to western Japan, where he traveled back and forth along the main Sanyō Road through the western provinces. As he passed beneath the famous White Heron Castle at Himeji, he had become so deeply immersed in his koan that he took no notice of the castle's beautiful shape soaring magnificently above him. Coming to the same spot many years later as an elderly priest, he recalled, "If I had continued on that pilgrimage like my fellow monks did, as a kind of sightseeing trip around the country, I would not be gazing up from my palanquin today at White Heron Castle." These youthful travels, leading him to well-known Zen teachers in temples throughout western and central Japan, continued for over four years.

On stopping over at one of these temples in the hills of Harima Province, he wrote a verse:

Water flows down from the mountain without ever ceasing.
When the Zen mind is like this, *kenshō* cannot be far away.

With that, he divested himself of all the writings, poems, books, and paintings that had accumulated in his travel pouch, even his writing brush and inkstone, and threw himself into his practice "as though his head was on fire."

In the spring of his twenty-fourth year, when he hung his traveling staff in the monk's hall of Eigan-ji in Takada in the northern province of Echigo, his practice was finally beginning to show signs of bearing fruit. He had entered a realm where everything, within and without, had become a concentrated lump of singlemindedness. He was like a mute trying to swallow a bitter gourd. Standing, he was unaware he was standing; moving about, he was unaware he was in motion; speaking, he was unaware he was speaking. The whole world seemed to be a single shrine of purest crystal, bright and clear, and he was sitting within it. Although rapturously absorbed in this resplendent realm, he was utterly composed, and yet amid this serenity was the deep and ponderous feeling of the quickening rebirth trying to emerge. He felt that if only someone would deal this crystalline clarity a single blow, his great self would suddenly explode and the wondrous realm of nirvana would spread out beneath his feet.

Keeping firmly in mind the words "The arduous striving of the ancient teachers endowed them with a radiance that could not help but grow and prosper," he shut himself up inside the shrine room of Eigan-ji, which was dedicated to the provincial lord, and began a weeklong practice session. Almost forgetting to sleep or eat, arousing his bodhisattva vow within the Vajra King Samadhi that cleaves through all ignorance, he pledged that if he did not achieve kenshō during this session, he would bite his tongue and bring his life to an end.

At dawn, the end of his retreat, Ekaku heard the boom of a distant temple bell rolling through the morning mist. Unaware what he was doing, he suddenly leaped up from his zazen cushion in stunned surprise: "It boomed out! *I boomed out!*" His self crumbled into pieces, the pure crystal enclosure in which he was encased shattering to the ground. Everything he saw—a tree, a blade of grass—they were all shining with a buddha's brilliant radiance. He waltzed mindlessly about in boundless joy, waving his hands wildly over his head, issuing peals of laughter, his face drowned in hot, ecstatic tears. He shouted out unthinkingly, "Yen-t'ou is safe and sound! Yen-t'ou is safe and sound!"

3

SHŌJU RŌJIN

YOUNG EKAKU, certain that no one in the past three hundred years had ever achieved such a splendid satori, was unable to stay still. Myriad thoughts rushed through his mind. He felt that no one could possibly understand the vast realm, greater than heaven and earth itself, he had experienced. He marveled at the universal blindness in others. "But isn't that all right too!" he reflected. "How could they possibly understand the unprecedented satori I have achieved?" His mind became filled with pride and arrogance. The very sight of other people grated on him. He was sure that if Shakyamuni or Bodhidharma should return to the world, his satori would surpass even their understanding. "The Buddha Dharma has fallen to earth," he cried. "Not a single person in the entire world possesses the true Dharma eye." On discovering that neither Shōtetsu, the head priest at Eigan-ji, nor the head monk, nor any of the five hundred other monks attending the meeting were able to counter his assertions, his arrogance grew apace.

Now at this very moment in the village of Iiyama deep in the mountains of Shinano Province, totally isolated from the world, near the birthplace of Kanzan Egen, the founder of Myōshin-ji, there lived a great priest named Shōju Rōjin. By great priest I do not mean that he wore the splendid robes of a high-ranking cleric or taught Zen in a magnificent monastery setting. Shōju was a maverick priest who devoted his entire life to furthering the Buddha's teaching while dwelling in a run-down grass hut so shabby that even a poor farmer or woodcutter would despise it.

We do not even know the secular name Shōju used before he entered the priesthood. He had a proper priestly name, Etan, as well as a splendid sobriquet, Dōkyō. But no one called him by these names. Nor did they refer to him by the honorific title Dōnin, "man of the Way." He was just Rōjin, "Old Man," and he was altogether unconventional. He took the name Shōju from the tiny hermitage he used for shelter. It was said he was the illegitimate son of Matsudaira Ensū, the lord of Iiyama Castle; also that he was a son of Saneda Nobuyuki, the lord of the Matsushiro clan, and that it was Nobuyuki who had placed him in Lord Matsudaira's keeping. Whichever is true, there seems little doubt that Shōju was brought up inside the walls of Iiyama Castle.

When Shōju reached thirteen, an eminent priest who was a favorite of the lord visited Iiyama Castle for a few days to give some lectures. The young boys in the castle each brought a sheet

of paper for the priest to inscribe. He wrote on them the name
of a particular Buddhist deity whom the boy was to regard as
his tutelary guardian. He wrote the inscriptions for them according to their ages, beginning with the oldest: "You are the
Bodhisattva Monju," "You are the Buddha Dainichi." "You are
the Bodhisattva Kokūzō," and so forth. Shōju's turn came, but
when he asked for a name, the priest, studying his face, declined.
"Within your own heart you have the Bodhisattva Kannon," he
said. "There is no need for me to write that down for you."

The priest's words puzzled and greatly troubled Shōju, "Why
am I the only boy who didn't get a name? How can I have a bodhisattva inside my heart?" He pondered over this in springtime as he
gazed at the cherry petals scattering in the spring breeze. He became lost in it while listening mindlessly to the patter of the autumn rain. "Had that priest lost his senses? Was his mind sound?
Was he besotted by a romantic involvement of some kind? But
even if his actions did make people feel dubious or sad about him,
or even abandon him, I don't believe he would change—I don't
think it would faze him in the least." Thoughts such as these must
have gone through young Shōju's mind.

In *A Tale of a Sexy Young Prostitute* (*Osharaku-gozen monogatari*),
a short work from his later years on the theme of love, Hakuin
wrote of someone who suffered distress in seeking the Kannon within her heart: "She was a young lass from the Nadaya
in Harima Province, aged sixteen, at the height of her seductive
beauty, as matchless in figure and looks, gentleness and refinement, as Lady Yang in T'ang China or Ono no Komachi in Japan.

15

On catching sight of her, even Shakyamuni and Bodhidharma would be caught joyfully clapping their hands. Since last spring she has been moping gloomily about. Everyone wanted to know the reason why. Was she pining away because of the work she was doing? Did she find it too much of a hardship? 'Neither hardship nor work,' was her reply. 'I have given myself to the way of satori. I will follow that path in earnest, do whatever it takes, sleeping or waking, sitting or moving about.'"

In the spring of his sixteenth year, Shōju and the maids and children of the feudal lord were bustling busily about, attending to the needs of an important guest of honor at Iiyama Castle. As Shōju was carrying a tray of food up to the guest quarters on the third floor of the castle, he slipped on the stairway and fell, upsetting the tray. At that very instant he awakened to his self-nature. Oblivious to his fall and the spilled food around him, he burst into peals of laughter. He had seen the Kannon in his own heart! How grateful he was! How happy he felt!

He ran to a nearby temple and told the priest what had happened. Unfortunately, the priest was unable to fully comprehend what Shōju was describing to him. But he did suggest a book that might help the young boy. He got out the book, *Bodhidharma's Six Gates* (*Shōshitsu Rokumon-shuū*), a collection of the teachings of Bodhidharma, the founder of the Zen school, and lent it to Shōju. On reading it, Shōju felt, "Everything I experienced and have been trying to say—they are all in these pages." His belief in the Zen path strengthened. His religious joy deepened.

At nineteen, on accompanying Lord Matsudaira on a trip to Edo, he sought out many of the leading Buddhist teachers in the city. Among those he visited was Zen Master Shidō Munan (1603–1676), who resided in Tōhoku-an, a tiny hermitage in the Azabu district. In time he became Munan's disciple and entered the Buddhist priesthood, receiving from him the religious name Etan. Acting as Munan's attendant for a number of years, he mastered the secrets of his Zen and struck to the root of the great Dharma. However, he had no ambition to remain amid the wealth and comforts of Edo or any large city, and he returned to his native Iiyama. There he spent the rest of his life, hidden in a small thatched hermitage in a state of total purity.

Shōju Rōjin was probably the only person in the entire country who could have tweaked Ekaku's proud young nose and rescued him from the dark hole of one-dimensional satori. Ekaku slipped away from the training session at Eigan-ji before it was over and, at the urging of his fellow monk Sōkaku Jōza, made his way secretly into the mountain roads of Shinano Province to seek an interview with Shōju. What every young religious seeker needs is an exemplary fellow seeker like Sōkaku Jōza. And what he must find is an authentic teacher like Shōju Rōjin. If he had not encountered Sōkaku, Ekaku would not have met Shōju Rōjin, and he might have spent the rest of his life among the ranks of the Zen demons, those pitiful beings who not only go astray but spread their poison to others as well.

4

BURSTING INTO TEARS

O N HIS FIRST MEETING with Shōju, Ekaku reverently handed him a sheet of paper on which he had written a verse setting forth his experience. "I ask that you overlook my lack of manners," he said, "but this is what I have succeeded in grasping." Shōju snatched the paper and crumpled it imperiously in his left hand, at the same time thrusting his right fist in Ekaku's face. "This is something cooked up in your head! Show me what you grasped down in your belly!" he barked with a fierce glare in his eye. But Ekaku was not about to concede so easily. "If my satori were such a mean and miserable thing," he said, "I'd puke it up like this, '*Ge . . . Ge . . . Ge . . . !*'" Without an instant's hesitation, Shōju thrust back, "How do you see Chao-chou's *Mu*?" "No way to get a grip on *Mu*," Hakuin countered with what he thought was a fine riposte. But Shōju was faster. His large hand, gnarled and knotted like a hard lump of pine resin and clay, grabbed the bridge of Ekaku's nose and wrenched it mercilessly. "I got a good grip on it, didn't I? *Hahahaha!*" And he pressed on: "How about the story of Nan-ch'uan's death?!" Shōju's two arrows, loosed in rapid succession, knocked Ekaku back, rendering him limp and drenched in nervous sweat. Shōju stood over him shouting, "Hole-dwelling bonze!" The angry abuse struck Ekaku like a hundred bolts of lightning, and Shōju threw him bodily out of the room.

It is easy to die the Great Death but difficult to regain one's life after that. It is easy to give up life but more difficult to make one's way through life. Outgoing *ekō*, transferring the merit acquired through practice to others, is not overly difficult, but returning ekō, going back into the world to work for living beings after attaining realization, is a very arduous undertaking.

Nan-ch'uan's Death is the koan that asks, "Where did Nan-ch'uan go after he died?" Although you may understand more or less the circumstances of Nan-ch'uan's death, when it comes to the question of where he went after his death, you won't get a free and totally unrestricted hold on that until you advance one step beyond the tip of a hundred-foot pole. One of the ancients said, "The deeper your satori is, the harder you must bear down!" You must not remain curled up inside a minor, self-satisfied satori, like one of those horn-turban mollusks that keeps its rock-hard lid clamped shut. The rebuke "Hole-dweller bonze!" was the iron mallet Shōju used to smash that tight lid. In truth, both Shakyamuni Buddha and Manjushri Bodhisattva, the buddha of the future, are right now still engaged in their Zen practice.

By the time he was thirteen, Hakuin knew the *Kannon Sutra* and *Diamond Sutra* by heart. Someone introduced him, at fourteen, to the *Kuzōshi*, the book of poetical phrases used in koan study; he memorized it completely. This was to be a great help to him later on. When the need arose, he said he could come up with choice poetical phrases "as easily as if I were pulling them out of my pocket."

When he was sixteen he read the *Lotus Sutra*. As his family members were devout followers of the teachings of Nichiren Shōnin, which are based on this sutra, no doubt Hakuin already had some acquaintance with it. He tells us that when he resolved to engage in Buddhist practice as a young boy, it was with the unlikely ambition of gaining the spiritual power "to enter a fire without being burned, enter the water without drowning"—words that appear in the *Lotus Sutra*. But at sixteen when he read in the *Lotus* about radiance appearing from the white hair between the Buddha's eyebrows and revealing all worlds in the universe; about the parables of the burning house, the rich man and his poor son, the jewel concealed in the robe, the five hundred phantom cities, and the medicinal herbs, he was disappointed and deeply discouraged. The sutra seemed to be made up of nothing but parables; it was like peeling an onion and never coming to anything of real substance. If this is the king of sutras, he concluded in disgust, wouldn't the Confucian classics, the writings of the Taoist sages, Noh chants, narratives for puppet shows, and kabuki chants be "the king of sutras" as well? It did not even mention authentic Buddhist practice. He cast the *Lotus* aside with disdain and did not take it up again for many years.

It was not until the autumn of his forty-second year that Hakuin brought the *Lotus Sutra* out again. He had now been the head priest at Shōin-ji for ten years and was in the prime of life, with a growing reputation as a teacher. While he was reading the "Parables" chapter of the sutra, the doleful *creek*-ing of a cricket under the veranda reached his ears. At that instant he understood the wonderful secret of the *Lotus Sutra*. Now, twenty-seven years after he had thrown it aside in disgust, he grasped for the first time the intrinsic truth of the *Lotus*. His biographies describe him as "bursting into loud sobs in spite of himself," but whatever the case, there is no question that the experience he felt at this time shook him to the core.

He, who had despised the *Lotus Sutra* as having no more religious authority than Noh chants or other forms of secular literature, now realized how fundamentally mistaken he had been, that the sutra's teaching did indeed lead people to the true Dharma. Lamenting yesterday's mistaken notions, elated at today's realization of the truth, he burst into tears. He understood for the first time Shōju's everyday behavior; and he understood that Shakyamuni Buddha, the World-Honored One, had never deceived him. He understood the true meaning of the *Lotus* teaching that there is only one Dharma vehicle, "not two or three." His heart overflowed with the Buddha's great compassion, compassion that declares "Now this threefold world is all my domain, and the living beings in it are all my children." He acquired a great, totally unfettered freedom in teaching others. Tears of profound emotion streamed endlessly down his cheeks as he grasped the truth that all living beings are originally buddhas, that the sole desire cherished by all buddhas who appear in the world is to make living beings awaken to buddha wisdom, that each of the parables in the *Lotus* stems from the same deep compassion of a mother chewing food before giving it to her child. Having joined the priesthood with the dubious aspiration of acquiring the strength that would allow him to enter fire or water without being harmed, he now found the gap between that dream and what he was now actually experiencing incomparably vast—greater than the difference between a tortoise and the moon.

It made him realize with greatest clarity that he had truly made the Buddha's great wisdom and compassion his own. How could he help feeling jubilant? How could he not burst into loud tears? Unthinkingly, he hummed a verse to himself,

A thin cotton robe, poor food,
Unable to ignore a cricket's cry,
Tears falling like rain.

The tears Hakuin shed on hearing the cricket trill beneath the veranda were in and of themselves the warm tears of the Tathagata's unconditional compassion for living beings: "I will never neglect your needs. It is you who will become buddhas." The Buddhist life should be like that of the Bodhisattva Never

Disparaging (Jōfukyō), who is described in the *Lotus Sutra* as one who prayed constantly for living beings, vowing, "I worship all, the poor and rich, the elderly and young." Isn't this lofty utterance also the basis of the democratic spirit we talk about today?

5

PLEASE TAKE A SEAT

WHEN YOU ARE invited to "take a seat," and a cup of fragrant tea and a piece of cake are placed before you, you will no doubt experience a pleasant, relaxed feeling. You settle comfortably into a soft chair, perhaps lighting a cigarette, sinking into your own thoughts. But if you are required to sit formally, with your legs folded under you, the experience will be different. You will probably feel a sense of constraint, as if sitting face-to-face for a scolding. When you are urged to take the special seat of honor before the *tokonoma*, and you sit solemnly as tea and sweets are set before you—that does not engender an altogether carefree state of mind either. Sitting can be a very serious matter.

The posture assumed when you sit in a chair is one that allows you to get up and walk around at any time. In that sense, it is a dynamic posture. In contrast, the posture you assume when

24

sitting on a Japanese-style cushion inclines you to remain as you are—to stay put. It has the disadvantage of promoting inactivity. I think this may help explain why Western civilization has a strongly materialistic, dynamic, energetic quality, while Eastern culture is to the last spiritual, impassive, solemn, and serene.

A well-known kabuki actor once said, "It is more difficult to make people who are seated in chairs cry than those seated Japanese-style. Bringing tears to someone who is standing is even more difficult than to someone seated in a chair." So perhaps even on an emotional level, sitting Japanese-style can be a matter of serious import.

This all suggests that the way in which you sit is of considerable importance. Might we not say that the people who created Western culture did their thinking seated in chairs, while those who gave rise to Eastern culture were stably seated in straight and upright posture?

Buddhism speaks of "four kinds of solemn attitude" (*shi-igi*), construed as referring to the four bearings the human body assumes: walking, standing, sitting, and lying down. Among the four, the seated posture undoubtedly offers the greatest stability and mental composure. Statues and paintings of Buddhist figures show them in different ways; there are both standing and seated buddhas and bodhisattvas, and also bodhisattvas depicted seated on elephants and lions, symbolizing their dauntless strength. As a rule, however, buddhas are shown sitting. The Buddha Dharma is a religion that began from a seated posture.

There are many ways in which to sit—folding one leg under

you and drawing up the other; cross-legged, tailor fashion; with your legs thrown out to the side; or with both legs folded under you, Japanese-style. The way buddhas sit is the posture known as zazen.

Simply stated, the way to do zazen is to seat yourself on a cushion, bend your right leg and place it over the base of your left thigh, and bend your left leg and place it over the base of your right thigh. You then place your hands, palms upward, above your left thigh with your thumb-tips touching. Hips and spine should be aligned straight and upright, with your chin and head aligned directly above them. It is essential that the body be positioned vertically in this way, like a five-story pagoda, each story placed above the one below it. The old teachers had a humorous way of explaining this: "Sit perfectly straight, like a bamboo trunk with all its joints removed, so that a copper coin on the top of your head falls with a clink into your anus." You allow your body to completely relax, letting all your energy concentrate naturally in the *tanden*, the "cinnabar field" below your navel. You leave your eyes partially open with your gaze loosely focused a few feet ahead. When your body is positioned in this way, you must then regulate your breaths. It is important that you breathe quietly and regularly. You exist and you do not exist. There should be no sounds, no gurks or wheezing in your throat; your breaths should not be hurried or disordered. Chuang Tzu said, "The true man breathes through his heels; the ordinary man through his throat."

Once you have regulated your breaths, you must next regulate your mind. This is the most difficult part. It means, briefly stated, to think of nothing at all; to sit in a state of *mushin*, "no-mind." And when you have settled your mind in this way, you must next regulate the external world. An example on a minor scale of regulating the external world is seen in aligning the geta when you leave them in the entrance hall; at a greater level, it is regulating the country and the world at large. You regulate your body, regulate your breathing, regulate your mind, regulate your geta, and regulate the world as a whole. I believe that the meaning of zazen may be summarized in the single word *regulate*. It is in this way that you become one and breathe in harmony with the great earth, and live timelessly together with it.

Buddhism is not a religion that stands unsteadily looking up at the sky, praising the earth and yearning for Heaven. It sits, deeply rooted in the great earth, gazing at it, its eyes cast downward, and proceeds to merge with it. From a Western way of thinking, the earth is a dusty place, defiled and sinful. Buddhism is a religion that plants itself solidly on the great earth, heedless of the dust, not brushing off the defilements, unconcerned with sins; it strikes deep, deep down into the self, seeking to tap the vital life welling constantly up within it.

Sitting in zazen makes the mind and phenomena one, fully integrating the self and the world, immersing the self in the harmonious life of the great all-encompassing universe. There is from the outset no inclination whatever to complicate this with logic or reasoning, using phrases such as "self and Buddha are one" or "heaven and earth are the same root as my self; all the myriad things are a single body with my self." It is a realm of absolute oneness, where "seeing, hearing, feeling, and the rest are not disparate or independent functions"; where "mountains and streams are not reflected in the mirror of mind." It is a realm of incomparable loftiness. As the *Blue Cliff Record* (Case 40) has it, "The moon, in the depths of night, sets in the frigid winter sky. Whose shadows could reflect coldly on the clear pool?"

6

THINKING QUIETLY

THE CHINESE USED the Sino-Japanese character *chan—zen* in its Japanese reading—as a phonetic equivalent of the Sanskrit word *dhyana*; it had no specific meaning in Chinese. It was interpreted to mean "quiet contemplation." Adding the word *za*, "sitting," to *zen* gives us *zazen*, "to sit and quietly contemplate." To contemplate what? Human life: What is human life for? Do we have human life in order to be happy? In order to suffer? What is happiness for? Am I being or nonbeing? What happens when I die? What is my relation to the world? How should I live my life? These are some of the matters for us to contemplate.

You often hear people saying that their everyday life is so busy they have no time to think about such matters, yet I believe there are times when it is necessary for us to quietly contemplate human life. I don't mean musing in bed, or strolling along, or smoking a cigarette. I mean lighting a stick of incense, if that is possible, and, seated in an upright posture, contemplating solemnly and serenely, setting your thoughts in order, engaging in deep and serious contemplation of human life. If your notions of human life are mistaken, then the precious human life you have received, which will not come again, will be spent in vain.

Cudapanthaka was a disciple of the Buddha who was dull-witted and had a terrible memory. He was not even able to remember his own name, so he had someone write it on a wooden tablet, which he carried around on his neck. Shakyamuni attempted to help the young man. Since Cudapanthaka could not remember teachings of any length, Shakyamuni gave him a brief set of instructions: "Do not create evil in any of the three karmas (words, thought, action). Do not cause injury to living beings. If you contemplate emptiness with right thought, you will avoid unnecessary suffering." Shakyamuni taught him these same words day after day. The children of a goatherd playing nearby soon memorized them by heart, but Cudapanthaka was unable to remember them. Finally at a loss, the Buddha told him to remember only the words "Brush away dusts, remove impurities." Even this Cudapanthaka found difficult. He would remember the first part, "Brush away dusts," but forget the following "Remove impurities"; or he would remember "Remove impurities" but forget "Brush away dusts."

For the next six years, whether he was sitting or standing, sleeping or awake, Cudapanthaka focused singlemindedly on remembering these words. As he did, the dust gradually cleared from his mind, defilements fell away, and then, suddenly, he realized a world in which there was no dust or defilement, neither afflicting passions nor enlightenment. He had attained the self-awakening of the Buddha himself, the realization achieved by the arhats. At that moment he experienced an incomparable joy, the light of wisdom shining radiantly from his eyes. It is a strange and remarkable thing. Even without learning, even if your memory is poor, if you sit quietly, singlemindedly contemplating the teaching you are given, satori will open within you of itself.

Many of Shakyamuni's shorter teachings were collected in the Agama group of sutras, the *Dhammapada Sutra*, and other early Buddhist scriptures. People achieved religious awakening by meditating on these utterances and making each of them their own. Later on, Buddhists in China also meditated on the sayings and doings of former teachers, finding they were more direct and struck closer to home than the old scriptural texts. In whatever age, Zen must be something that moves and functions in tune with the temper and spirit of the times. Why did Master Chao-chou say, "The cypress tree in the garden"? What was Yun-men's aim in uttering "Every day is a good day"? As you continue sitting quietly and meditating on these questions, you become able, without even knowing it, to enter Chao-chou's world and to attain the ground that Yun-men attained.

This being so, these teachers' words came to assume the role of a passport to pilot a student through the barrier into satori, so they came to be known as *koan*, the Chinese word for "a public record" or official document issued by the law court. A true grasp of these teachers' words ushers you into a true, impartial, universal view of human life.

What is of the greatest interest is that as you continue to sit quietly focusing on the same thought, you enter a psychological state in which you are thinking of nothing at all. You grasp the unique wisdom that you possessed at birth, wisdom shining serenely as though silently illuminating itself alone. To correctly contemplate human life is, after all, to open the eye of wisdom and grasp that you are thinking of nothing at all. All human beings, whoever they are, must enter the Buddha's own self-awakening, grasp the same realm the ancient Zen teachers grasped, and become open to a truly universal view of human life.

7

THE FUNDAMENTAL SOURCE OF THE TRADITIONAL JAPANESE ARTS OR WAYS

I N JAPAN, people speak of the oneness of swordsmanship and Zen, poetry and Zen, tea and Zen, haiku and Zen, the game of Go and Zen, baseball and Zen, farming and Zen, medicine and Zen. Zen may indeed be the source of these various traditional ways.

When Eugen Herrigel, a German professor of philosophy, was invited to teach at Tōhoku University in Sendai in the nineteen-thirties, he was already keenly interested in Japanese Buddhism, and especially Zen, so he decided to avail himself of the opportunity to engage in Zen practice. On consulting a Japanese colleague at Tōhoku University, he was apprised of the difficulties he would face. "Zen terminology and sayings are hard even for a Japanese to understand. For a foreigner, it would be well-nigh impossible. To begin with, you don't know Japanese, and I don't think there are any Zen teachers who can speak German or any other foreign language. It would be difficult to find someone who could interpret for you, but even if you found someone, how is he going to translate those mystifying Zen terms for you? You would be better off studying one of the traditional Japanese arts or ways. If you can master one of them, I am sure it would help you understand Buddhism, and Zen as well. The traditional arts embody the Buddhist teachings, so you should find studying them a shortcut to understanding Buddhism and Zen."

Dr. Herrigel followed this advice, looking into the traditional arts or "ways," finding that tea adepts spoke of the onenss of tea and Zen. It was the same with masters of haiku, Noh, calligraphy, and painting. The ultimate secret of the way of *kendō*, Japanese swordsmanship, is said to be *kenzen ichimi*, the oneness of sword and Zen. In a teaching Zen Master Takuan (1573–1646) gave the swordsman Yagyū Munenori, he wrote, "In speaking of the immovable wisdom of the buddhas, the word *immovable* does not mean remaining inert and insensate like a stone or tree. It means the mind moving at will in any direction whatever, forward, backward, left, or right. 'Immovable wisdom' is the mind functioning without the least constraint or hesitation." This represents the furthest reaches of Zen as well as the ultimate secret of the art of swordsmanship.

As Sen Rikyū, one of the originators of chanoyu, wrote, "To perform the tea ceremony in a small room is to practice and attain the Way by virtue of the Buddha Dharma." The realm of *wabi*, the very soul of the way of tea, emphasizes a life of simplicity and poverty, enabling you to encounter things in their true "suchness," is in itself the tranquil realm of Buddhist nirvana.

In the art of flower arrangement (*kadō*), Zen is to be found in the flowers. The Mishō school of flower arrangement enunciates its position in this way: "This room, the board on which the flowers stand, the vase, the branch holder, the water, the shears, the arrangement of stems and grasses—they are all flowers, with the aspiration being that the mind will become a flower as well." This describes a state of samadhi in which there is nothing in heaven or earth that is not a flower. Someone who has passed the koan of Chao-chou's *Mu* will unconsciously break into a smile on reading such words.

When we consider that celebrated Japanese painters such as Kanō Motonobu, Kanō Tan'yu, and Ike Taiga opened up unique dimensions in the art of painting through their practice of Zen; and that outstanding Zen painters, such as Mu-chi of China and Kei Shoki and Hakuin of Japan, were men who had attained a profound realm of totally unhindered freedom; I think we can presume the existence of "the oneness of painting and Zen" and also, by extension, the existence of "the oneness of poetry and Zen."

Zen is present in the Noh plays. Scholars stress the importance of the words *kore wa* (literally, "this is"), a standard phrase chanted by a Noh actor in announcing himself on the

35

stage. Often the actor at the opening of a *kyōgen* play chants, "*Kore wa kono atari ni sumu* (I am someone who dwells around here)." In uttering these initial words, the actor must present himself egolessly as the character he portrays. Any form or shadow, even the slightest hint, of the person who chants them must disappear and the performer—the *shite*, or chief actor; or the *waki*, or supporting actor—must emerge, chanting clearly and brightly. Thus each phrase uttered in singing the Noh chants is itself the singleminded practice of the Zen Way and communicates directly the degree to which the reciter has overcome his ego-self. The Noh teacher Takabayashi Sensei of the Kita school, who spent many years studying Zen in the training hall of Kyoto's Myōshin-ji, has said that he regards Hakuin's *Song of Zazen* as a kind of Noh chant. All of this suggests, I think, that each of the so-called Japanese traditional arts or ways is deeply rooted in Buddhism and Zen.

After Dr. Herrigel familiarized himself with some of these traditional ways, his wife decided to study flower arrangement and *sumi-e* or ink painting, while Herrigel himself, who already had engaged in the sport of archery in Germany, elected to practice Japanese *kyūdō*, the traditional Japanese art of archery. He was fortunately able to locate a fine teacher in Sendai, and through his Japanese colleague he gained an introduction to him. The teacher did not accept foreign students. He said he had tried teaching several foreigners but found that all they could think of was hitting the target and showed no interest in learning the spirit at the heart of *kyūdō*. Herrigel finally convinced the teacher that he was different, that he was interested above all in the inner spirit of the art, indeed that he was eager to practice Zen itself. The teacher finally relented and accepted Herrigel as a student.

The teacher began by having Herrigel shoot arrows at a bundle of straw about two feet high set up about twelve feet away. "You must have no consciousness of the arrow leaving the bow!" he cautioned. "It must occur unconsciously, so that the arrow flies off naturally of its own accord." To Herrigel, who as a philosopher specialized in theoretical thought, this seemed irrational. He argued using all the logic and reasoning at his command, but his teacher's response to all his questions was a serene tranquility. "I hold the bow and shoot the arrow, but the arrow flies off of itself without my being conscious of it?" said Herrigel. "That is ridiculous! If that is true, then who is pulling the bow? Do you mean someone else is doing the shooting?" "Yes," replied the teacher. "The self that is not the self. "If you can grasp that *self*, you will understand Buddhism and Zen as well."

For two years Herrigel did nothing but practice loosing the arrow from the bow. In time he managed to arrive at the point where he drew the bow but did not draw it at all. He reached a stage where the arrow flew from the bowstring on its own. Now his teacher allowed him to shoot at a real target, set up at a distance of about sixty feet, but cautioned, "You mustn't think about hitting the target!" Another exceedingly irrational statement.

"Archery is a matter of shooting at a target," thought Herrigel, "Why would you try to not think about hitting the target?" He attempted to resolve his doubts with his teacher, but the teacher would not budge from his original statement. "If you face the target in a state of no-mind where self and other are one, if you assume the correct attitude and posture, even though you don't think about hitting the target, the target will come to you and be hit on its own."

Although Herrigel followed his teacher's instructions diligently, he was unable to attain a state of no-mind. He always ended up aiming at the target. Finally, all his steadfast resolve gave out. "I'll never be able to understand either archery or Zen," he said, "I'm ready to throw in the towel." "It can't be helped," the teacher replied, "Let me try one final expedient. Come and visit me tonight."

When Herrigel went to the master that night, the master lit some incense and told Herrigel to set it beside the target. In its light the target was faintly visible. The teacher took two arrows and ascended to the archery platform and released one of the arrows. It struck the center of the target. When he unloosed the second arrow, it too flew straight to the target. When they went to retrieve the arrows, they found the second arrow embedded in the first one; it had split it in two.

The teacher pointed to the arrows and said, "How do you explain this? Even if someone thinks about hitting the target as you do, isn't the target oblivious of that? You may have the idea that the first arrow struck the center because of the skill I acquired standing here and shooting arrows all the time. But what about the second arrow splitting the first one in two? It shows that if you make your mind perfectly clear, then even without trying to hit the target, the target will be hit. That is my explanation. You are free to do as you like."

Herrigel continued to struggle in earnest for several years, and he finally received his teacher's certification as a kyūdō student of the fifth rank. He returned to Germany and eventually published the well-known *Zen in der Kunst des Bogenschiessens* (English title: *Zen in the Art of Archery*), which relates how he gained an understanding of Buddhism and Zen through the study of archery.

This realm in which you grasp the self that is not the self, where the target comes to be hit of itself without your aiming at it, the world of the oneness of self and other—this is the realm of *zenjō*, the Sanskrit dhyana. The Sixth Patriarch explained *zenjō* in this way: "*Zen* is being free of forms externally, *jō* is being undisturbed within." This mental state is one that appears throughout all traditional forms of Japanese art and culture.

I believe that *zenjō*—using the word in a broad sense—is always present in human life at its finest, and that a truly good and genuine life emerges only from within zenjō. In other words, the zenjō of Mahayana Buddhism is zenjō that is rooted in the realities of everyday life.

8

"AROUSE THE MIND WITHOUT FIXING IT ANYWHERE"

SHAKYAMUNI BUDDHA is the founder of the Zen school and of the Buddha Dharma as well, although the second part of this statement may be easily misunderstood. Appearing twenty-eight generations after Shakyamuni, the Indian monk Bodhidharma traveled to China where he came to be regarded as the First Patriarch of Chinese Zen. Zen Master Hui-neng, usually referred to as the Sixth Patriarch, appeared six generations after Bodhidharma. Hui-neng was born of peasant stock in the south of China. As a youth, he eked out a living while caring for his mother by gathering firewood in the mountains and selling it in the market. One day when he delivered a load to a person's home and was waiting to be paid for it, he heard someone reciting a sutra inside the house. The words "Arouse the mind without fixing it anywhere" reached his ears. His mind must have been ripe for the experience because he had a sudden awakening

41

on hearing the words. The householder later introduced him to the Fifth Patriarch, Zen Master Hung-jen. He became Hung-jen's student and later received his Dharma transmission, becoming the Sixth Patriarch of the Chinese Zen school.

The Sixth Patriarch defined *zazen*, seated meditation, in this way: "Sitting (*za*) means not giving rise to thoughts in the face of any and all external realms, good or bad; *zen* means remaining undisturbed internally as you see the self-nature." He also said: "Sitting means our consciousness not giving rise externally to discriminatory distinctions with regard to the world's myriad phenomena—good and evil, beautiful and ugly, being and nonbeing, illusion and enlightenment, sin and salvation, loss and profit. Zen means the consciousness internally self-awakening to its true nature and not straying from that true nature—which can be called absolute nothingness." I think these words grasp zazen, not conventionally or uncritically but in an essential way.

Sitting, then, is not a matter of endeavoring to think of nothing at all; it is a realm where thinking of all kinds has disappeared. Zen is not taking great pains to keep the mind from working at all; it is the mind not leaving its original nature—like a well-trained dog that stays at home and does not go dashing off. To be sitting and quietly thinking is to enter a clear, transparent realm free of all such attachments and preoccupations. Zen Master Dōgen called zazen "the Dharma gate of ease and comfort" (*anraku no hōmon*). I think if you start telling people to think of nothing at all and make the mind immovable, they may easily conclude that they should try to become utterly insensate and inanimate, like a stone or tree.

Lord Date Masamune once acquired a famous teabowl that he had long cherished. One day as he was holding it, gazing at its beauties, it slipped from his hands and would have fallen to the floor if he had not caught it. His clumsiness perturbed him. Although the bowl had not been broken, the same could not be said for his mind. "How shameful," he thought, "that my mind, which has remained composed through countless battles large and small, should be unsettled by a single teabowl." Taking the bowl, he threw it into the garden, where it smashed to bits against a rock. Keeping the mind calm and unwavering amid the confusion of armed conflict was the mental state essential to the samurai. It is also the ideal of zazen practice. But that does not mean becoming unconcerned and unfeeling like a stone or a tree. In such a state, a samurai could never survive the heat of battle. Let me return to the words of Zen Master Takuan quoted in the previous talk:

> In speaking of the immovable wisdom of the buddhas . . . the word *immovable* does not mean remaining inert and insensate like a stone or tree. It is the mind moving at will in any direction whatever—forward, backward, left, or right. *Immovable wisdom* is the mind functioning without the least constraint or hesitation.

"Immovable wisdom," then, describes a mind that moves freely in all directions without stopping or hesitating. In everyday terms, it would be like riding a bicycle through a busy downtown center. You must negotiate your way through the crowded streets, paying full attention to the streetcars, buses, trucks, taxis, motorbikes, bicycles, and pedestrians you encounter so you don't collide with them, at the same time remaining oblivious of everything else. This is what is meant by immovable wisdom: the mind flowing freely in any direction without any stopping or hesitating—what the *Diamond Sutra* calls "arousing the mind without fixing it anywhere."

Leaves and buds and grasses become fresh and radiant thanks to the nutrients they obtain from water. And then they blossom into flowers. We must not forget the plant metabolism that is always secretly at work. Streams flow on, their water never striking twice against the same bank. All the things in the universe are constantly negating the self while constantly creating the self anew. Within this process there is neither birth nor death; there is nothing but the beautiful flow of life. Such is the principle of the natural world. On the other hand, only human beings, who have been called "thinking reeds," indulge themselves in pleasure when they encounter pleasure, are dashed by sadness when sadness comes, are immersed in endless yearning and regret. It is all a sickness of the mind that is truly pitiful.

The famous words in the Confucian *Great Learning*, "Renew yourself one day, renew yourself each day, and continue to renew yourself," connote a life lived fully and earnestly, at each thought-instant a new thought, each new thought radiant and clear. This should be the natural mode of human life—

laughing from the core of your being when you laugh, crying from the core of your being when you cry, becoming angry from the core of your being when you are angry. Moreover, if you can live so that your thoughts are purified, one after another, by vanishing into oblivion without a trace, then "every day is a good day."

Takuan's "immovable" is a mind utterly unstirred, from the highest heaven above to the floor of hell below, its movement a completely untrammeled activity that penetrates through the three worlds of past, present, and future and encompasses the universe in all directions. In other words, its movement is immovable; its immovability is in constant motion. Zazen is a matter of attaining this crystalline mind, unimpeded and free of hindrances and attachments of any kind.

9

NATIONAL TREASURES

LAST MONTH a special exhibition of newly designated National Treasures opened at the Kyoto National Museum. These are works judged to be outstanding even among Japan's many important cultural properties, works to be preserved and protected as cultural assets of the highest order. Indeed, they are the treasures of the world as a whole. My own temple, Myōshin-ji, is represented by its ancient bell as well as Josetsu's painting *Catching a Catfish with a Gourd*, housed in the Taizō-in subtemple. I heard from the priest of Ryōan-ji that the famous Kizaemon Ido teabowl preserved in the Koho-an subtemple of Daitoku-ji, which visitors must pay a hefty fee to view, is also being shown at the exhibition.

The current exhibition includes some forty works from the Kyoto area. In viewing them I noted the existence of two cultural currents, the Heian and Muromachi. Heian culture, which was oriented toward Shingon Buddhism, is represented by works from the esoteric Shingon temples Jingō-ji and Daigo-ji; Zen-oriented Muromachi culture mainly by works preserved at Daitoku-ji. Among the Daitoku-ji works were paintings such as Mu-chi's triptych of Kannon Bodhisattva, Monkey, and Crane; the Jingō-ji paintings included the portrait of Minamoto Yoritomo, the founder of the Kamakura shogunate. There was the famous painting of Kujaku Myōō, "the Peacock Wisdom King"; Kōbō Daishi's letter to Saichō (*Kaze Shinbo*); the *Anthology of the Thirty-Six Poets* (*Sanū-rokunin Kashū*) from Nishihongan-ji; and calligraphy by the Sung dynasty Chinese Zen priest Yuan-wu. All of them were most splendid works. I was glad to have had the privilege of seeing them and came away with a feeling that I myself had grown and deepened, had been cleansed and purified. However, there was one exhibit that literally stopped me in my tracks. Gazing at it, I became unwittingly riveted to the spot, my body trembling in awe. It was a piece of calligraphy by Daitō Kokushi, the Zen priest of the Kamakura period who founded Daitoku-ji in Kyoto.

My first and immediate interest was not the Chinese characters that made up the calligraphy. I felt that I was personally encountering Zen Master Daitō himself. Without knowing it, I bowed my head and for a long time did not move from the spot. Everything else forgotten, I experienced something that filled and overflowed my heart. The Chinese Zen teacher Huang-po said that his teacher Ma-tsu's shout rendered students deaf for three days. That is how I felt. Even seeing that calligraphy, I thought, had given me a new perspective on life.

Just as I was about to go and call on the Ryōan-ji priest so I could thank him for having urged me to see the exhibition and to explain my feelings about it to him, I received a telephone call from Professor Akamatsu of Kyoto University, telling me that this was the last day the Daitō calligraphy would be shown. Everyone seemed to feel the same way I did about the calligraphy. I understood why the owner would want to have it returned before the exhibition ended. I also understood why Professor Akamatsu was urging me to see it while I could.

Last month when I was in Tajima in northern Hyōgo prefecture, I met the head priest of Tsūgen-ji. He said he was planning to go to Kyoto to attend the exhibition of National Treasures at the Kyoto National Museum. When I told him the exhibition had just ended, he said, "What a shame. A painter friend in Kyoto sent me a letter telling me about a wonderful example of Daitō Kokushi's calligraphy that was being displayed and urging me by all means to see it." Once again I was struck by the way Daitō's calligraphy seemed to evoke a kindred response in all those who saw it.

What is it about Daitō's calligraphy that makes it so special? It is not merely because of its age—it was written six hundred years ago in the Kamakura period—or because the brushwork is skillful. I think it is because the writing embodies a true greatness of spirit. The Chinese characters, written in black ink, throb with an energy that insinuates itself deeply into the viewer's heart and mind; one cannot help being moved. When the human spirit is deepened or elevated to this degree, we marvel

48

at it naturally. Come to think about it, was not this spirit—the spirit of Zen—the matrix in which the culture of the Yoshino and Muromachi eras would later quicken and burst into flower? We may call it Buddha or more simply the life spirit. It is something we all possess from the time we are born. Self-awakening to this—being self-awakened to it—is the religion we know as Buddhism.

From long in the past, Zen seekers engaged in difficult and prolonged training, probing under enlightened teachers into life itself: "What is the great meaning the Buddha Dharma has transmitted?" "Show me Zen that has no shape or form." "Reveal the formless spirit." The master may respond in various ways. At times he will spit out a single sound, "*Kaa!*"; at times he will deliver twenty or thirty blows with his staff; at times he will raise up a single finger; and at times he will glare menacingly at the questioner. There are no other ways that the master can show them Zen. In the end, the only way to express Zen, the formless spirit, is through the medium of art. This is where Zen's affinity with the traditional Japanese arts or ways comes in. It is a causal affinity, in which Zen is the source of these arts. Daitō Kokushi's Zen calligraphy is a prime example. The National Master's heart and mind—his Zen—is even today vitally alive, pulsing within those Chinese characters he brushed in black ink.

To me, the fact that Daitō's calligraphy is deemed a Japanese National Treasure indicates that Zen itself is a National Treasure. Non-Japanese will readily agree that traditional paintings and sculptures should be ranked as National Treasures, but will they be able to appreciate the merits of *bokuseki,* Zen calligraphy, such as Daitō's? I believe they will, because these are not merely works of art; they are the spirit of the Zen master himself.

In this way, zazen can be truly seen as a seedbed from which the loftiest spirit emerges and is fostered—a treasure for all the world's inhabitants. Zen Master Hakuin extols the practice of zazen in *Song of Zazen* using lines of easily understood Japanese verse.

I could go on like this praising Daitō's calligraphy, in what some might regard as a kind of self-flattery, but I will now bring my prefatory remarks to an end and turn my attention to *Song of Zazen* itself.

10

POINTING STRAIGHT AT THE MIND

"ILLNESS IS CURED naturally, the physician merely aids the process." These are the famous words of the ancient Greek physician Hippocrates, the father of Western medicine. Shakyamuni taught using precisely the same method: "Extraordinary! Extraordinary! Living beings all possess the virtues of the Tathagata's wisdom! They fail to realize it only because of their delusions and attachments." Hippocrates enunciates the fundamental principle of physical health, Shakyamuni that of spiritual salvation.

Not even the most skillful physician can save a person whose vital life force is exhausted. In the same way, the greatest religious teacher cannot lead to buddhahood someone who lacks the buddha-nature. Healing a seriously ill person at death's door is contingent on the vital life strength deep within them.

None of a physician's medicines can do more than make that strength work to greater effect. The unenlightened sunk deeply in sin and worldly passions achieves peace of mind and buddhahood because the buddha-nature is inherent in them from birth. A teacher can only help encourage them to self-awaken to that intrinsic nature. Hence it can be said without exaggeration that the brief line *All beings are from the first buddhas* in Hakuin's *Song of Zazen* embodies the fundamental principle of the Buddha's Dharma, and that if you truly understand these words, the Buddha's Dharma is yours.

Great teachers beginning with Shakyamuni who have transmitted the Dharma down through the centuries exerted all their effort making this simple truth known to as many people as possible. Of all the Buddhist schools, Zen had the clearest doctrine of all—"Pointing straight at the mind of man, seeing into the self-nature and attaining buddhahood." No recourse to expedient means, just straight and direct pointing to your fundamental nature, clearly revealing it, and becoming Buddha straightaway.

After Kanzan Egen, the founder of Myōshin-ji in Kyoto, completed his practice under Daitō Kokushi, he disappeared into the mountains of Ibuka in Mino Province to engage in post-satori practice and "nurture the sacred embryo." For eight years he devoted himself to helping the local villagers, returning each night to his grass hut and devoting himself to zazen. When Daitō died, Emperor Hanazono, in accordance with Daitō's final wishes, initiated a search for Egen, circulating a description of him throughout the country. Finally discovering that Egen was living in Mino Province, Hanazono dispatched the counselor Kanroji Chūnagon to summon Egen to the palace.

Egen made various excuses to refuse the emperor's request, but in the end, unable to go against his teacher Daitō's final instructions, he relented and returned to the capital. The simple villagers of Ibuka were astonished. Completely unaware that the beggar monk living among them was a celebrated priest, they had treated him as a menial servant, working him hard. They felt deeply ashamed. Saddened to see him leave, they gathered to send him off and accompanied him for many miles along the way.

They declared that they would go with him all the way to the barrier station at Seki, nearly half the distance to Kyoto. Master Egen produced his ink case, took a piece of paper from his robe, and wrote the words "The Seki station is here." "My fellow villagers," he said, "the Seki barrier is here. Now please return to your homes." Thus persuaded to return to their village, they reluctantly bade him farewell.

Among the villagers who had accompanied him was an elderly couple who had always been particularly friendly to him. As they were saying farewell with tears in their eyes, they told him, "We deeply regret that we had such a holy priest in our midst and were unable to receive his teaching. Would you please give us a few words in parting?" Knowing how earnest they were, Egen readily granted their request. He told them to come closer to him and had them sit facing each other. Then he reached out, grabbed their topknots, and bumped their foreheads together. "Ouch!" they both exclaimed. "There!" said Egen. "That's it! Now don't forget it!"

The "Ouch!" you utter when you strike your head against something was not learned at school from your teacher or from your parents or from books. It comes straight from your own mind. You understand it perfectly on your own. You understand it without any help. No one told you to say it. It is not something you thought about doing either; it was uttered without thinking or questioning. Not thinking of anything, not considering anything, is the buddha-nature, the fundamental nature and mind of human beings. It is, in the full sense of the word, nothingness (*Mu*). It was from *Mu* that the "Ouch!" appeared, without pondering or deliberation of any kind.

This *Mu* (absolute nothingness) is not something that is created or established, and it is not something you attain. It is not a thing of beauty or defilement. It does not increase or decrease. It is truly and absolutely unborn and undying. Hence we provisionally give it the name "buddha-nature." Thanks to this *Mu*, we see and hear, weep and laugh, sleep and wake, and are able to lead a totally free existence without any problem whatever—this is what is meant by becoming a buddha. It is also the meaning conveyed by the phrase quoted above from the *Diamond Sutra*: "Arouse the mind without fixing it anywhere."

Zen Master Shidō Munan, the teacher of Hakuin's teacher Shōju Rōjin, alludes to this meaning in his verses. For example,

Buddha is the name
　For what remains alive
After the body

Has thoroughly died.
Become a dead man

While you are living,
Do as you please,
Then all is right.

There is no jeweled lotus seat
In Buddha's Land of Bliss
Aside from knowing you have
No self or body while you live.

Zen Master Lin-chi, the founder of our Rinzai Zen school, said, "Above the mass of red flesh is a true man of no rank who is always going in and out of your face gates. To those who have yet to confirm this true man in themselves, I say: *See! See!*" The true man of no rank is himself the fundamental nature in all people, and grasping this nature is the meaning of the Zen phrase "seeing into the self-nature and attaining buddhahood." The fundamental nature is not something that appears suddenly from doing zazen. It is not received from Amida Buddha when someone recites the Nembutsu. Since it is something all are originally born with, Hakuin says, *All beings are from the first buddhas.* Utterances such as Kanzan Egen's quoted above, which address themselves directly to the mind itself with no unnecessary flourishes, make very clear that "pointing straight at the mind of man," the adage said to epitomize Zen, is an extremely appropriate one.

11

THE ETERNAL

THERE IS ANOTHER well-known saying of Hippocrates: "Life is short, art is long." Human life is as fleeting as the morning dew or evening mist, and yet the pursuit of truth in learning and the infinite joy of art that takes place within that brief span shine radiantly with eternal life.

Vita brevis, ars longa. Within the brevity of human life an endless joy is experienced by those who set their minds on the path of learning and by those who find meaning for existence in their devotion to art. But however long-lived art may be, it is not eternal or immortal. Certainly as long as human beings exist, they will continue to hand down a common fund of knowledge, and they will continue to cherish their great artistic treasures. Yet how long will human beings continue to exist? How long will the earth go on? Human existence is, after all, transitory as well. Set against the permanence of the universe, they are no more than shadows in a dream.

Our world will one day come to an end. Of vastly greater importance, however, is Shakyamuni Buddha's wisdom in penetrating to the truth that the birth and death of worlds is something that takes place endlessly, over and over. Shakyamuni went into the mountains, casting all worldly ties aside, and meditated for six long years, finally entering enlightenment on seeing the morning star and discovering the true life that is unborn and undying.

In analyzing the basic substance of the world, what is the smallest component that can be found, something that defies further analysis? Is it the atomic or subatomic particles of modern science? Buddhism has coined terms such as *rinkyo* and *gokumi* to describe particles of infinitesimal size, which it regards as the basic components of the universe. Generally stated, it maintains that while all phenomena are born and perish, the essential substance constituting them is unborn and undying. In this, however, something remains in the basic substance of the universe, both material and spiritual, that does not lend itself to such an easy explanation. Buddhism calls this the world of suchness, also the Dharma Body of the Buddha Vairocana. It believes that the phenomenal world remains in constant flux within the universe, turning through births and deaths for all eternity, but if we ask the ultimate purpose of this state of constant change, it lies in bringing the highest virtues inherent within it into play. It gives to these highest virtues the name Amida Buddha, the Reward Body of a buddha that is acquired as a result of meritorious deeds performed over countless past lives.

The name Amida Buddha has two meanings: Tathagata of Unimpeded Light, and Tathagata of Boundless Life—"Boundless Life" because Amida Buddha is the fundamental substance of the universe; "Unimpeded Light" because he represents infinite merit or ultimate worth. Amida is an ineffable spiritual essence that is unborn and undying. Reciting *Namu-Amida-butsu* means becoming one with this spiritual essence and being incorporated into its boundless life.

What could be more rewarding or have greater worth than that?

But though we can readily grasp that our physical body is one with the substance of the universe, in spite of everything there is something that prevents us from simply uniting with it. The many impurities at the source of the consciousness of the ego-self, the unaccountable emotions of anger, jealously, greed, ignorance, passion, and guilt—these keep us from becoming one with Buddha. How are we to deal with them?

Shakyamuni, a person who had succeeded in clearing these impurities away, is called the Great Taming and Subduing Hero (Skt. *Purusadamyasārathi*; literally, "one who tames people's emotions and leads them to enlightenment"). It is one of his ten honorable epithets. Since he is a being who appears from the world of suchness for the express purpose of saving living beings, he is also called the Tathagata, one who has "thus come," or perhaps "one who has come from thusness." Since he is a buddha who manifests himself in the actual historical world in response to the troubles and sufferings of human beings, he is called the Buddha of the Manifested Body (*Ōjin-butsu*). The Buddha's three bodies—the Dharma Body, Reward Body, and Manifested Body—express things in their genuine reality, their true form and function in the universe. As ordinary unenlightened people can see no resemblance whatever between such exalted buddhas and themselves, it seems inconceivable to them that they could become buddhas—and yet Shakyamuni taught us, with great power, that we can.

When Shakyamuni awakened on seeing the morning star on the eight day of the twelfth month, his first words were, "Extraordinary! Extraordinary! Living beings all possess the virtues of the Tathagata's wisdom! They fail to realize it only because of their delusions and attachments."

"Extraordinary! Extraordinary!" is an exclamation of great wonderment. Wise sages do not typically display emotion, but here we see Shakyamuni Buddha, the wisest mortal on earth, marveling in this way, so there is no doubt that he felt it to be truly extraordinary. The reason? Because we ordinary, unenlightened men and women are buddhas! The Buddha's wisdom and compassion are inherent in us all! It was as though Shakyamuni had come suddenly upon a diamond while searching through a rubbish dump. It is stranger, and in fact a greater miracle, than a lump of gold appearing from a crock of night soil. There was good reason for the Buddha's great surprise.

Is there anything more fortunate, more desirable than human life? We believe that we are creatures overflowing with evil passions and we are fearful of our sinful karma, but such things do not really exist. They appear by chance, like clouds, mist, or fog, and after a time they vanish. Shakyamuni taught us that the true form of our mind is the unborn, undying buddha-nature, and wisdom and compassion; that the three bodies of the Buddha—the Dharma Body, the Reward Body, and the Manifested Body—are in truth the authentic states of our own mind.

Just as there is no difference between space inside a test tube and space throughout the great universe, Shakyamuni's buddha-nature and our buddha-nature are one and the same. In the Dharma universe of true suchness, there is no self or other. Shakyamuni Buddha proclaimed to us for the first time this great declaration of human emancipation: *All beings are from the first buddhas.*

12

LIKE A MIRROR

THE WORDS *God* and *Buddha* are often used in somewhat dubious ways, suggesting, I believe, how very difficult they are to grasp. The Japanese word *kami*, "god," uses a Chinese character whose original meaning is not "god" but "heaven" or "demon" or "spirit." And although the word *kami* is used for the indigenous Japanese kami as well as for the Christian and Islamic Gods, there are between each of them great differences in meaning.

A great many explanations of the etymology of the word *kami* have been offered. One authority explains that the word *kami* means "up, upper part, higher as opposed to lower," asserting that this is how it came to be used for an exalted being of the highest rank, a being possessing virtue and power excelling ordinary human beings. Another authority says that *kami* is a variation of the word *kabi*, meaning "mold," slime mold being the earliest life-form to appear and so the basis of all subsequent terrestrial life. Another scholar holds that the word *kami* is a contracted form of the word *kakurimi*. He cites a verse by Emperor Meiji:

Communicating with the mind
　Of the kami that cannot be seen
Must truly take place in our
　Sincerest, most genuine mind.

He claims that *kami* indicates something shapeless and formless, hence set apart or hidden, and that *kami* is a contracted form of the word *kakurimi*, a being isolated or set apart from others in some way. Yet another specialist holds that the word *kami* is contracted from *kagami*, "mirror," pointing out that Amaterasu Ōkami, the most important of the Shintō deities, entrusted the sacred mirror Yata no Kagami to her grandson Ninigi no Mikoto, telling him, "When you regard this mirror, it should be with the same devout reverence you show in worshipping me." A mind as pure and unsullied as this mirror is kami.

　There are other theories as well. Hakuin's leading disciple, Zen Master Tōrei, was born into a family of Shintō priests in the village of Gokōsō in Ōmi Province. On finishing his Zen practice under Hakuin, he sequestered himself in the book repository of the Ise Shrine for three years to engage in a thorough examination of the Shintō teachings. His study led him to conclude that the word *kami* derives from *kagami*, "mirror." If that conclusion is correct, it would mean that Buddhism and Shintō share some elements in common. As an example, we might cite the fact that Buddhism refers to the Buddha's primal wisdom as the Great and Perfect Mirror Wisdom.

There are no tricks or artifice about a mirror. It is mindless and totally impartial. If a flower comes before it, a flower is reflected, and if a bird comes before it, a bird is reflected, both exactly as they are. A mirror reflects all things that come before it without any discriminating whatever; and when they depart, the images vanish without a trace and the mirror returns to the state of emptiness or no-mind. This mirrorlike mind, immaculately pure, free and untrammeled, is called kami. It is also called Buddha.

In front of a mirror, everything is equal. A mirror does not make you look more beautiful because you happen to be rich or make you look inferior because you are poor. Before a mirror, rich and poor, powerful and insignificant, men and women, old and young are all perfectly equal. Towering Mount Fuji and a tiny sesame seed, the water in the Pacific Ocean and the water in a cup, a diamond and a glass bead—all are reflected equally. There is no distinguishing between great and small, beauty and ugliness, high and low, rich and poor. A mind that is pure and undefiled, free of contrivances of any kind, impartial and selfless as a mirror—this is the meaning of kami, and also the meaning of Buddha.

In 552, the thirteenth year of Japanese emperor Kinmei's reign, King Songmyong of Paekche sent a Buddhist image, Buddhist scriptures, and other presents to the Japanese court. The emperor was deeply moved on seeing a Buddhist image for the first time. "The radiant countenance of this buddha sent to us from a kingdom to the West is something I have never seen before. Should we worship it?" he asked his assembled courtiers.

Soga no Iname, the leader of the powerful Soga clan, replied, "Countries throughout the world worship such objects. It would be good for us to worship this buddha." Mononobe no Okoshi, the chief of the Mononobe clan and a rival of Soga no Iname, voiced opposition to the idea. The emperor thereupon gave the image to Iname, telling him to worship it. But when a pestilence suddenly appeared and spread throughout the populace, Okoshi declared, "We have aroused the ire of the kami by worshipping a foreign deity." He ordered his men to burn Iname's residence to the ground. The buddha image was thrown into Namba Pond.

Not long afterward, peasants saw light glowing from the pond one evening as night fell. They cast a net to discover the cause, and they pulled up the image of the buddha. On examining it they found traces of the conflagration that had razed Iname's residence. Everyone became excited when a person exclaimed, "*Hotoborike! Hotoborike!*"—"It is still warm! It is still warm!" The Japanese word *hotoke*, "buddha," came to be believed, by a rather far-fetched folk etymology, to be a contracted form of the word *hotoborike*.

Another theory, citing a line from an old verse, suggests that *hotoke* means *hodokeru*, "to untie," as in a knot: untying the knots of the evil passions, delusions, and attachments that confine and restrict and thereby attaining the realm of untrammeled emancipation. This is no doubt just another ingenious folk etymology.

Although the etymology of the Japanese word *hotoke*, "buddha," is uncertain, a traditional theory that it derives from the Chinese *fu-t'o-jia* seems to me a reasonable assumption. *Fu-t'o* transliterates the Sanskrit "buddha," and since *jia* means "house," *fu-t'o-jia* is "a house in which Buddha is worshipped" or simply "a Buddhist." Perhaps from this latter meaning—"a Buddhist"—the word came to refer to Buddha itself.

In the original Sanskrit, the word *buddha* means "the self-awakened," one who has truly understood their true self. The true self is as pure and undefiled, selfless and impartial, as a mirror, a state of mind in which self and others are one. When we are born into the world, all of us possess this splendidly selfless mind. We do not acquire it at school or learn it from books. It is the originally pure and undefiled heart and mind we possess inherently from the moment we are born. Hakuin's *Song of Zazen* expresses this as *All beings are from the first buddhas.*

13

WATER FLOWS

CONFUCIUS ONCE STOOD on the banks of a great river and said, "See how it flows on like this, never stopping day or night." "Water conforms to the shape of the container" goes an ancient Chinese proverb. The *Flower Garland Sutra* speaks of "the cool refreshing Bodhisattva moon moving enjoyably through the utterly empty void, Bodhi revealing its light in the pure water of living beings' minds." One of my favorite Zen couplets is the well-known *Shadows of bamboo sweep the stairs without stirring a single particle of dust. / The moon penetrates to the floor of the clear pond leaving no trace on the water.* The following lines by a Sung master excellently express the furthest reaches of Zen: *Seated in a place of practice, you are like the moon and the water, / Your mind reflecting faultlessly the myriad flowers of emptiness.* And Zen Master Hakuin writes, *All beings are from the first buddhas, / Their kinship is like water and ice.*

The analogy has been drawn since ancient times between water as the fundamental substance and waves as phenomena. It is plainly articulated in lines such as, "There are no waves apart from water, no water apart from the waves. There are no phenomena apart from the fundamental substance, no fundamental substance apart from phenomena." In this same sense, we living beings do not exist apart from Buddha endowed with the Dharma Body of ultimate reality, and Buddha in turn does not exist apart from we unenlightened beings.

Although Hakuin's words in *Song of Zazen*, *Apart from water there is no ice, / Apart from beings, no buddhas*, may have a metaphysical ring, what they assert has, I think, somewhat of a broader implication. There is no essential difference between water and ice, and not only between water and ice; as the old verse says, *Rain, hail, snow, and ice are different, but in the end are all the same valley stream.* Though precipitation takes various different forms, those forms all consist of the same components—two parts hydrogen, one part oxygen. They are exactly the same and yet they are altogether different; altogether different yet exactly the same. And within this relation there is profound meaning.

Let us examine how water and ice differ. To begin with, water is warmer than ice. Water is shapeless; ice is not. Water flows; ice does not. Water spreads everywhere, into all places, freely harmonizing with all things; ice does not spread or harmonize in this way. Water nourishes plants and trees, it sustains fish, and is, as a rule, life-giving. Ice is harmful to plants and trees, injurious to fish, and generally works to destroy. Although water and ice are said to be one and the same, in their forms and the ways in which they function they are remarkably at odds. What I find most interesting about them is their dissimilarity, which makes them appear to be totally different things, while having exactly the same components.

The same comparison applies to buddhas and ordinary men and women. They are exactly the same and yet they are altogether different; altogether different yet exactly the same. How are they different? First of all, while a buddha's heart has the warmth and compassion of a mother for her child, a living being's heart is cool and detached, without a great deal of time to think about others. While a buddha's mind has neither shape, color, nor form, a living being's mind is filled with kinks and lumps—"Me, me." The mind of a buddha always moves freely, utterly unimpeded, like water flowing on endlessly without ceasing. The minds of living beings attach to food and clothing, property and wealth, alcohol and sex, prestige and fame, and countless other things as well. Their minds are constrained and restricted, unable to act freely.

In the same way that water finds its way into all places, harmonizing with all things, the buddha-mind finds its way into the minds of those who are troubled or suffering, adapting compassionately to the conditions of the most indigent and the most unruly and lawless alike. But a strong, stubborn streak in the hearts of living beings causes conflict among siblings, hostility between parents and children, making it difficult for them to live together in the same house. Although the mind of the buddha embraces, affirms, and emancipates all beings in the same way that water brings its benefits, ordinary people coldheartedly inflict damage on others, at times even murdering them in order to advance their own ends. The minds of buddhas and ordinary unenlightened people are like snow and ink, like the moon and a turtle, to all appearances as totally different as two things can be. But that is not so. They are one and same.

Recall once again the words Shakyamuni spoke upon attaining enlightenment: "Extraordinary! Extraordinary! Living beings all possess the virtues of the Tathagata's wisdom! They fail to realize it only because of their delusions and attachments." He exclaims that while living beings are all born with the Buddha's own wisdom and compassion, because they do not awaken to this fact and mistakenly believe they have a "self," attaching to it and cherishing it above all else, Buddha's wisdom and compassion cannot manifest themselves.

National Master Bukkoku wrote in a verse,

Do not suppose the light appears after the clouds lift;
The pale morning moon was in the sky from the first.

If the ice of intruding thoughts and attachments melts, the water of the buddha-nature will flow freely, collect in a calm, clear pool in which the bodhisattva's refreshing moon will rest its perfect sublime shape.

The world of Buddha is moreover a pure, unhindered realm. The moon leaves no trace of having rested there, the water shows no sign of having harbored it. This freely flowing life is also what is being expressed in the Zen phrases quoted above: *The moon penetrates to the floor of the clear pond leaving no trace on the water* and *Seated in a place of practice, you are like the moon and the water, / Your mind reflecting faultlessly the myriad flowers of emptiness.* Life that flows as freely as water—it is this to which we give the name Buddha.

14

ICE MELTS

THE CHINESE ZEN MASTER Ma-tsu Tao-i (709–788) was a Dharma grandson of Hui-neng, the Sixth Patriarch. Inheriting the Sixth Patriarch's teaching style, he took it even further and ended up creating a uniquely Chinese Zen. Ma-tsu was an imposing figure. He "walked with the slow, ponderous gait of an ox, his eyes had the glint of a glowering tiger." He was a formidable priest from whose forge fully eighty-four Zen masters emerged.

One of Ma-tsu's favorite teaching phrases was "This mind itself is Buddha." Otherwise stated, this is Hakuin's *All beings are from the first buddhas*, which has also been stated as "The mind of the unenlightened person is, as such, Buddha." This saying is briefer and more trenchant than Bodhidharma's "Pointing straight at the mind of man, seeing into the self-nature and attaining buddhahood." Ma-tsu's saying is simpler than the Sixth

Patriarch's "Arouse the mind without fixing it anywhere." Chinese Zen appeared from that brevity and simplicity. Ma-tsu used the phrase "This mind itself is Buddha" throughout his long teaching career, and it became well known in China. In time it was on everyone's lips. So he felt obliged to change it — to "No mind, no Buddha."

The phrase "This mind itself is Buddha" is an important one for the Zen school, though Ma-tsu was not the first Zen figure to use it. It had already appeared in *Inscription on the Mind King* (*Hsin-wang ming*), a work by the famous Zen layman Fu Ta-shih (497–569) dating back to around the time Bodhidharma arrived in China. In full the passage reads: "The mind is itself Buddha; Buddha is itself mind. Every thought is the buddha-mind, the buddha-mind thinking of Buddha."

Actually, the first appearance of the phrase was not in a Zen work at all but in a sutra of the Pure Land school, the *Sutra of Meditation on the Buddha of Immeasurable Life* (*Kanmuryōju-kyō*). Commenting on the phrase in his *Kyōgyōshinshō* (*Teaching, Practice, Faith, and Realization*) the Shin sect founder Shinran wrote,

> "The mind itself is Buddha" means there is no Amida Buddha apart from the mind of faith. It is, for example, like fire taking hold in a piece of wood and being unable to leave the wood. Because it is unable to leave the wood, the fire continues burning it until the wood is finally consumed completely and becomes totally fire.

So even Shinran, a proponent of the Pure Land's "other-power" teaching, acknowledges that Buddha does not exist apart from the mind. Shinran chooses to use the analogy of fire and wood instead of water and ice. Fire is produced on coming together with wood, and the fire that appears does not exist apart from wood. By virtue of its not existing apart from fire, wood goes on to become fire.

Living beings are not born from buddhas; buddhas are born from the minds of living beings. Buddhas thus born do not exist apart from living beings. Living beings by virtue of not existing apart from buddhas are assimilated into buddhahood and go on to become fully attained buddhas.

To return to Hakuin's water and ice analogy, his line "*Apart from water there is no ice*" should logically be followed by "There are no beings apart from Buddha." Yet the fact that —although by no means failing to notice this—he chose instead to write *Apart from beings, no buddhas* deserves special notice.

Ice not existing apart from water may seem to us a common everyday reality, but in other parts of the world there is a different reality. In the Arctic or Antarctica, ice is found everywhere you look, but there is no fresh water. If you want water, you have to melt some ice. It is not possible in today's world of the latter-day Dharma for human beings to worship Buddha. If living beings want to encounter Buddha, their only recourse is to discover Buddha within their own minds. There is no other way they can worship Buddha. Thus the saying, *Apart from beings, no buddhas.* Like wood producing fire and the fire being inseparable from the wood, when water is made from ice, the ice gradually melts and the volume of water increases, and the unmelted ice that still floats in the water in no way obstructs the water.

This is what the Pure Land teaching means when it says that you attain liberation with your afflicting passions intact, that your sins or karmic hindrances do nothing to obstruct your liberation. Just like wood finally becoming fire and ice finally becoming water, when the time comes for the afflicting passions to become enlightenment and sin and evil to turn into acts of virtue, even if you yourself do nothing, it will happen of itself.

Among Shinran Shōnin's *Kōsō Wasan* (*Hymns of High Priests*) are these two verses:

> Your karmic obstacles become a body of merit,
> Existing in a relation like that of ice and water;
> Where there's much ice there's also much water,
> Where obstacles are many, virtues also abound.

> It is taught that a person who takes delight
> In shinjin is no different from the Tathagata;*
> A mind of great faith is the buddha-nature,
> The buddha-nature is, in itself, the Tathagata.

The lines *A mind of great faith is the buddha-nature, / The buddha-*

* *shinjin* = mind of faith.

nature is, in itself, the Tathagata are taken verbatim from the *Nirvana Sutra.* The pure mind that affirms unconditionally the Tathagata's wisdom and compassion must itself be the Tathagata.

The perfectly clear state of a mind firmly established in great faith is in no way different from the clarity of the buddha-nature in someone who has cast aside all discrimination and achieved self-awakening. The buddha-nature itself is Buddha. We learn of the Buddha's boundless compassion, and when this ardent compassion melts the ice in our hearts, then for the first time "the mind that resolves to recite the Nembutsu arises in us," opening up the realm of the mind of great faith (shinjin). Doing zazen and becoming one with heaven and earth, hearing "*Kaa*" when a crow cries and "*Woof*" when a dog barks, we awaken to the buddha-nature in ourselves, in the realization that our mind never was a restricted, unfree lump of ice, and in that way we experience the joy of *All beings are from the first buddhas* and grasp the truth of *Apart from beings, no buddhas.*

15

"LOWER YOUR BUCKET!"

All day I sought the spring but saw no spring,
Straw sandals in shreds, Mount Lung hung in cloud.
Returning, I passed beneath a flowering plum,
Its branches were overflowing with the spring!

SINCE SPRING has come, the poet went out thinking he
was sure to find it somewhere, but after looking for it all
day, he never once got even a glimpse of it. This verse by the
Sung poet Tai I brings to mind the well-known Japanese children's song *Haru ga kita* ("Spring has come"): *Spring has come,
spring has come. Where has it come? Here in the mountains, here in the
village, here in the fields.*

Straw sandals in shreds, Mount Lung hung in cloud. Although I
combed through the mountains and valleys searching for the
spring, my efforts were in vain. I wore out my straw sandals and

exhausted myself in the bargain. *Returning, I passed beneath a flowering plum.* Returning home at dusk, reaching the entrance gate downcast and weary, I passed beneath the plum tree. One or two plum blossoms had burst open and were emitting a fragrant scent. *Its branches were overflowing with the spring!* Why, it is there in these flowers! I needn't have taken the trouble to seek it far away. It was right here, at home, all along.

One implication of this thought-provoking verse is, of course, that looking for the spring is as foolish as pursuing the Way, the truth, buddhahood. "Spring" is an essentially abstract concept, not something to be found as a result of seeking it. The plum blossoms are plum blossoms; they are not spring, and yet there is no doubt that where plum flowers are blossoming, spring is there.

Where on this earth can Buddha be found? In the great monasteries on Mount Kōya or Mount Hiei? At Zenkō-ji temple in Nagano? Perhaps at Mount Wu-t'ai or Mount Potalaka in China. Perhaps he can be found in Burma, or Thailand, or Ceylon. But even if you strapped on a pair of iron sandals and traversed the entire earth, I don't expect you would encounter a living buddha anywhere you went. Perhaps on returning home after all your searching you would find your grandmother sitting before the Buddhist altar reciting the Nembutsu with her hands pressed together in gasshō. Then you would know that Buddha had been right in your home all along.

The painter Yamamoto Daiji, a friend of mine, was in Fukui prefecture during the severe earthquake that struck that area in

1948. He happened to be in the city of Fukui when the quaking started, walking down the street near the department store in front of the train station. Telephone poles along the streets were thrown to the ground, and he was pinned beneath one of them. Fortunately the pole had first struck against a piece of fire protection equipment, for otherwise he would have been crushed. He couldn't remember how he extricated himself, but he said he ran to the Kuzuryū River and sat for several hours on the riverbank. It was growing dark when the aftershocks began to subside, so he got up to return home. When he did, he realized that the riverbanks thronged with people. The paths were filled with a great many carts and bicycles and people carrying baggage, making walking difficult. As he slowly made his way through the crowds, he saw an old lady with a topknot done up in the "tea whisk" style sitting quietly facing the setting sun with her hands pressed together in gasshō. He told me that the moment he saw her, he felt as though he had been struck in the head with an iron club. "This is it!" he thought, realizing at that instant that he was encountering something he had long forgotten. He said he had never been so deeply moved.

Returning, I passed beneath a flowering plum, / Its branches were overflowing with the spring! No matter where you seek, you will never be able to worship a living buddha, but in truth do we not discover Buddha when we perform gasshō, do zazen, or recite the Nembutsu. Just as plum blossoms are not spring but spring is undoubtedly found where plum blossoms are in flower, zazen is not Buddha, nor is performing gasshō or reciting the Nembutsu—nevertheless Buddha is undoubtedly present in those activities. This truth is even more striking if you succeed in attaining the peace of shinjin's believing mind, or even the awakening of satori, for in that case your peace of mind or satori are in themselves the living Buddha.

Shinran refers to this in his verse:

It is taught that a person who takes delight
In *shinjin* is no different from the Tathagata;
A mind of great faith is the buddha-nature,
The buddha-nature is, in itself, the Tathagata.

In *Song of Zazen*, Zen Master Hakuin says, *Apart from water there is no ice, / Apart from beings, no buddhas. / Unaware Buddha is right at hand, / Beings pursue him in far-off places.* Seeking Buddha in far-off places because you do not realize it is close at hand is like searching for your spectacles when they are on your face, looking for your shoes when you are wearing them, or complaining of thirst while sitting in the middle of a lake. No, it is even closer at hand. It is like a man—call him Kembei—who goes around asking, "It there anyone here named Kembei?" How transcendentally absurd that the consciousness engaged in the seeking is itself none other than Buddha.

Many years ago, a Japanese boat steaming up the Amazon River ran short of fresh water. The captain signaled to a passing English ship going downstream, "We'd like to take on some fresh water if you can spare it." "Lower your bucket over the side!" replied the English ship. Doing this, the Japanese crew-men found that the river water was sweet and fresh. Crossing the vast expanse of the great river-sea with nothing but water as far as the eye could see, the Japanese fell under the illusion that they were still in the ocean, though they had in fact entered the Amazon River. It is *like someone surrounded by water / Continually complaining of thirst.*

16

THE PARABLE OF THE
RICH MAN'S SON

Like a person born to great wealth
Wandering out into a beggar's life.

THESE LINES from Hakuin's *Song of Zazen* allude to a story in the "Belief and Understanding" chapter of the *Lotus Sutra*. I am writing this while traveling, without a copy of the *Lotus Sutra* at hand, so I am afraid I will have to relate the story from memory.

Many years ago in India, the only son of a very rich man wandered from his home, and he either lost his way or perhaps was abducted by scoundrels. His father immediately mounted a search for him, which extended far and wide, but no trace of the boy was found. Five years passed, ten years passed, with the rich man constantly thinking of his lost son. Growing forlorn and dejected, he lost all interest in life. Then one day a ragged beggar appeared at the gates of the rich man's house. After receiving something to eat, he shuffled off. From the upper floor of his residence, the rich man noticed the beggar walking away, and in a sudden flash of perception he knew that the beggar was his long-lost son. "Bring that beggar here!" he called out, then rushed down the stairs and dispatched four or five of his men to go after him. On catching up with the beggar, they grabbed him by the hands and shoulders, stopping him in his tracks. The beggar, alarmed and distressed, began shaking from head to foot. "Please let go of me," he pleaded. "I will never come here again. I am a beggar, but I have never taken anything that belonged to someone else." "Don't worry," the servants replied. "Our master just wants to see you. Come with us. No one will hurt you."

"No," the beggar said, refusing them. "Why would a person who lives in such a great house want to see me?" he asked and begged them to set him free. Thoughts about the wealthy person in that huge house, whom he imagined as great and powerful as a king, made him dizzy, and he fainted to the ground. Not knowing what to do, the servants returned without him and reported what had happened to their master. Greatly distressed, the rich man felt an overwhelming sense of pity for his son, who had made his way back to the family home at last but was not even aware of it. His own father was crying out to him, but he was unable to respond. What could have brought about such a wretched state of affairs?

So that he would not lose contact with his son, the rich man had one of his servants dress in a beggar's filthy rags and make friends with him. When he felt the time was right, the servant said to him, "Well, brother, I have some work that I think might be right for you. It is not difficult, just a matter of dipping the night soil from the privy. When you finish your work, your time is your own and you can do as you like. You'll have a room, food, and clothing too. You'll even get a bit of pocket money. It's just the work for you. You don't want to go on like this without anywhere to live."

The son's interest was piqued by the servant's proposal and he accompanied him to the rich man's house. They slipped in through the back entrance, and the son was given a room to sleep in and proper clothes. His worries gradually faded, and he became a member of the rich man's household. He worked cleaning the privies for four or five years, becoming thoroughly familiar with his new surroundings. He was told, "You don't have to keep cleaning the privy. Why don't you do some work in the gardens as well? We'll give you a better room and increase your allowance." So he worked in the gardens for four or five more years. Then he was told, "We've been watching your work. You are an excellent young fellow. You shouldn't be wasting your talents in the garden. We want you to come into the house and take charge of the young boys and girls who work there. You can arrange the flower settings and change the artwork displays. You will be given better clothing too. And we'll double your allowance."

After working in the rich man's residence for five or six years, the young man was told, "You have become a member of our family. You are on familiar terms with the master. From now on, we would like you to serve as his assistant and attend to his personal needs." From then on, the young man never left the rich man's side, although he still had no inkling that the man he assisted was his father, that he was the heir to his great properties and untold wealth. However, as the rich man grew old and knew that his time on earth was nearing an end, he summoned his family, his ministers and friends, his officials and notaries, and informed them of his final testament.

"I can no longer conceal the fact that this young man who has served as my personal assistant is my own son and sole heir. When he was very young, he wandered away and for many years he lived a vagrant life, forgetting his birthright. But beyond any doubt whatever, he is my true son and legitimate heir. I have submitted evidence of various kinds in proof of this fact. Therefore, after I die, I want to bequeath this house and all my wealth to him."

In this way the young man learned for the first time that he was the rich man's son and would inherit his position and estate. It is difficult to conceive the hardships that the rich man endured in his efforts to bring his son back home.

17

OPEN YOUR EYES

WHEN SHAKYAMUNI attained enlightenment and became a buddha, he joyously exclaimed, "Living beings all possess the virtues of the Tathagata's wisdom!" In Hakuin's words, *All beings are from the first buddhas.* When Buddha uttered those words, the multitude who heard him were astounded. They all fled. "Unbelievable! We've never heard such a teaching! We, with our deep sins, are buddhas? With our malicious, prevaricating, avaricious, vain, egoistic hearts? Please, master, don't deceive us with flattering words. We are hopelessly ignorant and deluded. Please don't confuse our minds with such nonsense."

Just as the young beggar refused to return when the rich man's servants went to bring him back to the house, the host of men and women that heard the Buddha teach with great compassion could not become convinced of his truth. Imagine how sad it must have made him. After giving some thought to the matter, he adapted his teaching by contriving what is called expedient means (*upaya*). His wisdom gave rise to compassion, his compassion to expedient means.

So, addressing his followers with a grave demeanor, he said,

All of you are sinners of the first order; you are hopelessly buried in defilement. There is no doubt you are destined for hell. You must repent your sins and rid yourself of defilement. For your future happiness, you must perform benevolent deeds, and you can begin by giving to the poor. You must follow closely the advice I give you. If people ridicule or belittle you, bear it with patience. Alcohol is harmful, so you must no longer drink it.

"This is a teaching we can treasure," they replied. "We must cleanse ourselves of sins. We must amass good deeds in order to attain salvation in the future. We will give to the poor and needy. This will be the cause of our own happiness as well. And we must patiently persevere. Alcohol is a noxious drink, so we will abstain from it. What a comfort the Buddha's teaching is! Shakyamuni is indeed a savior for unenlightened people like us."

The young beggar secured a place in the world by dredging filth from privies. The Buddha's followers experienced peace of mind by cleansing themselves of sinful impurities.

After teaching these simple instructions for a number of years, Shakyamuni proceeded to contrive another expedient teaching:

You think you have a self, sins, a world, and morality. In other words, you believe that all of these exist. But you are mistaken. In this great universe, your self, your world, and your sins all arise through causes and conditions and perish through causes and conditions. All things in this world flow like water in a river or stream; nothing abides forever. All is emptiness. Your self, your world, your sins—they are all like dreams and illusions, foam, the haze rising from the heat. Everything is nonexistent. To realize this and live completely free of all attachments is human life's greatest fortune.

Again the members of the assembly were beside themselves with joy. They set about following the new instructions. "It is a truly invaluable teaching. Shakyamuni is indeed our great guide and teacher. All things arise in accordance with temporary causes and conditions and perish in the same way—how true are his words." All things are empty. There is nothing whatever to worry us or trouble our minds. All we have to do is realize that truth and our minds will be bright and clear." This is in no way different from the young beggar who was freed from his privy-cleaning chores and discovered happiness in the daily work of caring for a garden.

Several years later, Shakyamuni gave his assembly another expedient teaching:

Until now I have taught you about emptiness, but that does not fully clarify the true nature of things. Emptiness is form, form is emptiness. Being is nonbeing, and nonbeing is being. The realm in which being and emptiness are one is the middle way, the true reality. The reality of this middle way is the true and eternal way.

Hearing this made his followers even more jubilant than before. They followed Shakyamuni's instructions faithfully.

This is where things start to get interesting. Being is itself nonbeing; nonbeing is itself being; the middle way transcending them both is the proper path for followers of the Buddha Way. Shakyamuni is a person—"a teacher to the entire human race and to gods"—who realized enlightenment in a profound self-awakening. His buddha wisdom is like a vast and bottomless abyss, totally beyond our human understanding. This is like the poor fellow who on entering the rich man's house was led to discover enjoyment in refined pastimes such as arranging flowers and works of art. Shakyamuni guided his followers in this way for several decades, closely observing their minds until they matured to the point that they were able to grasp the genuine principle. Then, finally, he put all expediencies aside and revealed the true teaching to them:

> The time has now come for me to reveal the true teaching to you. Listen carefully, listen very carefully. The Tathagata will now teach you the plain and unadorned truth. All buddhas who have appeared in this world have done so to make living beings open the buddha-eye—to re-

veal the buddha-eye to them, to awaken the buddha-eye in them, to have them embark on a life in which the buddha-eye fully opens. Open the buddha-eye. If only you can accomplish that, this world just as it is will become a land of bliss, and all of you will become buddhas, just exactly as you are.

Hearing this, the Buddha's followers became convinced that they could become buddhas. But however much they believed this in theory, in actual practice they found it extremely difficult to attain true self-awakening. This is just like the young man spending his days managing the rich man's wealth and property, completely unaware they were his own but finally coming to know, in continuing to live and work in proximity with him, that the rich man was his true father.

What untold difficulties the World-Honored One experienced as he strove to guide beings to liberation. The parable of the rich man's son, which he used to instruct his followers, expressing the noble hardship the rich man suffered in trying to induce a son who had sunk to the level of a beggar to accept his birthright and return home as his heir, is a story that must have brought tears of profound gratitude to their eyes.

18

"IT'S A BAD OMEN"

THE JAPANESE WORD *innen,* meaning causes and conditions, is originally a Buddhist term, expressing one of Buddhism's most important philosophical concepts—that of *engi,* dependent origination, the interdependence of all things in the universe. This principle has entered deeply into Japanese life. We use it today it in a number of ways in our colloquial speech, in the sense, for example, of "destiny" or "fate," appearing in phrases such as "You should accept this as your destiny" or "The fate of the parents is visited on the child." Wedding speeches often refer to bridegroom and bride "brought together today, uniting their two families through a propitious destiny." Another common phrase is *engi ga warui,* meaning "it is a bad omen, a sign that something bad is likely to happen in the future." Shakyamuni, however, was moved to declare, "I became a buddha and attained satori on realizing the teaching of dependent origination," so for him, both innen and engi were among the most fundamental principles of Buddhism.

Shakyamuni's follower Shariputra, said to be first in wisdom among the ten major disciples, was originally the teacher of a heretical sect. He had 250 disciples. One day when Shariputra was visiting the Venuvana bamboo grove near the city of Rajagriha, he happened to encounter a solitary ascetic whose face shone with a transcendent joy and tranquility. The ascetic was perfectly composed and self-possessed, moving with a casual, unhurried grace and dressed in clean but extremely poor garments; and he walked gazing quietly down at the ground. Deeply impressed, Shariputra went up to him and asked,

"What kind of practice do you engage in?"

"I am a disciple of Shakyamuni," he replied.

"Shakyamuni? I haven't heard that name before. What does he teach?"

"Shakyamuni was a prince of the kingdom of Kapila," the ascetic answered. "Last year he achieved enlightenment and attained buddhahood. He now resides in the monastery at Venuvana, and he always preaches the doctrine of dependent origination. I took his words as a koan: 'Things arise according to conditions, and they perish according to conditions as well; all things are empty, they have no being,' and was able to achieve enlightenment."

Shariputra was astonished. He thought he had mastered all the known teachings. He had studied all the writings he could lay his hands on. Yet this was the first time he had heard the words *dependent origination*. Likewise totally unknown to him were the teachings, "Things arise according to conditions, and they perish according to conditions as well; all things are empty, they have no being," but he thought they were splendid. He and his friend and colleague Maudgalyāyana mulled things over and decided to take their followers (each had 250 disciples) to join Shakyamuni's assembly, which, now in its second year, had grown to over five hundred.

The religions in Shakyamuni's lifetime taught that we are created by a god or gods and governed by their command, and this is taught today as well. But the principle that the world and its beings are neither created or governed by a god or gods nor as a result of natural or random forces but are born and perish according to causes and conditions, had never been heard until Shakyamuni taught it. It is a principle that is not found elsewhere, except, I believe, in modern science.

If god created the world, the world must have had a beginning. However, I think there will probably never be an end to this world. But it is unreasonable to say that the world has a beginning but has no end. If there is no end, there must be no beginning either. In other words, the world has neither beginning nor end, but continues arising endlessly through causes and conditions, through cause and effect.

In the Japanese word *innen*, literally "causes and conditions," "cause" refers to a direct cause, and "conditions" to indirect or secondary causes that foster or develop the direct cause. All things arise and perish through the combining of a direct cause with indirect causes. Here is a grain of rice—a direct cause.

With the addition of soil, water, sunlight, heat, and other indirect causes, the grain germinates and becomes a seedling, a rice plant, and in autumn when it ripens, a grain of rice.

The world itself operates in this same way, coming into being according to dependent origination, causes and conditions. It exists for a period of time and then perishes into nothingness. This is repeated over and over from the beginningless past on into the infinite future. That is, it was born, it will continue to exist for so many billions of years, and then finally it will be destroyed and return to nothingness once again. The word *nothingness* may be understood as meaning something like what modern science calls a nebulous state. This process, repeated over and over and over, is what Buddhists call transmigration, *rinne* in Japanese. It is often compared to a six-spoked turning wheel, with each of the six spokes standing for one of the six destinations or realms of the world of illusion.

When Japanese want to castigate someone with particularly abusive language, they may use *gokudo-me! Konchikushō!* Or *kono gaki!* In literal translation these terms refer to a "hell dweller," a "beast," and a "hungry ghost," the inhabitants of the three most unfortunate destinations into which beings transmigrating through the six ways of existence (*rokudo*) are reborn.

Lying above these three is the realm of the *asuras*, which is characterized by continual contention and strife. Above that is the realm of human beings, in which it is possible to feel shame and engage in self-reflection (shame and self-reflection being what eventually lead us to the realm of Buddha). Above the human realm is the realm of *devas*, or heavenly beings, who lead existences of continual pleasure, knowing no suffering or pain whatever, though because of that, it is also a realm in which no self-reflection takes place. Living beings move endlessly through these six realms of rebirth—devas, humans, fighting spirits, beasts, hungry ghosts, and hell.

19

UNDERSTANDING
HOW A CAT FEELS

Dr. Daisetz Suzuki has recently returned from teaching and lecturing in America. A few days ago, for the first time in over a year, I had the opportunity of meeting and talking with him. During his stay in America, he told me, he was most frequently asked about the concept of transmigration. "Does Buddhism really teach the ridiculous notion that when a human being dies, they are reincarnated as a cow or horse, or a dog or cat?" He said that his usual response was something like this: "I don't know about the future, but in the past I think I have been a horse, a cow, and various other beings as well. I'm fond of cats; for many years now I have kept them as pets. I can understand quite well the feeling of a cat when it is mousing. A mother cat often flicks her tail to keep a kitten under control, and I understand her feeling when she does that. Maybe this indicates that I can discern the cat's feelings because I was born as a cat in a previous existence. For that matter, I understand the feelings of dogs, horses, dragonflies and butterflies, plants and flowers as well, so perhaps I have been born as many other things."

The idea that we are born and die over and over, which first appeared in India over three thousand years ago, has today become a subject of psychic research. Although reincarnation is perhaps a legitimate subject of scientific investigation, it does not seem to me to have much to do with religion. Religion is a matter of truly understanding our own self and freeing ourselves of illusion in this world and the next.

The six realms or ways through which Buddhism says beings transmigrate may be conceived as spiritual realms lying in the future, also as stopovers on a journey of cosmic evolution. They could be understood as six progressive steps taken in our normal daily life, and also, most obviously, as the content of that life. At times in our daily life we may become hopelessly angry. At times we may feel prompted to stand up and challenge someone about some matter or other. When these emotions arise, we fall into the realm of the asura, or fighting spirit. At other times, blind passion flares instinctively in our heart, making us act in ways that later cause us shame and regret at having been seen in such behavior. At such times we descend into the realm of primal ignorance or perhaps the realm of beasts, two other unfortunate destinations in the six paths.

There may also be times when we are tormented by a fervent desire that makes us thirst for something that is beyond obtaining, or we crave avidly for something that would not satisfy us even if we were to gain it. When that happens, we descend into the path of the hungry ghosts, or *preta*. On quietly mulling our conduct later, we may be tormented with remorse: "I'm afraid I went too far this time." We may continue to worry ourselves in this way until we lose our appetite and are unable to sleep. To me this suggests we have fallen into the one of the realms of hell.

Immediately after this, we might go around blithely humming a popular tune completely oblivious of our difficulties and discontent with secular life. Now life is pleasant and agreeable; we are able to enjoy works of literature and art. This resembles the lives of unbroken enjoyment led by the heavenly beings in the deva realms.

Finally, there is the realm of human beings in which we now exist. I believe that the distinguishing characteristic of the human realm is our ability to feel shame. Human beings have a mind that can reflect on itself. It is only from this self-reflection that the precious Bodhi-mind can emerge. The most desirable rebirth in all these six paths is thus the realm of human beings. That is the reason Buddhism is so emphatic about the value of human re-birth—"A human body is extremely difficult to receive, and I have now received it!"

Our actual life, which we live day by day, is thus moving through the six transmigratory paths or realms. The workings of the society in which we animate these tendencies are also a manifestation of the six realms. In any event, all of it is, in the end, no more than a realm of delusion. Thus Hakuin writes,

The causes of rebirth in the six ways
Arise in the dark paths of ignorance.

The dark paths of ignorance (guchi no yamaji) describes a blind and benighted existence that is unexamined and void of reason.

But when did these dark and mournful ways of karmic transmigration begin? What is the cause of our delusion? Christianity teaches that it began when our common ancestors Adam and Eve ate the forbidden fruit. Buddhism holds that it results from our primal ignorance *(avidya)*—that is, a basic lack of self-awareness with regard to existence. And it explains the true reality of all forms of existence, beginning in this lack of awareness and ending in the sufferings of birth, old age, and death, through the principle of the twelve links of causation (Skt. *nidana*).

The Twelve Causations were an important doctrine in early Buddhism. *Pratyeka* or "private" buddhas were said to achieve enlightenment simply by perceiving clearly the truth of the Twelve Causations. Here is a list of the Twelve Causations, the links of cause and effect that elucidate the origins of the condition of birth-and-death to which all living beings are subject. My comments appear in italics and parentheses:

1. Ignorance *(from ignorance of spirit, primal ignorance)*
2. Action or volition *(blind activity arises)*
3. Consciousness *(individuality comes into existence upon conception in the womb)*
4. Names and forms *(in the womb psyche and body)*

5. Six enterings *(form eyes, ears, nose, tongue, tactile body, and mind)*
6. Sensations *(developing from birth, they contact and experience the external world)*
7. Desire for pleasure *(receive outside influences of every kind)*
8. Egoistic desire *(learn to attach to external objects)*
9. Grasping *(grasp and attach to them)*
10. Existence *(learn a sense of possession)*
11. Birth *(cause awareness of existence)*
12. Old age and death *(end in cessation of existence)*

Ignorance and volition are *causes* arising from the past. Consciousness, names and forms, and all the rest, up to and including old age and death, produce the *effect* of one's present suffering. The twelve links of causation or cause and effect thus chart the journey of human life, beginning with causes in fundamental ignorance, then birth into the world, and finally the suffering experienced as we grow old and die.

20

HAPPIER THAN
THE MOON

SOME YEARS BACK, when Queen Elizabeth was still a royal princess, she is said to have whispered to a friend. "I am happier than the moon." Bright, heartwarming words, worthy of a royal princess and perfectly in character. Born with grace and elegance, Elizabeth grew to womanhood without experiencing a single want whatever, took as her husband one of the world's most eligible bachelors, and succeeded to the throne and wealth of the great British Empire, wearing exquisite clothes and precious jewels of her choice, eating sumptuous food, and engaging in splendid pastimes. Yes, the words "I am happier than the moon" seem quite well suited to the English queen.

Even so, I think that the youthful Shakyamuni could have said that he was "happier than the sun." He was born the crown prince of an Indian kingdom, possessed rank and riches of the highest order, excelled in all things, was conversant with the

highest knowledge of his time, and proved unmatched in ath-
letic prowess. He married the surpassingly beautiful Yasodhara,
who bore him a fine young son. At separate palaces for each of
the four seasons, he enjoyed at his pleasure amusements and di-
versions of every kind.

Now what does a human being seek who has already attained
a life that caters to all his desires? We ordinary mortals, pressed
by the exigencies of everyday life, never have everything we need.
We do not even have time to consider such fancies. But if we
did have a life that was lacking in nothing whatever, what would
we hope for or desire? Perhaps we would desire not to grow
old, to avoid death, or to live forever. The question of how long
this present happiness will last would probably worry us day and
night.

Come to think of it, each and every one of us is like an in-
mate on death row, not knowing when the death sentence will
be carried out. When faced with the abyss of death, what help
will the pleasures of our dreamlike, dew-like human life end up
being?

If material wealth alone thwarted human suffering, Shakyamuni would no doubt have used his great wealth unstintingly to
that end. However, his problem could not be resolved through
such means. No matter what he might have come up with, it
would have been no use whatever in producing a life for human
beings that transcends birth-and-death.

This seems to me to show that Shakyamuni was a bit wiser
than Princess Elizabeth. In order to obtain happiness greater

than the sun itself, Shakyamuni ended up casting everything aside like a worn-out sandal and entering the mountains. What he earnestly sought there was freedom from the suffering of old age and death. Like the arhats who would come after him, Shakyamuni sat down and meditated in the shade of the Bodhi tree and contemplated the principle of the twelve links of causation.

I think he quietly contemplated the twelve causes over and over: Where does the suffering of old age and death come from? It comes from the self-awakening of life. Where does the self-awakening of life come from? From a sense of possession. Where does the sense of possession come from? From acquiring something. Where does acquiring come from? From desiring something. Why do we desire something? Because we see it. Why did we see it? Because we have perception. Why do we have perception? Because we are furnished with six sense organs. Why are we furnished with six sense organs? They are conferred in our mother's womb. Why were we in our mother's womb? Because our mother conceived us. Why were we conceived? Through the actions of our father and mother. Why did our parents engage in these activities? Through unconscious or unknowing instinct.

Continuing to contemplate deeply the twelve causes in this way, the fundamental source of the suffering of old age and death is seen to be our unawakened instinct, primal ignorance. Therefore it is this unconscious, unknowing instinct or primal ignorance that is the root source of karmic transmigration. This unawakened state gives rise to further unawakening, setting in motion cycle after cycle of ignorance, volition, consciousness, names and forms, the six enterings, sensations, the desire for pleasure, grasping, taking and holding, being or existence, birth, old age and death—repeated over and over as we wander endlessly the darkness of the six paths. Hakuin's *Song of Zazen* expresses this as:

> *The causes of rebirth in the six ways*
> *Arise in the dark paths of ignorance:*
> *Leaving one darkness, you enter the next,*
> *Never breaking free of birth-and-death.*

We human beings are destined to pass from one unawakened state to the next as we continue our journey transmigrating endlessly through the six paths. Is there no way we can gain salvation? No way to free ourselves from this unawakened state?

Pratyekabuddhas, the sages of Hinayana Buddhism, renounce sexual passion and enter the mountains to engage in difficult ascetic practices, subsisting on a single grain of rice each day. Overcoming ignorance and the afflicting passions, they enter a state of self-realization and discover a realm of true freedom where ignorance and passions can never trouble them again.

But is it possible for us to practice such difficult austerities? Rather, is there any real need for us to practice them? Is the human instinct that evil? Have we not multiplied, continued to exist, and created and maintained cultures throughout the world thanks to our human instinct?

Is there no path that will allow us to attain salvation while remaining in society, having a family, working at a job; no means of self-realization without entering the mountains, engaging in ascetic practice, and turning our back on society? Is there no way to achieve self-awakening with our worldly passions remaining as they are? The Buddha's Dharma cannot be something of benefit to only a small group of people possessed of special gifts or talents. The path that fulfills all the essential requirements in the questions posed above is the Mahayana, or Great Vehicle.

21

A BICYCLE IS THE
GREAT VEHICLE

IN CONSIDERING Mahayana Buddhism, I turn to the *Lotus Sutra* once again, a story from the "Parables" chapter.

There was once a rich man of a certain country who lived in a large, rambling old house so spacious and filled with so many halls and rooms that it was difficult to look after them all. Neglected, decaying old storage rooms became the lairs of raccoons and badgers and scorpions. One day, a fire of unknown cause broke out in the house. The rich man, greatly alarmed, dashed outside. He immediately remembered that his sons were still inside the house and ran back inside, where he found them engrossed in their games, quite unaware of the conflagration around them. The rich man ordered his sons to leave, but the young children had no understanding of fire and were so utterly engrossed in their games that they showed no interest in heeding their father. The rich man could have picked two or three of them up in his arms and carried them outside, but he had so many children that it would not be possible for him to save them all.

Thereupon the rich man devised the following expedient means (*upaya*). He told his sons, "Why don't you go outside? You'll find the kind of playthings you like—goat-carts, deer-carts, and oxcarts—outside the gate. Go and play with them." Children like things they can ride on. If you ask them, "What kind of present do you want me to bring you?" most boys will ask for toy cars or trains or airplanes. In the past, when you asked a young boy what he wanted to become, he would likely tell you he wanted to be a general. But these days a boy will more often reply that he wants to be a bus driver. In any case, young boys seem partial to vehicles of one kind or other.

Hearing the rich man's promise of carts, his sons dashed out of the burning house in the nick of time and were saved from death. The rich man had lied about the goat-carts and deer-carts and oxcarts, so they found no carts waiting for them outside the gate. It was a blameless lie, having saved their lives. Moreover, instead of giving them a goat-cart, deer-cart, or oxcart, their father presented them with a great white oxcart splendidly adorned with precious gems.

In this story, which is known as the parable of the burning house, the rich man is Shakyamuni, the children are living beings, and the burning house is our impermanent world. Living beings are children, cherished by the Buddha, so absorbed in their pleasures and divertissements they make no attempt to free themselves from the burning house, the impermanence of this world. Hence the Buddha employed expedient means in preaching to the three kinds of disciples in his assembly: sravakas, pratyekabuddhas, and bodhisattvas. Each group gladly received his teachings, practiced in accordance with them, and succeeded in escaping the sufferings of the burning house, the threefold world of unenlightened beings.*

This teaching alone would have brought ample happiness to his hearers. But in his final teaching at the meeting of the *Lotus Sutra*, Shakyamuni set forth the true and genuine path itself, dispensing with all expedient means. Even without engaging in ascetic practices, he taught, if we can simply open the eye of the mind, we will all become buddhas. He preached the wonderful teaching that if we attain buddha-wisdom and open the buddha-eye, seeing everything with that eye, then even without severing ourselves from ignorance, our evil passions just as they are, we become buddhas. We call this precious instruction the teaching of the one supreme vehicle—the Mahayana, or Great Vehicle.

Shakyamuni compared followers of the three vehicles—sravakas, pratyekabuddhas, and bodhisattvas—to a goat-cart, a deer-cart, and an oxcart, respectively; and the Mahayana teaching to a

---

*The threefold world is subdivided into the world of desire, whose inhabitants have appetites and desires; the world of form, whose inhabitants have neither appetites nor desires; and the world of formlessness, whose inhabitants have no physical form.

great white oxcart. Even today, people in India regard a white cow as the most hallowed of living beings. Just last year the Indian government presented the ancient Buddhist temple Zenkō-ji in Nagano prefecture with two white oxen as an expression of the Indian people's deep affection for Japan as a Buddhist country.

The "Great White Oxcart," the Mahayana, is a splendid vehicle of unsurpassed excellence pulled by a large, immaculately white ox, but that does not in any way suggest a vehicle of great size able to transport large groups of people. As one of the ancient teachers wrote, "The Mahayana is the vehicle for buddhas and great men." Just after the Pacific War ended, when I was still residing at Tenryū-ji on the western outskirts of Kyoto, representatives from a bicycle company in the city of Sakai in Izumi Province came to the monastery and asked me to give them a talk. The transport union in Kyoto happened to be on strike at the time, bringing the streetcars to a halt, so I talked about that.

The Mahayana school uses the terms *Mahayana* (Great Vehicle) and *Hinayana* (Small Vehicle). Some compare the Mahayana to a train that can transport large numbers of people, and the Hinayana to a bicycle, which you must ride alone. But during a railway strike, nothing is less practical than a great vehicle of this kind, while those who have bicycles are unaffected and are able to proceed to work or school at their convenience.

Buddhism does not teach idleness or indolence. It isn't

premised on any notion that you can enjoy yourself as you please because eventually someone will come along and save you. Even Shinran, who advocated rebirth in the Pure Land through the other-power, wrote, "When the thought to say the Nembutsu arises within you in the belief that you will be born in the Pure Land through the inconceivable power of Amida's vow, at that very moment the blessing of being taken under Amida's protection and never again abandoned is secured." The moment the mind gives rise to the thought to say the Nembutsu, you are saved. But the thought must arise in you; so long as it does not, you will not be saved.

So the cart of the Great Vehicle, or Mahayana, is not a conveyance like a train or trolley that large groups of people board with great noise and commotion, relying on others to take them to their destination. Rather, we should think of it as a bicycle of splendid faith. Each person receives it individually, and each person takes hold of the handles and peddles forward on their own, and moreover they do so in congenial and harmonious association with everyone else who rides their own bicycle. In other words, the Mahayana creates a host of bicycles and tries to get them to as many people as possible so that everyone can mount and ride the vehicle themselves.

The people from the bicycle company seemed quite pleased with these remarks and left behind a substantial donation to the temple.

The Great Vehicle does not teach us that we are saved by doing away with ignorance and freeing ourselves from birth-and-death. The Great Vehicle teaches us that we can lead a free and vigorous life in the midst of birth-and-death, our ignorance remaining just as it is, and yet be untroubled by ignorance and birth-and-death.

22

A LAND MOST SUITED
TO THE MAHAYANA

THE PAPER CURRENCY in use today in Japan, both one-hundred-yen and one-thousand-yen notes, bears the image of Prince Shōtoku, the celebrated crown prince and regent of seventh-century Japan. The one-hundred-yen note has the image of Prince Shōtoku and the octagonal Yumedono Hall of Hōryū-ji on the back and a full view of Hōryūji on the front. The one-thousand-yen note has the prince on the front and Yumedono Hall on the back. I do not know why the Bank of Japan decided to use Prince Shōtoku's image, but to me the fact that they did is deeply significant, and gratifying as well. Of course, the value of Japanese currency has now decreased quite a bit. In the old days you could get considerable use out of a thousand-yen note. Now a Prince Shōtoku doesn't go nearly so far.

All Japanese carpenters used to belong to the *Taishi-kō*, or

Prince's Guild, and have revered Prince Shōtoku through the centuries as their patron saint. This is altogether fitting in view of the fact that the prince founded Hōryūji, which has the oldest extant wooden buildings in the world. The old Kawaraya-ji at Yōkaichi in Shiga prefecture, long affiliated with the Myōshin-ji branch of Rinzai Zen, is the site of the kilns that produced the first roof tiles in Japan. According to tradition, Prince Shōtoku had these tiles transported by boat to the Yamato and Namba regions to be used for temples and other construction projects he was engaged in around the capital.

Prince Shōtoku is credited with having carved the oldest Japanese sculpture, an image of Yakushi Nyorai, "the Healing Buddha," done for his father, Emperor Yōmei, when the latter had fallen ill. The oldest surviving Japanese painting, until it was destroyed by fire last year, lamented by people around the world, was a fresco on the wall of the Hōryūji that Prince Shōtoku founded. He is said to have also written the oldest Japanese historical work, no longer extant, as well as the oldest written text, the *Sangyō Gisho* (*Annotated Commentaries on the Three Sutras*), the holograph manuscript of which is still preserved.

In view of this, it does not seem an overstatement to say that virtually everything related to early Japanese culture—politics, literature and religion, astronomy and geography, history, even the balance scale and measuring rod—originates with Prince Shōtoku. Historical researchers, using modern scientific principles, are said to have debunked many of the statements found in the early Japanese records, but I believe that these accounts, dating from Prince Shōtoku's time, are not really at great variance with historical fact.

Indeed, it would not be an exaggeration at all to call Prince Shōtoku the creator of Japanese culture. Today, at a time when Japanese are raising a great hue and cry about their culture and the need to establish themselves as a peace-loving nation, Prince Shōtoku is the historical figure above all others to whom they should look. It is altogether just and fitting that he has been revered from ancient times as a *shōnin*, or "saint," spoken of as the Shakyamuni Buddha of our country. He established and spread the Buddhist teachings in Japan in the belief that they were the most desirable foundation for the nation. The Japanese people have long revered his words, "Japan is a land most suited to the Mahayana."

From among the more than 5,040 scrolls in the Buddhist canon, Prince Shōtoku selected three sutras—the *Lotus, Vimalakirti,* and *Srimala*—and lectured on them before Empress Suiko. He added his annotations and commentary to these sutras, and the handwritten text of his *Sangyō Gisho (Annotated Commentaries on the Three Sutras),* as the work is known, is preserved today in the Imperial Household Collection. In considering his choice of these three works from the entire canon, we can only marvel at Prince Shōtoku's exceptionally deep knowledge and perceptive grasp in evaluating the doctrinal aspects of the sutras.

The *Lotus Sutra*—said to be the crowning achievement of the Mahayana—the *Vimalakirti Sutra*—containing the teachings of the celebrated lay teacher Vimalakirti—and the *Srimala Sutra*—

preached by the Indian queen Srimala—all affirm the actualities of daily life, in line with the Mahayana teaching that all things are aspects of ultimate truth (*shohō jissō*). The *Lotus* preaches that benefiting society by working and producing things is not at all contrary to the Dharma teachings—rather that it is, as such, a religious life. It is the Mahayana that offers salvation to laypeople with families, working at jobs or trades with their afflicting passions just as they are.

The heads of the Mahayana bodhisattvas are not tonsured. Kannon, Fugen, Monju, and Seishi are all depicted with good growths of hair. For some bodhisattvas, the hair is shown hanging down; for others, it is dressed in a topknot; and for yet others, it is a stylish coiffure resembling a permanent wave. They wear necklaces, bracelets, and other forms of jewelry. Although not ladies or matrons, some are seen with diaphanous veils over their heads. All of them exemplify the layperson, a Buddhist who has not been fully ordained as monk or nun.

Layman Vimalakirti preaches in the *Vimalakirti Sutra*, "Not abandoning the principles of the Way and yet revealing yourself in the activities of a common unenlightened person—this is what is meant by quiet sitting." The Mahayana bodhisattva puts the Buddha Dharma into practice as a member of the laity. Prince Shōtoku did not enter the priesthood, although he believed in and deeply worshipped the Three Treasures of Buddha, Dharma, and Sangha. He remained a layman throughout his life, but when lecturing on the sutras he wore a Buddhist surplice over his ordinary clothes and did not in any sense abandon his quest for the Way. For him, the work of governing the country was itself the Buddha Dharma, the Buddha Dharma was the governing of the country. No doubt it was his example from which the concept of "the emperor's law is the Buddha's law" emerged.

Jizō is the only bodhisattva who appears in the guise of a Buddhist monk. Having vowed at the outset of his career to liberate all who have fallen into the seas of karmic suffering, Jizō enters into all six realms of transmigration to bring salvation to the living beings there. Could it be that he could not save the unenlightened trapped by their grievous sins and raging passions in the three evil destinations as a bodhisattva decked out with jewels and sporting a fancy coiffure; that he had to take the form of a priest, one who has renounced the world and overcome desires and evil passions? Even though living beings saddled with afflicting passions can understand the truth of the Mahayana teaching, they may still yearn for the example of the pure life of the renunciant who has left worldly desires behind. Herein, I believe, lies the reason why the Shin sect founder Shinran could not fully renounce the state or condition of priestly life even as he lived as a layman.

If you seek to learn Mahayana Buddhism's basic principle — salvation as a layperson with evil passions intact — I think you will find it summed up in the two Chinese characters that make up the word zenjō, "samadhi" or "meditative concentration." The Sixth Patriarch explained the characters in this way: "Zen is being free of forms externally, jō is being undisturbed within." In fact, zenjō and zenjō alone opens the Dharma eye that sees and affirms all things as true forms of reality. The freedom implicit in these two characters is the source of the high degree of cultural life that human beings have attained; we can regard all the various forms of Japanese culture and the traditional arts or Ways as being based on the truths that derive from them. That is why Hakuin says,

How great the dhyana of the Mahayana,
No praise could ever exhaust its merits!

23

THE SECRET ART OF
TURNING IRON TO GOLD

W HEN I TURNED FOURTEEN, my elder brother took
me to Tokyo to continue my education. My father
wanted me to study law, and as a young man I shared that ambition. However, in my second or third year in middle school I
began mulling over human life and the various problems it gave
rise to. I remember in particular some words of Confucius I
came upon while reading the *Analects*: "In hearing lawsuits, I'm
no different from other people. But what we need is for no lawsuits to exist!" This shook my aspiration for a career in law. No
doubt, I could hear lawsuits and make correct decisions as well
as anybody, but now I wanted and deeply hoped for what Confucius spoke of—the kind of peaceful society in which there
was no need for such things as lawsuits.

Using that same line of reasoning, I felt that if I became a
physician, I could help the sick as well as anyone, but what I

really desired was a world without sick people. I was confident I could hold my own as a soldier on the battlefield, but what I really wanted was a world without war. I could become a businessman and make money like other young men, but my real aim was a world without poverty. Graduating from middle school, I watched my friends setting out to achieve such aims by continuing their diligent study. I, however, no longer knew what to do with my life. Several of my closest friends went on to the first higher school, present-day Tokyo University. I envied those promising young students in their characteristic white-striped caps. It wasn't their entering the university I envied but their strength of purpose, their mental fortitude that enabled them to go forward with their lives without harboring any doubts.

It was from that time that my religious quest began. While constantly seeking to discover what I should do with my life, I wandered around Tokyo, at times stoutheartedly, at other times more like a stray dog that had lost its home. I made my way to various religious institutions, the Seinen Kaikan (YMCA) in Kanda, the Fujimizaka Christian Church, Buddhist groups like those at the Chūō Bukkyō Kaikan, and the Shin sect's Gudō Kaikan in Hongō. I studied at Rinshō-in, a Rinzai temple in Yushima. I even visited the Shinsei Kyōkan, a new church established by the "prophet" Miyazaki Toranosuke.

At the time, the priest Kawaguchi Eka had returned from Tibet and was lecturing on Shantideva's *Bodhicaryāvatāra* (*Way of the*

Bodhisattva) in Hongō in Tokyo. In this work, which Ekai had translated from the Tibetan, I read,

> If you covered the entire world in cowhide, people could walk everywhere barefoot. It is not possible to do that, but if you put seven inches of cowhide on your feet, it will be the same as covering the whole world in cowhide. To make the entire world the ideal place you want it to be is probably not possible, but if you arouse the mind of Bodhi—if you vow to offer all you have for the sake of humankind, putting on the shoes of patience and perseverance—the whole world will immediately become an ideal world answering to your desires. Once the ordinary unenlightened person gives rise to the Bodhi-mind and devotes himself to helping all beings, he becomes a buddha. Discovering a means of turning iron into gold would be a truly miraculous feat, but it is an even greater miracle for an unenlightened person to become a buddha.

Reading these sacred words over and over with deep emotion, I concluded that the arising of the Bodhi-mind that is pledged to the salvation of living beings is the most precious thing in human life. I determined that the matter of paramount importance in my own life was to become a disciple of Buddha, and I entered the priesthood. Since then, thirty years have passed, so long ago now that it seems like a dream.

My Zen teacher, Seki Seisetsu Rōshi of Tenryū-ji, often said to me,

> Everyone who takes the tonsure and hangs a surplice over his shoulders gives himself to the Buddha—it's as though he wrapped himself up as a gift package, decked himself out with a strip of dried abalone (*noshi*) and twisted red cord (*mizuhiki*). His body is no longer his own, it has been given to the Buddha. So he must not treat it carelessly and allow himself to get sick or catch cold!*

Seisetsu Rōshi, though expressing himself in an unusual way, was indicating a life in which a person dedicates everything to Buddha. Whether you are a layperson or a cleric, to lead such a life, arousing the mind of Bodhi and dedicating everything— body and mind and belongings—to Buddha and all living beings, is the path of the Mahayana bodhisattva.

It is also a life that is sustained by donations from others. Today we speak of this as *o-fuse*, "donations," which a person, the donor, enfolds in white paper and gives to a temple priest. But the original meaning of *o-fuse* is not so narrow. All giving or donating is o-fuse, and there is both monetary giving and Dharma giving. Bodhisattva clerics, who are not engaged in business or industry, engage in religious practice and donate the Dharma

---

* Gifts decorated with strips of dried abalone and narrow slips of colored paper are presented at various congratulatory events.

thus attained. Lay bodhisattvas who run a business or industrial operation donate the wealth they earn.

Buddha put the greatest emphasis on the spirit of giving in his preaching to the early Buddhist community, and it became an important doctrine and essential component of the Mahayana thought that evolved in later times. I, too, want to do what I can to emphasize this spirit of giving. Human beings have eyes so they can see others. So I think it would be a good idea to lead our human life thinking solely of how to be of service to others. Some might argue that to think only of others will make it difficult for us to make our own way in the world, but that is not so. Although our two eyes allow us to do little more than survey the world, in society at large there are a thousand, ten thousand eyes observing us. Do you think they will just stand by and abandon bodhisattvas who are dedicating their lives solely to society?

It might be argued that Buddhism abandons our basic rights as human beings. Yes, I believe that it true. Buddhism abandons all things, including all human rights. However, the world is a strange place. The further you go in abandoning your individual rights, the more generous will society be in granting you the most generous human rights and respecting them. It is nothing less than a miracle. One of my friends from middle school days paid me a visit and said, "You are the most successful person in our class." Even assuming his words were true, that I was what people call "most successful," what a contradiction to describe me this way—someone whose deep doubts about the principle of social success and rising in the world had led him to throw everything aside and enter the priesthood. Here I was doing everything I could to cast all things aside, to give them up, while society was doing its level best to keep on giving to me!

24

THE WEEK OF THE
HIGAN FESTIVAL

Weeklong Higan (Other Shore) festivals during which Buddhist services are performed are held twice yearly, at the spring and autumn equinoxes. The term *haramitta* that appears in the following essay in connection with the *Heart Sutra* is the Japanese transliteration of the Sanskrit *paramita*, other shore.

A N ELDERLY LADY from my native place in Aichi prefecture came and asked me, "Oshō San, what does *haramitta* mean?"

"*Haramitta* means 'reach the other shore,'" I replied. "You sure ask difficult questions."

"Well, there you are," she said. "I had thought that the words in the *Heart Sutra, issai kuyaku . . . haramitta,* referred to full bellies (*haramitta*), that it was my job (*yaku*) to get the priests to eat (*ku*) everything (*issai*) I put on their food trays."

This is not dialogue from a comedy routine. The lady in question spoke those words in earnest. It is an example of the very limited level of understanding that good men and women of deep faith have about Buddhism today. Should we be satisfied with this? Is Buddhism that difficult to comprehend? Is it all right for people to be ignorant of it because it is too difficult? Perhaps we should try to recast the teachings so as to make them easier to understand. In any case, we cannot overlook the fact that we Buddhist teachers have been remiss in our duty to educate the general public. The continued failure to address this problem, which dates back to the beginning of the Meiji period, appears to have left a large blank in the Buddhist world, one that will no doubt grow even worse in the future.

The Sanskrit word *paramita* has traditionally been translated as "reach the other shore" or "go across to the yonder shore." In a country like Japan, whose biggest rivers are of only moderate size, going to the other shore is usually no great matter, there being little real difference between the other shore and this shore. But in countries with great rivers like India and China, it is easier to see how the yonder shore might become an object of longing.

Twice I have been laughed at by the Yangtze River. Once on accompanying Seisetsu Rōshi on a trip to China during the war, we took a plane from Peking to Shanghai. The trip took about seven hours, with a brief stopover at Nanking. The Rōshi was always chaffing me for dozing off, and I remember falling sound asleep on the plane as well. "*Oi! oi!*" the Rōshi called out, wakening me. "Look! It's the Yangtze River." Rubbing my eyes, I stared down from the window at a large river, although there was no way for me to tell if it was the Yangtze or not. It didn't look much larger than the Yodo River back in Japan. "It looks small, doesn't it?" I said. "Blockhead!" barked the Rōshi with a laugh.

On our return to Shanghai, we boarded a boat for Nagasaki. We set out from the wharf and before long were heaving in a strong, muddy flow, the shoreline having disappeared. "Rōshi, are we in the Yellow Sea now?" I asked. "Blockhead!" he barked, laughing again. We hadn't left the Yangtze; we were in the tributary Huang-pu River. So the Yangtze River made me the butt of two bursts of laughter. It seemed so wide and vast, over thirty miles from one bank to the other. I found it very plausible that the Yangtze's yonder shore could become the object of longing.

There was nothing on this shore but ceaseless war all year long, but if you crossed to the other shore, perhaps you would find it was sheltered from such conflict. People on this shore engaged in horrendous acts of robbery, murder, swindling. But on crossing to the other shore, you might find a place where everyone was a good citizen. Here starvation, sickness, poverty, and suffering were the rule; over there, a land of happiness and good fortune may be waiting. The other shore is an ideal world, a place we yearn for.

There is a village at the southern tip of Wakayama prefecture that has come to be known as Amerika-mura, "American Village," because so many of its inhabitants had left to live overseas since the Meiji period. Villagers who gazed out from their earliest years over the endlessly billowing waves of the vast Pacific were probably filled with endless yearning for the other shore of America and Canada. Upon growing up, I don't suppose they gave much thought to the nearby cities of Osaka or Kyoto; instead, they went overseas. The other shore is an ideal country, the Pure Land, a paradise, nirvana.

From early times, Buddhist Higan ceremonies have been performed in Japan during weeklong festivals twice yearly, at the spring and autumn equinoxes. As suggested by the popular saying "The summer heat and winter cold last until Higan," the two Higan weeks in the spring and autumn both fall at a time when the weather is at its best: neither too hot nor too cold, days and nights exactly the same length, the sun rising due east and setting due west—a time when all things have attained to the moderation of the Middle Way. Two weeks enjoying the most moderate weather of the entire year, a time when everyone tries to make this world manifest the attributes of an exemplary ideal land—such are the Higan ceremonies of spring and autumn.

When the Higan week arrives, men and women who have been immersed in the busy routine of daily life will, at the very least, visit the graves of their ancestors, clean and tidy them up, and purify their hands with water and offer incense and flowers. They will take time off from their work to visit the family temple, listen to the priest's homily, and elevate the fundamental virtues in their relations with one another. During this week they pledge not to take life, steal, lie, grow angry, or voice complaints. *O-sushi* is prepared, each family according to its means, and also *o-hagi* (rice balls coated with sweetened red bean paste). Merit is obtained by offering portions to the Three Treasures—Buddha, Dharma, and Sangha—and to one's ancestors; food is shared among family, friends, and others in attendance.

People making a common effort to create a bright and peaceful buddha-land on earth, an ideal world without strife, resentment, or envy—this is the meaning of the weekly Higan observances. It is unclear when the ceremony was first celebrated in Japan, but since it is recorded that Prince Shōtoku ascended the Western Gate of Shitennō-ji temple, in present-day Osaka, on the day of the autumnal equinox and worshipped the Pure Land in the West, I think we can say that the first Higan observances probably date from around the prince's time.

Groups have appeared in recent years promoting Safe Driving Week, Fire Prevention Week, Reading Week, Be Kind to Animals Week, and the like, encouraging citizens to exercise restraint and cooperate in these areas. But the fact is, Japanese were already observing an event well over a thousand years ago that today might be named Religion and Culture Week. I hope we can make the most of this fine weeklong event with its long history, so that the Higan Festival, living up to its wonderful name, will be a truly meaningful time. I think that only by applying the Higan week's ideals in our individual practice can the Buddha's Dharma be restored to its inherent greatness.

25

MIRACLES

AROUND THE TIME Shakyamuni attained his enlighten-ment, there was an extremely wealthy man named Ana-thapindada living in the city of Sravasti. As he was generous in providing charity to orphans, the poor, and old people without means of support, he was referred to as "the rich man who do-nates to orphans and widows." He wanted very much to build a Buddhist temple in Sravasti so he could invite the Buddha to reside in it. He began by having the Buddha's disciple Shari-putra select a suitable site for the temple. It was decided that a villa owned by Royal Prince Jeta was the best possible location. Anathapindada went to the prince and tried to convince him to sell the property, but the prince refused to consider parting with it. On repeating the offer several more times, Prince Jeta finally agreed to sell it, but only if Anathapindada would cover the en-tire surface of the property with gold.

Although the prince did not believe such a condition could actually be fulfilled, Anathapindada proceeded without the least hesitation to do as the prince had requested and had the property sheeted with gold. Prince Jeta was left with no choice but to sell him the land. When he asked Anathapindada why he went to such lengths to acquire the property, Anathapindada replied that he wanted it to build a temple for Shakyamuni. Deeply moved by Anathapindada's selfless ambition, the prince offered to donate the forested areas of the property and the trees themselves, which it had been found impossible to cover with gold.

In this way the Jetavana monastery came to be built. Its original, much longer name contained allusions to the contributions of the donors Anathapindada and Prince Jeta, but as this came to be deemed too lengthy, it was abbreviated to Jetavana.

Anathapindada was a deeply religious man, and he possessed unparalleled wealth. A devout follower of Shakyamuni's teaching, he offered donations to the poor and oppressed, to orphans and to elderly people who were all alone in the world. But his resources were not unlimited and people needing help were endless, so his enormous wealth eventually ran out. In his final years, he was obliged to release his many servants, and together with his wife assume a quite precarious existence.

Although quite sure that his storehouses were empty, he searched carefully through them anyway to see if something might have been overlooked. He discovered a box of sandalwood, which he sold, using the proceeds to buy four measures of rice. He was relieved that he and his wife now had enough food for five or six days. But one day when Anathapindada was away from the house on an errand, their old friend Shariputra came to the door on a begging round. Without a thought, Anathapindada's wife gave him one measure of rice. Soon afterward, Maudgalyāyana and Mahakashapa also came around holding out their begging bowls, and to each of them she also gave a measure of rice.

Now they had only one measure left, but she felt happy in the knowledge that they still had two days' worth of food. Next, Shakyamuni appeared carrying his begging bowl, and Anathapindada's wife, without considering the consequences, gave him the remaining measure of rice. She accompanied Shakyamuni to the gate and bowed deeply in reverence to him as he left. Then, returning to her senses, she realized what a terrible mistake she had made.

"Donations should be given in accordance with one's circumstances. I did a careless thing and now we have no food for ourselves. My husband will be returning soon, and he will be hungry. I don't have even a grain of rice to offer him. How terrible! There is no excuse for what I did." She threw herself to the floor in tears.

When her husband returned home, she told him everything and begged his forgiveness. His reply filled them both with joy: "You did a fine thing. Anyone can give a donation of rice when they have enough for themselves. A true donation is one that is given when you have nothing to give. I am particularly grateful that you gave to the Buddha. We must dedicate our lives to the Three Treasures of the Buddha's Dharma. Stop crying. It's only a few measures of rice. Perhaps we can find something else. I'll go and take another look in the storehouse." When he went to the storehouse door he was unable to open it. Finally forced to break it open, he discovered that it was packed to the rafters with gold and silver, jewels, bales of rice, and fine sleeping mats, just as in former days. Anathapindada was once again a very rich man, with ample resources to offer donations freely to all those in need.

It is a fable, of course. But how should we interpret it? It surely does not mean that the Buddha made Anathapindada wealthy in return for four measures of rice. Should we regard it simply as a miracle? If so, then it was a miracle that occurred without worshipping or petitioning either gods or buddhas. Some might get the idea that it teaches, if only you continue offering donations to the needy, great miracles like this will occur. Or they might come to the following conclusion: "This is not a miracle. The gold and other valuables that reappeared in the storehouse are not material goods but spiritual treasures. To give everything you own so that nothing, not even food, is left means you will be truly wealthy in a spiritual sense. The joy of giving is more precious than treasures of gold and silver." This final explanation is the most intellectually satisfying, but since human beings do not exist on a spiritual plane alone, I suspect it may be a bit too inclined to the spiritual side of things.

The epithet Most Honored of All Two-Legged Beings is sometimes used for Shakyamuni, the "two legs" being wisdom and happiness or good fortune. When Shakyamuni attained the perfection of wisdom, it was simultaneously and intrinsically combined with consummate happiness and good fortune of the highest order. This means that if human beings perfect their character, they will be furnished naturally with their material needs without even having to seek them.

Explained more objectively, despair and material poverty occur because human beings become overly attached to material things. If they did not attach to material things and gave unselfishly to one another, no one would suffer distress and this world just as it is would become the "other shore."

26

A MIND THAT
DOESN'T THIRST

SOME FIFTEEN HUNDRED years ago, twenty-eight generations after Shakyamuni Buddha, the Indian priest
Bodhidharma took Zen's mind-to-mind transmission to China,
where he came to be recognized as the First Chinese Zen Patriarch. Apparently, he traveled by sea, setting out from the Bay of
Bengal, sailing around the Malay Peninsula, and making landfall
in southeastern China on the coast of Kuangtung Province. The
entire trip seems to have taken about three years to complete.

At the time, China was divided into two kingdoms: the Liang state to the south of the Yangtze River, and the Wei state to
the north. Emperor Wu, the ruler of the Liang state, was a devout Buddhist. He constructed many temples and gave generous
help and encouragement to the priesthood. He was also a formidable scholar and would sometimes don a Buddhist surplice

and lecture on the sutras. People came to refer to him as the Buddha-Mind Emperor.

When Emperor Wu learned that an eminent priest of royal birth was soon to arrive from India, he immediately dispatched an envoy to invite him to the palace. And Bodhidharma, for his part, also probably looked forward to meeting this Monarch of the Buddha-Mind.

The emperor began by asking Bodhidharma the question, "What teachings have you brought to educate living beings in this land? Eminent priests have come to our kingdom from India with marvelous Buddhist scriptures; surely you have brought some as well. I am excited at the prospect of reading them and would be deeply grateful if you would show them to me. What sutras you have brought?"

A courteous inquiry, to which Bodhidharma gave a simple and uninspiring answer: "I have not brought a single word."

The emperor, somewhat taken aback, changed the subject, saying, "I have established temples, provided for the priesthood, copied sutras, and created images of Buddha. What kind of merit do such acts have? Constructing great temples in which many monks now live and practice, giving donations to the poor and indigent, having many Buddhist statues made, copying the sutras and having others do the same, have made some people call me the Buddha-Mind Emperor. Do you think in performing these acts I have accumulated some merit?" Bodhidharma's reply was unsparingly harsh: "No merit whatever."

To the very end, Emperor Wu never had the slightest inkling of the vast divide separating him from this eminent priest from a distant land. Irritated, frustrated, and having completely misconstrued Bodhidharma's essential point, he pressed on and asked, "What is the first principle of the holy truth? That is, if creating Buddhist statues, transcribing sutras, building temples, and providing for the priesthood have no merit, then what value does Buddhism have? Does it have any value?" Although the emperor was set on continuing his attack, Bodhidharma calmly replied, "Vast emptiness, nothing holy whatever. Buddhism has nothing—not a single particle anywhere on earth."

Emperor Wu, now drawn deeper into the labyrinth, unleashed his final arrow. "Who, then, is the person who stands before me? If Buddhism doesn't have anything of value, then is the eminent Buddhist priest who stands before me now also without value? I don't believe that is true, but how would you answer that?" At this point, the emperor seems to have become rather unsettled. Bodhidharma answered quietly, "*Fushiki*"—literally, "I don't know."

With that, the meeting ended and Bodhidharma took his leave of the emperor. He boarded a small reedlike skiff and crossed the Yangtze River to the state of Wei. He entered Shao-lin temple on Mount Sung near the city of Lo-yang, remaining there for nine years. He sat facing a cliff doing zazen while guiding the practice of the monk Hui-k'o, who later succeeded him and became the Second Patriarch. Among Bodhidharma's many famous sayings: "Cease all external relations. Do not have a thirsting mind within. When the mind becomes like an enclosing barrier cliff, use it to enter the Way."

"Cease all external relations" means to stop constantly pursuing good and bad, praise and censure, success and failure in the external world. "Do not have a thirsting mind within" means being unhindered and unconstrained by one's emotions and desires, gladness and sadness, abhorrence and attraction, by the constant tendency to make decisions: Is this one good, or is that one? "When the mind becomes like an enclosing barrier cliff, use it to enter the Way" means if you maintain a continuous state of no-mind so that you thrust right through the cliff, satori will come of itself and you will enter into true and genuine life. But to construct temples, to provide for the community of monks, to create images of Buddha, to transcribe sutras, and to calculate the number of good deeds you have performed cannot be what Bodhidharma means by "cease all external relations." Thinking that you have acquired great merit for doing such things, that it has increased people's respect for you, or that you will thereby be granted entrance into paradise when you die—these are but instances of "a thirsting mind within." You will never be able to gain an understanding of Zen in that way, and so a true and genuine life will always remain unattainable. It was that mentality Bodhidharma was censuring when he told Emperor Wu, "No merit whatever."

When you give people charity or donate to a public project of some kind, you must immediately forget about it. If you keep it in mind, emphasize what you have done, or boast about it, even though you may have performed a commendable act, because you have at the same time indulged in illusory thought and aroused the afflicting passions, your deeds will have no merit at all. The Christian Bible teaches this as well: "Do not let your left hand know what your right hand is doing."

It is through the act of giving that we are able to rid ourselves of our deep-seated attachment to material things and the desires and regrets that go along with it, and arrive at the other shore of enlightenment, or satori. This is the paramita of giving, the first of the six paramitas or perfections of wisdom. Giving openly and unselfishly, with the mind free of any thought of giving, is the giving of the other shore.

27

SPECKS OF DIRT
ON A FINGERNAIL

UPHOLDING THE BUDDHIST precepts means observing
the teachings and prohibitions set forth by Shakyamuni
Buddha. Among them are the bodhisattva's ten grave precepts,
the forty-eight minor precepts, the 250 precepts for a *bhikkhu*
(fully ordained Buddhist monk), and the five hundred precepts
for a *bhikkhuni* (fully ordained Buddhist nun). These precepts
are all described in some detail in the Buddhist scriptures. Most
important of them all are the five basic precepts: the prohibitions against killing, stealing, engaging in sexual misconduct, lying, and consuming intoxicants. These are basic precepts that all
laypeople must, as Buddhists, observe. The first one—the precept against killing, the taking of life—is especially important.

Everyone has seen the pictures depicting Shakyamuni's death
and entrance into nirvana. The Buddha is shown lying at the
center, his head pointing to the north, his face to the west, sur-

rounded by a host of tearful bodhisattvas and other disciples. His attendant, Ananda, who for over twenty years never left his side, is shown prostrate and weeping sorrowfully.

Arranged before these assembled figures are an elephant, lion, tiger, cow, horse, dog, pigeon, peacock, snake, turtle, even a centipede—they are weeping mournfully together with all other living beings. While I don't suppose all these creatures were on hand to attend Shakyamuni's wake, I do believe that the artist who conceived this depiction of his death was well acquainted with the spirit of the Buddha. Shakyamuni's compassion was unconditional, extending to all living beings, so they would naturally mourn his passing.

It is said the Buddha always carried a small pouch with him when he traveled, to strain water before drinking it so he would not injure the tiny living creatures in the water. When he walked, he carried a staff with a metal ring tip that would make a jingling sound, alerting the insects along the way so he would avoid harming them.

The fact that Shakyamuni held the life of a single insect in such deep regard gives even greater meaning to his admonitions about the value of human life, not only teaching us to refrain from taking another's life but also showing us that we must not treat our own life carelessly. Because the Buddha's heart and mind exists in all living beings, the act of taking any life is equivalent to taking the Buddha's life.

Walking one day with his disciple Ananda, Shakyamuni stopped, reached down, and took a pinch of dirt from the ground. Putting it on his thumbnail, he said, "Ananda, which do you think is greater in quantity, the dirt on this fingernail or the dirt on the ground?" "The dirt on the ground is greater, Tathagata," he replied. "Yes, that is true," replied Shakyamuni. "All the beings who live or have lived in this world are as numerous as the grains of dirt lying over the earth. But those who have been privileged to receive human life are as few as these grains of dirt on my fingernail. They must treat their human life with the greatest care and make sure they use it to realize the rare and precious meaning contained in it."

The oceans are filled with an inexhaustible variety of fish, as numerous as the gradations of color in the ocean water. On earth are birds and insects beyond count, so many that they sometimes blacken the sky. Animals in great variety dwell in the hills and mountains. Compared with all these countless beings, only a precious few are born in human form—they truly are like specks of dirt on the Buddha's fingernail. Even the primitive Peking man (*Homo erectus pekinensis*), who is said to be the closest ancestor to modern human beings, did not appear so long ago in the total scheme of the earth's immense history, and human beings' appearance on earth came after an extremely long evolutionary journey. Stars and planets in inconceivable number glitter in the sky, but how many of them can harbor life? Amid this near infinity of time and countless numbers of planets, those beings who receive life as human beings are truly, as the Buddha said, fewer than the particles of dirt on his fingernail. How can anyone afford to waste such a precious gift as human life?

Hardly a day passes that is not darkened by newspaper reports of suicide or lurid murders. Why do people today place such little value on their human life? Have they really lost all sense of reason, love, and hope? Are the admonitions found in the Buddha's precepts at all present in our lives?

Have moderns not heard of this precept against killing, which seems to be such an obvious truth? Have we, Buddha's disciples of today, forgotten even such a basic and precious teaching? It is a matter that should give cause to deep self-reflection. Even members of the Buddhist priesthood took part in the last war, swayed by fine words about a "holy" or "righteous" struggle into mistakenly believing it was permissible to take human life. Did they not sell the most precious of the Buddha's precepts to the devil? With the Buddha's own representatives failing to preach or uphold his admonition "Do not kill," it is no wonder that moral conduct fell by the wayside, nor is it surprising that society played an implicit role in it.

The argument that self-defense and military preparedness are necessary to protect the nation is a plausible one, but that does not mean we priests should not teach and promote the Buddha's precept against taking life. It would be a terrible misfortune for all humankind to be deprived of that noble cry from the depths of the Buddha's soul. I think we are obliged to cry out not only to those in our country but to people throughout the world, "Do not kill!" We must do everything we can to put an end to war. I think that if Japan joins hands with the other Asian Buddhist countries and puts this precept of the Buddha into actual practice, we might soon bask in the radiant happiness of a peaceful world.

28

A STRAIGHT
UNSWERVING PATH

I THINK THERE are few people who have not heard of Albert Schweitzer, the theologian, organist, philosopher, and physician revered today as the "saint of Africa." Born a German citizen in Alsace in 1875, considering himself French and later taking French citizenship, Schweitzer is one of the most well known and revered philosophers of the twentieth century, and he was greatly acclaimed as a medical missionary in Africa.

As a young man, Schweitzer loved taking part in wrestling matches with his friends. Once, when he threw an opponent to the ground, the boy got up muttering darkly, "If I ate beef twice a week like you do, you wouldn't beat me." Those brief offhand remarks made a strong impression on young Schweitzer. "It's true," he thought, "I didn't beat him; it must have been the meat I've been eating." This event played a large role in setting the future course of his life. Schweitzer received a degree in Protestant theology at the university and went on to become a Lutheran minister. He later studied medicine at the University of Strasbourg, taking a doctor of medicine degree in 1899.

Dr. Schweitzer came to believe that the property he owned was not something he as an individual really possessed. Society had merely placed it in his care. Nor did he achieve the position or learning he had acquired on his own; they were gifts society had accorded him, and he was obliged to return what he had been given by putting it to practical use for the welfare of humankind.

He divested himself of all his possessions in his native Germany and went to the remote village of Lambaréné in what is now the West African country of Gabon. There he established a hospital, living together with the tribal people of Lambaréné, ministering to their physical ailments while providing them with spiritual comfort through his preaching of the Christian gospel. Today, even as I write these words, Dr. Schweitzer continues to devote his life to the primeval peoples in western Africa.

From this it seems to me that underlying Dr. Schweitzer's life and work is a way of thinking that is rather more Buddhist than Christian. The self does not really exist; it is an accumulation of many different forces. This is the Buddhist doctrine of causes and conditions. Since "I" do not exist, my existence depends on the temporary union of causes and conditions. Within this, there is only the experience of feeling thankfulness and humility and being of service to others.

Bodhidharma taught, "Not giving rise to thoughts of getting or acquiring within the self-nature's mysterious, incomprehensible dharma of unattainability is what is called the precept of not stealing." This means that the precept of not stealing is a matter of becoming certain beyond any doubt that there is nothing in the world that you can regard as your own.

We fancy the notion that things belong to us. This is my house, this is my land, this is my car, this is my wife, these are my children, this is my self. We clearly define the boundary between our possessions and the possessions of others. For most Japanese, the idea of not stealing is doubtless a matter of not taking a single twig or blade of grass that belongs to someone else. But that is only a question of personal property—what someone has registered at the Recorder's Office. Considering the matter in much greater depth, it is found that there is in fact *nothing* we can call our own. Everything in the natural world, in the human world, even our physical body itself is in a state of constant flux, changing from instant to instant—completely beyond our grasp.

Toyotomi Hideyoshi (1537–1598), who rose from a lowly position, a servant whose sole duty was to care for his master's sandals, to become the ruler of all Japan, wrote the following death verse:

My life, which emerged
   Like the morning dew
Is fading like the dew!
   Even Naniwa's splendor—
A dream within a dream.

Riches and rank, beautiful women and power, are nothing but a dream within a dream. How could we possibly presume to possess anything in this world forever? The things of the world are exactly as the Buddhist sutras describe them: "Dreams, illusions, shadows, mist, lightning flashes." When Zen Master Ikkyū died, he left this verse:

My four chief constituents
    And my five basic elements
Only on loan to me till now,
    This month, on this very day,
I return lock stock and barrel.

Even our own body and our thought processes are borrowings; we have them on loan. There is not a single particle of dust we can call our own. When we die we must return everything, and nothing is excepted. To know this and live by it fully and completely is what is meant by "not stealing."

There is nothing in this world either to possess or to be possessed by, nothing to control or be controlled by. There is only the truth of causes and conditions. When we clearly understand this truth, a life of freedom and serenity opens up for us. The "haves" of this world should possess an attitude that allows them to regard their wealth and possessions as something that has been entrusted to their keeping, something they could at any time return unhesitatingly to society. As for the "have-nots," do we not find it inspiring to observe them steadfastly treading their own paths with independence and self-reliance, unmindful of others' wealth and possessions, without trading on others' sympathy? For both haves and have-nots, not stealing means being unswayed and unhindered by either the notion or the passion of acquiring and possessing things—which, in fact, both groups think and possess equally. I believe that genuine sharing can really take place only when such a pure and honest viewpoint prevails.

Truly, truly, we possess nothing whatever in this world. We possess life itself only as something altogether ungraspable, and we are not able to truly realize this until our life moves in that ungraspable manner, as smoothly and unhesitatingly as flowing water. All that is discernible in this flow is the vigorous, creative life itself.

Here is a verse by Saitō Mokichi (1882–1953), a celebrated poet of the Taishō period:

Walking along
A straight road
In the red glow
Of a setting sun—
Such was my life.

I think this expresses the truth that if you live life to the full, intensely, with radiant passion, you are living the Buddha's teachings; that treading such a straight, unswerving path through life, purely and simply, is tantamount to observing the Buddha's important second precept of not stealing.

29

TRAINING HALL WITH THE MOON REFLECTED ON THE WATER

The title of this essay comes from a line in an old verse: *Sitting in the training hall, the moon reflected on the water. Seated in a place of practice you are like the moon and the water, your mind reflecting faultlessly the myriad flowers of emptiness.*

THE STORY KNOWN as "The Old Lady Burns Down the Hermitage" is found in the *Kattō-shū* (*A Collection of Entangling Vines*), an old book of koans that has been used by generations of Japanese Zen students.

There was an old bodhisattva-like woman in Hakuin's day who lived near his temple, Shōin-ji. Apparently quite advanced in her Zen study, she had worked many years with various teachers of note, listening to their lectures (*teishō*) and having personal interviews (*sanzen*) with them, and she could drive a Zen monk with even five or six years in the training hall into a tight corner if he wasn't on his toes. You come across old ladies like this from time to time in the Zen records. What is interesting is that usually they take up Zen study as young women rather than in old age. By the time they've gotten along in years, they are very tough customers indeed. No one can lay a hand on them.

The lady in "The Old Lady Burns Down the Hermitage" koan seems to have had a fondness for Zen monks. For many years she allowed one of them to reside in a small hut next to her home. A clever young girl who was living with the old lady took the monk his meals. One day the lady told the young girl that after she set down his food, she should throw her arms tightly around him and ask, "What do you feel now?" The girl did as she was told, and the monk replied, "Nothing whatever—like a withered tree on a cold cliff."

The young girl returned to the hermitage and reported the monk's response. The old woman was furious. "For twenty years now I've taken care of that worldly little bonze," she exclaimed. "How foolish I've been!" She drove the monk away and burned the hermitage to the ground, raving about it having been hopelessly defiled.

What could the young monk have said that would have satisfied the old lady, saved him from being driven off, and kept the hermitage from being burned down? The aim of the koan is for the Zen student to produce an answer in place of the young monk. However, I think this monk showed exceptional mettle in being able to say "like a withered tree on a cold cliff" when the young girl grabbed hold of him. I don't think he could have uttered those words unless he had a great deal of hard training under his belt. Why, then, did the old lady drive him away and burn down the hermitage?

As desire for food and sex are the most powerful human instincts, detaching yourself from them requires extraordinary effort. It takes years of diligent practice, exertion so severe and uncompromising it has been described as gouging out raw flesh and as bleeding yourself dry. Attaining that stage is the goal of Hinayana Buddhism. Yet how much does all this effort that we put forth benefit human life? This young monk did his level best, warding off the girl by making himself like a cold cliff, but was he able to utter a single word to help save her, a living human being standing there before him?

Mahayana Buddhism is not like this. In the Mahayana the concern is first of all to grasp the buddha-mind, leaving the afflicting passions as they are without making any useless effort to get rid of them. If you grasp the buddha-mind, the afflicting passions are sublimated as a matter of course. For the monk in the story, this means, in short, that he should have admonished the young girl for her behavior.

The *Kannon Sutra* puts it this way: "Any living being beset by lusts and cravings can shed those desires by always holding Kannon Bodhisattva reverently in mind." Kannon Bodhisattva is the buddha-mind, and anyone—no matter how strong their lusts and cravings may be—will shed them naturally if they keep Kannon constantly in mind. Shedding desires does not mean cutting them off but becoming free of them even as the desires remain as they are.

Like the exquisite white lotus blossoming from the mud without being the least defiled by it, the buddha-mind bursts into bloom amid the afflicting passions — that is how the desires and passions are shed.

Try to rise up high above the clouds,
Where nothing ever hides the moon.

These lines from a poem by the Zen master Musō Kokushi tell us that since you are always living beneath the clouds, they may hide the moon from you. Go above the clouds, where they cannot obstruct the moon, and it will always be there shining constantly. Since you live perpetually buried in afflicting passions, you are always troubled. But rise up to a higher place above those passions and desires and no matter how many arise, they will not obstruct you.

The Kyoto artist Nohara Ōshū (1886–1933), in spite of being an adept in the art of swordsmanship, was terrified of thunder and lightning. The faintest rumblings in the sky would send him into his room, where he would hide under the mosquito netting shivering with fear. One summer after the cable car had been installed on Mount Atago, west of Kyoto, some of Ōshū's friends decided to take him to see it. He was quite reluctant to ride on the cable car, but they succeeded in persuading him to get in and take it to the top. When they were finally sitting in the teashop on the summit, low rumblings of thunder were suddenly heard. Lightning flashes appeared. Ōshū gazed miserably down from the teashop window, certain his direst fears were about to be realized. Then his composure immediately returned when he saw that the lightning flashes and thunder were occurring far down the mountainside below him. Clapping his hands together, he said, "No matter how eccentric thunder and lightning may behave, they certainly will never strike upward. I don't think anything has made me as happy as seeing them below me down there."

I find this story very amusing. Being engulfed in evil passions, we constantly struggle to escape them. It requires great effort. To succeed, we must become like "a withered tree on a cold cliff," like "the dead of winter with no sign of warmth." But if we can rise above the evil passions, then "nothing can give us more enjoyment than the evil passions." The *Heart Sutra* teaches, *There is no primal ignorance, and there is no exhausting of primal ignorance.* Ignorance is not something that actually exists, and is it not something that perishes, either. For the mind to be indifferent to whether evil passions exist and remain unattached to either their existence or nonexistence—this is what is meant by prajna wisdom. As Bodhidharma taught, "Not giving rise to thoughts of love and affection within the self-nature's mysterious, incomprehensible Dharma of nonattachment is what is called the precept against sexual misconduct."

There is an old poem:

THE MOON REFLECTED ON THE WATER

The moon without a thought
  of reflecting on the water,
The water without a thought
  of reflecting the moon —
The Pond of Hirosawa.

In the same way that the pond has no thought to reflect the moon and the moon no thought to be reflected on the pond, the mind remains unswayed by the afflicting passions even as it is immersed in them — such is the essential truth of our bright and marvelous self-nature. A life that is unobstructed either by the afflicting passions or by enlightenment upholds the third of the Buddha's precepts, the precept against sexual misconduct.

30

THE TRUE PERSON

ONE OF CONFUCIUS's disciples once asked him, "What is the most important thing in governing a state?" "Soldiers, food, and trust," he replied. The disciple again asked, "If you had to do without one of these, which would it be?" "I would do without the military," Confucius answered. "And if you had to do without one of the other two?" "I would do without food," he replied.

In governing a country, the people's trust is of paramount importance. Rulers who can provide food and secure the peoples' trust will be able to govern even without soldiers. Even if food is lacking, if they have the people's trust, they will be able to get by. But without the people's trust, they will soon find it impossible to govern.

Confucius often emphasizes this point. In government and secular life, including family matters, social intercourse cannot function at any level without the presence of sincerity and mutual trust. I have heard stories of Japanese who traveled abroad since the Meiji period falling into disfavor by declaring to people in the countries they visit that they have no religion. People in foreign lands find this surprising, since lacking religion suggests to them being somehow deficient in sincerity and trustworthiness.

What, then, are we to believe in? Is there anything in this world of ours we can place our trust in? What kind of self can we cultivate that others will be able to rely on? What is human sincerity? Shinran said, "The ordinary person weighed down with evil passions, the world as impermanent as a burning house, and everything else as well—these words are all devoid of meaning . . . utterances bereft of truth. The Nembutsu alone is true." It seems to me we have no choice but to acknowledge that there is nothing in the world we can truly rely upon. The newspaper often carries reports of occurrences of the most woeful nature—a family washed away in a torrential storm while happily eating dinner together; a family lying side by side in their beds found in the morning buried under a mudslide.

We ourselves are the proverbial burning house, impermanence itself. The fifteenth-century Shin priest Rennyo refers to a "pink healthy face in the morning, white bones by nighttime." Nothing is certain in the natural world, in human society, in our own lives, not even in our own minds. We read of a woman who kills her husband, mutilating his body and throwing the limbs into a river. We may think, "What a terrible woman. A devil! What could she look like?" But she turns out to be a quite ordinary human being—a schoolteacher, a person whom her children and her husband regarded as very kind. Right up until the morning that she murdered her husband, even one hour before, she would probably not have dreamed of committing such a horrible crime. Surely it was an impulsive act, a sudden urge so irresistible that it overwhelmed her.

Shakyamuni said, "The mind is like a venomous serpent, a ferocious beast, a ruthless bandit." Indeed, the human mind is a dangerous customer—it is as though you are hugging a viper to your breast or hand-feeding a rapacious wolf. We must hold ourselves fortunate that we have not perpetrated some terrible crime only because our mind has not been deluded by circumstances and led us to perform such an act.

As a matter of fact, there is one thing that is true and sincere in this world where nothing whatever can be relied on—the mind that makes us press our palms together in gasshō and recite *Namu-Amida-Butsu*. It is the mind of "absolute faith alone is true"; the mind Prince Shōtoku spoke of when he wrote, "Everything in this world of ours is provisional and transitory. Buddha alone is true." We can rely only on the Nembutsu, only on the realm of total faith. Expressed otherwise: the only thing we can rely on is our discovery of the eternal Buddha in ourselves.

In his *Hymns of the Pure Land (Jōdo Wasan)*, Shinran writes,

Sutras preach that a person who delights in
A mind of resolute faith is identical with Buddha.

The mind of great faith is itself the buddha-nature,
The buddha-nature is no other than the Tathagata.

Reciting the Nembutsu is attainment of the mind of absolute faith, the mind of absolute faith is the buddha-nature, the buddha-nature is the Tathagata or Buddha, the buddha-nature is the true and real self. If you find the word *buddha-nature* too hard to understand, we might simply call it "dignity of character."

The human personality is not masculine or feminine. It is not rich or poor, learned or unlearned, patrician or plebeian, young or old, good or evil, buddha or unenlightened, being or nonbeing, large or small, red or white, round or square, living or dead. It is something altogether ineffable, so we must resort to words such as *absolute* or *dignified*.

Bodhidharma taught, "Within the Dharma of unexplainability, not giving rise to the idea that you can explain things is what is called the Buddha's precept against speaking what is untrue." Discovery of the truth unexplainable in words is the state of satori, the territory of genuine belief. It is only from here that the authentic life can emerge in which you do not utter what is untrue in speech, mind, or body. That is the meaning of the fourth of the Buddha's precepts, the precept against prevarication.

31

BRING ME SAKE!

IN A CERTAIN country village, a family of my acquaintance had a young son who went about singing, "*Sake nomuna, sake nomuna*" (Don't drink sake, don't drink sake). I felt the words were perhaps linked to the fact that he was attending kindergarten at a Christian church in the village. Listening intently to the young boy's singing, I was surprised and amused when he suddenly began singing, "*Sake motte koi, sake motte koi*" (Bring me sake! Bring me sake!). Now, it may be just a case of worldly ignorance on my part, but my impression is that while in the past, Buddhists may have chanted "Don't drink sake, don't drink sake," today, given the decline in this latter day of the Dharma, you are much more likely to hear, "Bring me sake! Bring me sake!" I am sometimes even made to wonder if the Buddhist community as a whole has not fallen into a childish lack of self-examination.

What should never enter a temple gate
Is now allowed free and full access,
Wherever you look is sad and lonely,
Moss spreading on garden rocks.

There was a time in my youth when I may have written such a verse, though I am not so inflexible as to reproach drinking in others simply because I do not drink myself. If drinkers want to imbibe, my heart fills with the desire for them to have a drink. To go off the rails, kick over the traces occasionally, is a very human trait, and an amusing one at that. At the same time, we must bear in mind that Buddhism explicitly proscribes drinking; and in becoming a follower of Buddha, we should at least acknowledge the Buddha's injunction against drinking intoxicants as one of his five basic precepts, whether we observe it or not.

A story is told somewhere of a sincerely committed student of Buddhism who strove with great earnestness to attain the Way. One day a friend from a distant province came to visit and stayed over with him. When the friend left on an errand, the student spotted an unusual-looking flask on the friend's desk. Pulling out the stopper, he found that it was a jar of very good sake. Its wonderful fragrance tempted him to place a few drops on his tongue. Marveling at the exquisite flavor, he kept sipping from the flask until he began to feel warm and relaxed, a vigorous strength quickening within him.

A chicken happened to stray through the fence into the yard

from the neighboring house. The student went out, grabbed it, and wrung its neck. A little later, the neighbor's young daughter came and asked him if he had seen her chicken. Inviting her into the house, he proceeded to rape her. Her enraged father went straight to the local magistrate, who had the student arrested. When interrogated, he refused to confess, saying, "I don't know anything about that. Nothing at all."

In the end, this student broke all the five basic precepts: against drinking, stealing, taking life, sexual misconduct, and telling falsehoods. I have no way of knowing if these events actually occurred or whether they are merely a skillful story someone made up to convey a moral lesson. The fact remains, however, that the reason this dedicated follower of the Buddha Way was led to commit so many grave transgressions was because he chanced to drink sake. As the Buddhist scriptures go into meticulous detail warning against the baneful influence of alcohol to both the individual and society, I will refrain from saying anything more about it here.

During the last century, the Sōtō priest Hara Tanzan and the precepts teacher Shaku Unshō were being treated to a meal somewhere. It was a truly strange pairing, for Unshō would never touch sake, and Tanzan was a guzzler, known to never refuse a cup. Tanzan, without the slightest hesitation, began downing one cup after another. Finally Unshō, who always vociferously denounced alcohol to his followers, seems to have felt compelled to say something, so he remonstrated with Tanzan. Showing utter unconcern, Tanzan retorted, "People who don't drink sake aren't human!" "If they're not human," countered Unshō, "what are they?" "A buddha," Tanzan placidly replied. Even Unshō could say no more.

From long in the past, great men and heroes, superlative artists, even eminent Buddhist priests have been counted among the sake lovers, so it is difficult to simply conclude that drinking sake is wrong. What is important is not to show that drinking is blameworthy but that it is wrong to lose one's reason and act in a disorderly manner because the mind becomes intoxicated. The Buddha prohibited the consumption of alcohol because of his deep pity and compassion for ordinary people, those who are neither heroes nor persons of superior talents, whose drinking makes them lose their sense of reason, renders them a pernicious influence in their homes and society, and finally destroys them.

And when the Buddha speaks of drunkenness, he is not referring only to alcohol, for inebriation appears in various forms. We can become so blind and reckless when highly intoxicated that we appear strange or abnormal to others—like a person completely bereft of self-awareness. When we become drunk with lust, greed, delusions, pride, literature or philosophy, God or Buddha, we lose our autonomy along with our reason and judgment. Mahayana Buddhism broadly views all varieties of drunkenness as violations of the precept against intoxicants.

Bodhidharma thus taught, "Not giving rise to thoughts shrouded in primal ignorance within the self-nature's mysterious, incomprehensible Dharma of original purity is what is called the precept of abstaining from intoxicants." He equates the precept of abstaining from intoxicants with "the marvelous subtlety of the self-nature not giving rise to ignorant notions within the originally pure Dharma." The "thoughts shrouded in primal ignorance (*avidya*)" belong to a blind, indiscriminate mental attitude or outlook. Momentary ephemeral ways of thinking, based on something apart from the true self-nature, are all shrouded in primal ignorance. One of the ancients cautioned against becoming attached either to Buddha or God, to the Dharma or to truth itself, when he said, "Do not dwell in the place of no-Buddha! Pass with all haste through the place of Buddha!" A popular Japanese saying expresses much the same thing: "In becoming a buddha, there's no need to become so fixed and stable that you resemble one of those stone statues at the roadside." A free, unhindered mind, moving like flowing water, not adhering to anything whatever, is one that does not consume intoxicants. This is what Bodhidharma calls "the pure mind of the mysterious, incomprehensible self-nature."

32

A LOCAL TRAIN

Hakuin's *SONG OF ZAZEN* now mentions *Charity, precepts, the other paramitas.* As I have dwelt on—some might say belabored—these two paramitas at some length already, I will focus here on the four remaining paramitas,* which the exigencies of the *wasan* verse form obliged Hakuin to omit. My own leisurely excursion through the *Song of Zazen* is totally free of such restraints, so I am able to savor each of the paramitas, one by one, like a slow-moving local train that stops at every station. I hope readers who accompany me on this journey will not find it too tiresome.

I think it can generally be said that modern men and women are lacking in patience. Rather than walk, they take a train. They

---

*Perseverance or forbearance (*kshanti*), zeal or diligence (*virya*), meditation (*dhyana*), wisdom (*prajna*).

favor a super-express train over a simple express, an airplane over a super-express. They become fidgety as they wait for the trip to get started. At that rate, they can't expect to live very long. People who desire a long life need to be a bit addle-headed. They should have a foolish streak in them. What good can come from busily rushing about like a bill collector all the time?

Tokugawa Ieyasu, the founder of the Tokugawa shogunate that ruled Japan during the Edo period, once asked the high-ranking Tendai priest Tenkai Daisōjō (who ended up living to be 108 years old) the secret of his long life. Tenkai replied, "Eating little, eating poor food, a daily hot bath, dharani chanting, and letting rip an occasional fart." His reply sounds like a passage from one of those comic *aho-dara* sutras ("dharani sutras for fools") that enjoyed wide popularity during the Meiji period.

I myself have been following the first of Tenkai's secrets for many years, eating sparingly of so-called unpalatable or unappetizing food. I agree completely that it is the healthiest of diets. I have not been to a doctor or taken medicine for thirty years. I still follow this same regimen, taking rice gruel or rice and vegetable porridge at the morning and evening meals, and at midday only boiled barley with rice and miso soup. I have no need to be concerned about such things as calories.

You, dear reader, consume too much palatable food, concerning yourself mainly with shoveling it down without due consideration to your body's ability to digest and absorb it all. This is sheer folly. You are like a person who stuffs a furnace full of kindling, creating nothing but fumes and smoke until finally realizing he doesn't know what he is doing. The secret of a healthy life is to not overburden your digestive organs so they will always have capacity in reserve; then your ability to absorb what you eat will always be in sound condition.

I read in the newspapers about experts who reach the conclusion after years of research that people in villages where too much rice is eaten are short-lived, while in villages where barley and yams are consumed they are long-lived. Beans are said to be good for you—and tofu. A daily hot bath is also beneficial. Most people are probably too busy and too careful with their purse to have a hot bath every day, but there seems little doubt that it is good for you. One of the dharanis* that Buddhists chant is the Dharani of Long Life. You are supposed to repeat it 108 times each morning. It is believed to be particularly efficacious for the sick, who are able to regain their health by chanting. This benefit is not limited to the Dharani of Long Life; any dharani, even a cryptic passage from a sutra will do the job. Chanting the sounds in a loud voice is a way to maintain your health. The well-known formulas *Namu-Amida-Butsu* of the Pure Land schools and *Namu-Myōhō-Renge-Kyō* of the Nichiren Buddhists are both dharanis.

Last year a "Nembutsu notebook" kept by Tokugawa Ieyasu was discovered in a temple at Nagahama in Shiga prefecture. It revealed that Ieyasu chanted ten thousand Nembutsu nearly

---

*Dharani = a mantra, magic formula, or spell.

every day. This is roughly equivalent to invoking the Nembutsu for over two hours daily. Most moderns would probably smile to read this, thinking it ridiculous for someone to sit chanting the Nembutsu for two hours beating on a *mokugyō*, or fish-shaped wooden drum. Nonetheless, I have little doubt that it is an effective way to maintain your health.

It is sometimes said that when it comes to music, Buddhism has less to offer than other religions; that it produces only monotonous, meaningless noises using very primitive instruments of Chinese origin. It strikes me, however, that if you find yourself coming in touch with the mystery of the great natural world upon hearing the sound of ocean waves, the wind rustling through pine trees deep in the mountains, a waterfall cascading into a deep pool, or the hushed patter of raindrops on a temple roof, shouldn't you also find the monotonous sound of those sutra recitations, a mere continuity of meaningless sounds, to be the greatest music in the universe? Or am I crying sour grapes?

Finally, a few words about Tenkai's amusing remark about an "occasional fart," which implies that when you have to pass gas, you should just do it without worrying about social decorum. If the Shogun Ieyasu had let out an occasional fart, those beneath him would probably have followed his example. The sounds would have been heard everywhere you went. Wouldn't that have been something?

A person as dedicated as Tenkai to staying healthy will probably live a long life. What everyone must guard against above all is, to quote a proverb, neither offering fragrant incense at the altar nor letting rip a malodorous fart—words applied to one who spends a life remaining completely indifferent, doing nothing either worthwhile or bad.

Physicians recommend that we dispel the gas and not let it stay trapped inside. Yet what is even worse is to keep mental gas bottled up in your head. Lapses of decorum—that is to say farting—can be quite embarrassing when done in the presence of others, yet to be thick-skinned enough not to care about it is doubtless one of the secrets essential to living a long life.

I find highly dubious the tendency modern people have of needing to explain everything by means of shrewd logic or reasoning. Of being quick to take their own lives when they feel that something is unsatisfactory. Of showing scant reluctance to take the lives of their fellow human beings. It is definitely not through reasoning that we are born into the world, and we should not feel compelled to be so submissive to the dictates of reason.

As we approach the New Year period, here is a *kyōka*, or "mad" comic poem, on the custom of buying on credit and encountering the year-end debt:

New Year's Eve, debts piled up,
   I'm crossing, I can't cross,
Can't cross, I'm crossing anyway.

Although people might succeed in extending the deadline for the payment of debts, a final accounting would always come at the year's end. All accounts had to have been settled at that time in order for them to "cross over" and continue a normal life in the coming year; they would otherwise be obliged to begin the New Year as a debtor.

Here is another verse on a New Year's theme, from *Lives of the Loyal Retainers* (*Gishi Meimei Den*), a work dealing with the celebrated vendetta of the forty-seven rōnin of Akō. When the assembled group set out in December to avenge their lord's death, they happened on their way to encounter the poet Kikaku, who composed a haiku alluding to their mission. After another poet "capped" this with two final lines, it became:

Human lives
Floating down
The river at the year's end;
Counting on a treasure ship
To appear the next morning.

Issa wrote this haiku on the day before the New Year:

In any event,
All is in another's hands —
The year's end.

Should we not see the old year out in this quiet, untroubled attitude? And should we not welcome in the coming year with the calmness that prevails among the ordinary people? Issa portrays this attitude in another verse:

> A time of happiness,
> About average for me —
> Thus is my spring.

In any case, I am afraid this essay on local trains became sidetracked along the way, then got shunted into some odd sidings, and has now jumped the tracks altogether! *Hahahaha!*

33

CREATING A
BUDDHA-LAND

THE NEW YEAR is upon us, although it is still winter by
the solar calendar. This winter I have been made to feel
the exceptional beauty in the natural world. The rice plants
ripened handsomely and have been harvested, the red autumn
leaves that glowed so splendidly have fallen to earth; and there
is the smell of freshly turned black soil, the frost-yellowed scal-
lions, and bright-green daikon leaves. Freshness and simplicity
everywhere I look, everything settled in its proper place.

The tea master Takeno Jōō (1502–1555) once cited this verse
from the thirteenth-century *Shin-kokinshū* (*New Collection of Poems
Ancient and Modern*) as evincing the spiritual state of wabi, the
true mind of the way of tea:

Gazing all around,
　　Seeing no flowers

Seeing no red leaves—
    A hut at the beachside
In the autumn twilight.

I have resided for many years at Tenryū-ji at Arashiyama in the
Saga area to the west of Kyoto city, a spot famous for its scenic beauty. I think winter is the loveliest time in Arashiyama. The
springtime cherry trees and the new green leaves are indeed beautiful. The summertime is also splendid, and the maple leaves in
autumn are truly magnificent. But nothing equals Arashiyama in
winter, when the leaves have fallen and the hillsides' delicate bones
emerge intermingled with the branches and twigs of the wood-
land trees. It is a quiet, restful season, with withered trees veiled
lightly by the tranquility of pale-pink mist. Nothing could be
more beautiful than Arashiyama at the onset of spring.

Last autumn, crewmen on a ship engaged in pearl fishery
returning from the Arafura Sea between Australia and New
Guinea reported seeing an island where fire burned constantly
throughout the year. A jungle fire had once broken out and
spread over the entire island. Once the fire consumed the plants
and trees in one tract of land, they would immediately shoot
back up and revert to jungle once again. The fire would then return, consuming everything in its path once again, never completely dying out.

Hearing this story, I felt thankful Japan is a country where
the change of seasons takes place in an orderly fashion. The
Buddhist word *nirvana*, meaning "the tranquility that reigns

after a fire has burned out," refers to a mind in which the flames of passion and desire, of hate and envy and strife have all burned themselves out. Their ashes have fallen to earth, leaving heaven and earth as still and tranquil as a winter landscape. Is such a state of mind not the most wonderful gift possible for the men and women of the modern world—people who are constantly burning with distress and vexation like the island fire?

The Asian spiritual tradition calls this "flexibility (or elasticity) of mind," *nyūnan-shin* in Japanese. It is from this mind that the standpoint of "oneness," which is at the ground of this tradition, emerges. Has today's Japan not moved much too far in the direction of a Western, confrontational way of mind that divides things in two and sets them at odds? Husbands and wives form an integral unit, as do parents and children, nature and human beings, society and the individual, buddha and unenlightened beings. I think true peace of mind can exist only in a world in which such unity prevails. The more the confrontational attitude increases, the greater the need for harmonious unity of this kind.

In sports, two teams struggle vigorously on the playing field. But isn't it the greatest sign of sportsmanship when in the heat of competition players still remember the warm fellowship they normally feel for members of the other team?

I came upon this verse in the newspaper. It was written by a grammar school boy:

Returning from school,
I first call out, "Mother,"

When I hear her "Yes,"
I take off my shoes.

It is such a pleasant verse, I committed it to memory. Just as the mother's love for her son is uncritical and unquestioning, the son's deep trust in his mother is unconditional. Yet by the time this purehearted and innocent boy comes of age, his trust in his parents will be lost.

Is not the possession of such blind, unquestioning faith a sort of divine wisdom? Does it not suggest God's wisdom that "causes the rain to fall on the good and evil alike"; the great compassion of the Buddha's words, "Do not fear evil, there is no evil that can obstruct the working of Amida's original vow"?

New Year's Day!
From my own wife
A formal address.

These lines indeed imply a daily life of harmony and respect born from this spirit of unquestioning tolerance. This first morning of the New Year, even yesterday's demon-faced bill collector has a completely different look in their eye as the two of you exchange "Happy New Year" greetings. Is this not the true and engaging spirit of the New Year? A world where we can embrace our enemies without any regret whatever in a state of no-mind resembling the magnanimity of the earth itself—this is the realm of the forbearance paramita.

When the venerable Purna, one of Buddha's ten disciples, set off to preach in a heathen land, he paid a visit to the World-Honored One, who said to him, "Purna, the people in that land are savage and lacking in refinement. When they see you, they may revile you and insult you in various ways. Are you ready for that?"

"World-Honored One," Purna replied, "the people of that country are sensible beings. Even if they did insult me, I don't think they would strike me with stones and broken tiles, and I am thankful for that."

"Purna, those people have extremely brutal natures. They may strike you with stones and tiles. What would you do at such a time?"

"World-Honored One, those people still have compassionate hearts, so even if they beat me with stones and tiles, I am thankful that they would not kill me with knives and swords," replied Purna.

"Purna, they are a ferocious lot. What would you do if they came to kill you with knives and swords?"

Purna said, "World-Honored One, at such a time I would be thankful for their compassionate hearts in saving me by freeing me from my body, which is a vessel of evil passions and evil karma."

The Buddha commended him, saying, "Excellent, Purna, excellent. With your magnanimous heart, it is good that you will be traveling to foreign lands and transmitting the Way," and sent him off on his journey. In working to create a buddha-land on earth, being ready to endure any hardship—this is called the forbearance paramita.

34

DOESN'T THE PINE TREE TAKE ROOT ON THE CLIFFSIDE?

SOME YEARS AGO, there was an eminent priest named Mōhō living at Tokugen-ji temple in Nagoya. As a young monk, Mōhō had spent seven years in the training hall at Tokugen-ji concentrating on the *Mu* koan—"*Mu. Mu. Mu.*" But he was never able to attain the breakthrough into kenshō, or enlightenment. Younger monks who had entered the training hall after him made steady headway, passing koans one after another, but Mōhō could not even get past the first *Mu* koan. Finally, thoroughly disgusted with himself, he decided to throw in the towel. "A monk as thick-headed as me doesn't stand much chance no matter what kind of practice he does." He stuffed his belongings into his travel pouch and set out for home.

He had begun his religious life at Kaizō-ji at Maisaka on Lake Hamana, one of the post stations on the Tōkaidō Road. How pleased he would have been to return to his home temple loaded with honors. But things didn't turn out that way, and he was obliged to make the trip empty-handed, his heart overwhelmed with sadness. To reach Maisaka on the opposite shore of Lake Hamana, he boarded a small ferry at the Arai crossing. He sat in a far corner of the boat, lost in thought, his arms crossed, his head sagging to his chest. Meantime, the ferryman, totally unmindful of his passenger, began loudly singing the folk song, "Doesn't the pine tree take root on the cliffside? If you put your mind to it, there's nothing you can't do."

Mōhō, who had been hunkered deep in thought, raised his head, swelling with sudden emotion as though he had received an electric shock. "That's it!" he cried.

When the ferry reached the shore, Mōhō stayed on board, even though his home in Maisaka was just a short walk away. He returned to Arai, then set out walking westward, staring straight ahead and boring into the *Mu* koan—"*Mu! Mu! Mu!*" Sure enough, he entered into deep samadhi. As he continued striding along, he tripped and fell into a paddy field. At that very instant he achieved a wonderful satori.

Covered with mud, he resumed his journey, beside himself with joy. Back at Tokugen-ji, he immediately requested an interview with Sōzan Genkyō (1799–1868), and Genkyō confirmed his enlightenment. Mōhō received his teacher's Dharma transmission and later succeeded him as head priest at Tokugen-ji, going on to become a famous Zen priest whose great virtues were recognized throughout the country. There is a popular saying: "Failing one step short of great success." In the practice of zazen, just as in secular activities, you must not throw everything away when you are still only halfway to your goal.

It is just as the old verse says: *If you keep pressing diligently forward without slackening, you will end up covering a thousand leagues, even if you plod as slowly as an ox.* A person who continues doing the same thing over a long period of time without ceasing will finally achieve success. People who try to make their way through the world by imitating others, contriving shrewd and clever means to achieve their ends, may seem to be getting along all right for a time, yet they will never succeed in their ultimate goal. Unrelenting perseverance of this nature is the meaning of the paramita of diligence (*shōjin*).

When National Master Musō, Kanzan Egen, the founder of Myōshin-ji, heard that National Master Daitō was in Kyoto, he immediately set out from Kamakura to seek the master's guidance, leaving in such a hurry that he found himself with a straw sandal on one foot and a wooden geta on the other. It is said that he walked the entire distance to Kyoto in that fashion, and that when he passed Mount Fuji he didn't even gaze up at the majestic peak. When Zen Master Hakuin was a young monk, the story of Zen Master Tz'u-ming jabbing his thigh with a gimlet to keep from falling asleep during zazen inspired him to return to the Zen practice he had abandoned. The actions of both these men show an exemplary dedication to the Way, the kind of uncompromising diligence that we number among the six paramitas.

The *Sutra of the Buddha's Bequeathed Teaching* (Ch. *Fo ijiao jing;*

Jap. *Butsu Yuikyō kyō)*, said to contain the final words Shakya-muni spoke to his followers before entering nirvana, sets forth his instructions to them like a mother addressing a son who is setting out on a long journey, explaining to him with great earnestness and in explicit detail all the various things he must guard against. Among his admonitions and words of advice, all of which are imbued with kindness and solicitude of the deepest order, we find these remarks on the persistent diligence neces-sary to attain the Buddha Way:

> You monks (*bhikkhu*), if you work assiduously to achieve diligence in your practice, you will find there is nothing difficult about it. Therefore, you must strive for all you are worth to achieve this diligence (*shōjin*). It is like a con-stant trickle of water boring a hole in a rock. If from time to time the mind of the student becomes lazy or inatten-tive in any way, it will be like someone trying to make a fire by friction but stopping to rest before he gets any heat. He wants a fire, but there will be no fire. This is what is meant by "diligence."

In the Tokugawa period, people made fire by striking steel against a piece of flint, producing a spark that ignited some kind of tinder, a bit of soft wood or bark. Before that, people used a friction drill inserted in a hole in a piece of wood. Putting a spindle in the hole, they revolved it by hand with the great-est possible speed until the spindle tip was red-hot, creating an ember. The ember was then put onto a piece of bark or tinder and blown into a flame. This sequence had to be done with the utmost diligence in a single uninterrupted burst of energy; if you stopped spinning the spindle to rest, you would fail to get the fire. Just so, if you keep taking a kettle off the fire before the water comes to a boil, you will never end up with any boiling water. Zazen works like that. The reason you do not reach the end of your practice even after years of trying is not the fault of zazen. It is because you have not bored completely through and penetrated down to the very source. You must reach the point where you "die the Great Death" (*taishi ichiban*) and "sever all your roots to life," because those roots tie you to primal ignorance. It is imperative that you bore completely through and choke them off!

In the *Gateless Barrier* koan collection, Zen Master Wu-men makes this point extremely clear: "Arouse this great doubt with your whole body, with all its 360 bones and joints and 84,000 hair holes, and bore straight into this single character *Mu*." "Boring into" (*san*; the word can mean literally "to hold close intercourse with") signifies achieving perfect intimacy. Wu-men tells students to throw themselves body and soul into the struggle and continue until they no longer know whether they are *Mu* or *Mu* is them; they have become totally one with it.

The nineteenth-century Pure Land teacher Shichiri Gōjun said, "Repeat the Nembutsu as diligently as though your mouth were stuffed with beans and you can't let a single bean pop out." Such a lukewarm utterance would never be tolerated in Zen. Zen says, "It's like a lump of red-hot iron you've gulped down but can't swallow or spit out. You try to vomit it up, but you can't. All you can do is push forward—'*Mu! Mu! Mu!*'—until eventually all the worthless knowledge and addle-brained ideas you have picked up to this point in your life vanish without a trace, and your oneness with heaven and earth emerges of itself. You will be like a deaf mute who has had a wonderful dream—they know what has happened and just sit there grinning away, joyously happy, utterly grateful, but unfortunately they are unable to disclose it to others." You must reach this point once yourself, or else I don't think we can say your satori is fully realized. The zeal you devote to achieving this is called *shōjin* (*virya*)—utter devotion to the religious quest—the fourth of the paramitas.

35

A SLIDING SHUFFLE

I PREVIOUSLY QUOTED the Sixth Patriarch's explanation of the word *zazen*, seated meditation: "Sitting (*za*) means not giving rise to thoughts in the face of any and all external realms, good or bad; *Zen* means remaining undisturbed internally as you see the self-nature." This seems to me a clear and succinct exposition of zazen. I often tell people that zazen is summed up in the single word *totonoeru*, "putting things in order." Putting one's body in order, one's breathing in order, one's mind in order. Adding "putting the world in order" makes it even better.

The protocol for putting the body in order is set forth in detail in the *Principles of Zazen* (*Zazen-gi*), a Rinzai Zen text that provides the essential standards for zazen practice. You should sit holding the spine erect and straight, hips above your crossed legs, spine above your hips, neck above your spine, head above your neck. This posture affords the stability of a five-story pagoda, each story resting directly above the one beneath it. It is the most comfortable as well as the most healthful posture for sitting.

Next you must put your breathing in order so that your breaths do not murmur in your throat, or become irregular—fast, slow, then fast again. Breaths should be quiet and regular, with mouth and nose producing no sound—the breaths are there and yet not there, they exist yet do not exist. Putting your breathing in order is important for your health and the serenity of your mind.

Now you must put your mind in order. Shakyamuni taught, "Living beings all possess the virtues of the Tathagata's wisdom! They fail to realize only because of their delusions and attachments." Illusory thoughts and attachments are the disease of the mind. When the abnormal backwash produced by such thoughts disappears, the mind becomes sound and healthy, and the Tathagata's wisdom and virtues shine forth of themselves. Cutting off illusory thoughts and attachments at the root source of the disease enables the mind to work properly. It is a question of not thinking unnecessary thoughts, not fixing the mind in one place, and letting things move freely and effortlessly—like flowing water. This is the sense of a line of verse by Zen Master Shidō Munan: *Not thinking of anything whatever, at all times, is learning to be a buddha.*

If your body, breathing, and mind all function harmoniously so that the buddha-nature shines forth in its essential form, you can say that you have by and large reached the goal of your zazen practice. However, I think that when you have put the true mind in its inherent order, a great and congenial harmony will also appear throughout the world, with nature and the things around you, home and household, finally the nation as well, settling into their proper and inherent order.

You will notice a plaque in the entrance hall of a Zen temple that is engraved with the words *shōko-kyakka*, "Look carefully down at your own feet!" Monks taking off their sandals and stepping up from the *genkan*, or entrance hall, to enter the temple do so facing backward so that the sandals left behind face toward the door. No one has to take the trouble of turning them around, and on leaving, the monks easily slip their feet into them, even at night when the entrance is dark. The sandals and other footwear in the entrance hall are thus always properly aligned, never found in a disorderly manner—"Look carefully down at your own feet!"

They say that even thieves will not enter a house if they see the footwear properly aligned in the entrance hall. Orderly footwear in the entrance hall means that the minds of those who live there are properly disposed as well. Footwear left out in a careless, haphazard manner reveals the occupants' cluttered state of mind as well. If the mind is properly regulated, the footwear will be tidy as well. Keeping your feet and footwear well regulated leads in time to a correct application of mind.

When the Tenryū-ji priest Hashimoto Gasan (1853–1900) went to Tokyo to meet Layman Yamaoka Tesshū for the first time, he carried a letter of introduction from his teacher Tekisui.

No student attendants were around when Gasan arrived, so Layman Tessū himself, carrying an iron kettle in his hand, appeared from the kitchen to greet him. When Gasan handed him Tekisui's letter, Tesshū put down the kettle, read the letter, and then beckoned Gasan to follow him. Gasan picked up the kettle and followed Tesshū into an inner room. Setting the kettle down on a brazier, he performed his greeting. After that first meeting, Layman Tesshū was heard to remark, "Gasan is a Zen priest who really comports himself like a Zen priest," and from then on he always held Gasan in high regard.

A kettle does not belong in the entrance hall; it belongs on a brazier. Endeavoring to set something in its proper place, putting it in good order, making it exist in the way it is meant to exist—that is Zen.

Recently I have been commuting almost daily between my temple in Kobe and the Myōshin-ji headquarters monastery in Kyoto. I am often stopped short when I get on or off the train, feeling ashamed to see the miserably unsettled demeanor of my fellow citizens' feet. Why are they unable to follow the rules, form into two lines, and quietly board a train or bus? Why must they get so excited, with each person vying to be first on the train even when it is virtually empty? Even when everyone can board calmly and find a seat without pushing or butting in front of one another? They can get on two at a time without any trouble, so why do three or four attempt to enter at once, jamming the doorway and making it impossible for other passengers to board? Why can't they stand quietly in line with their backs straight and erect and board the bus in a dignified manner? When everyone leans forward, pushing against the person in front, the line turns into a confused human mass, good for nothing but blocking entrances.

Each of Japan's large bus and train stations serves as a genkan, or entranceway, into our country. But what I have observed there every day is the chaotic coming and going of my fellow citizens' undisciplined and ill-mannered feet. Would a thief be discouraged from entering here?

Have a single person begin shouting about the urgent need for rearmament, and others will rally to them and without any rhyme or reason start rushing around and yelling their approval. Let someone agitate loudly for revolution and the riot is on. Half the people will be running rampant, voicing support for the notion. It is clearer than the light of day that Japan is today on its way to repeating its previous errors on the Korean peninsula, once again turning itself into a stomping ground for foreign troops. Even if this does not happen, the country could still be snatched away from us without our even being aware of it. What I want for my fellow Japanese today are not lofty ideals or morality. I want for them to "look carefully at their own feet," for them to plant those feet firmly on the earth and quietly consider the appropriate course for the Japanese as a people to follow.

A sumo wrestler enters the ring *suri-ashi*—that is, moving his feet forward in a sliding or shuffling manner without changing the height of the center of gravity. A Noh performer moves his feet in the same fashion. I think walking with the soles of the feet firmly gripping the earth—not walking unsteadily on the toes or balls of the feet—is an inherent Japanese characteristic. A mind constantly retaining its equanimity, not becoming agitated or unsettled no matter what circumstance it encounters, is what is meant by the paramita of concentrated meditation (*dhyana*).

36

THE OTHER SHORE
OF WISDOM

THE APPEARANCE of the Rinzai teacher Bankei Yōtaku
(1622–1693) in the Edo period was a very welcome turn
of events for the Zen school of the time. He taught the school's
essentials using simple language that could be easily understood
by ordinary people. He told them, for example, that their mind,
their fundamental nature (he also referred to it as "the pure
mind of the self-nature"), is like a mirror. Nothing whatever
exists in the mirror; and because of that, it reflects all things.
Any person or object coming before it is reflected; and when the
person or object is no longer present, the reflection disappears.

Although the mirror reflects persons and objects, it does not
produce anything or bring anything into existence. It merely reflects their image. And when the person or object is no longer
there and the image vanishes, nothing has perished. This unborn and undying mind is our original nature. It reflects a beau-

tiful flower, but that does not mean the mirror is beautiful; it reflects filthy dog droppings, but that does not mean it is filthy. This is what the *Heart Sutra* means about *all things being not stained and not pure.*

In entrusting yourself to Amida's original vow, taught Shinran, "No other good is necessary, for there is no good that surpasses the Nembutsu. Neither should you fear evil, for there is no evil that is greater than the Nembutsu, the working of Amida's vow." Being far beyond such goods and evils, the buddha-nature's intrinsic dignity can neither be defiled by any evil, however foul, nor enriched by any good, however wonderful. A mirror does not increase in weight when it reflects something or decrease in weight when the image vanishes. This, teaches Bankei, is the meaning of the *Heart Sutra*'s words: *not increasing, not decreasing.* The same sutra's lines about *unborn, undying, not stained, not pure, not increasing, not decreasing,* it can be said, describe the fundamental nature—the absolute essence—of human being.

To say the mind is like a mirror might evoke the image of a shiny round object existing in the mind or heart, yet it is only a metaphor—there is, in reality, nothing at all. It is for that reason people resort to words like *emptiness* or *nothingness.* The Sixth Patriarch's "There is from the first not a single thing" alludes to this. Zen Master Shidō Munan expresses it in verse:

Once you know surely
    What it is to be living,

Though you laugh or cry
   There is nothing at all.

It is because we are alive that we laugh and weep, but when it comes to the question of who executes this weeping and laughing, they are as ungraspable as that mysterious person in the old verse:

   A cricket
In a withered field—
   A churring voice,
Yet no figure seen.

But if we suppose that because of this there is nothing at all, then why, oh why, do we laugh when something strikes us as funny and weep when something seems sad?

   I offer once again Zen Master Bankei, who explains it very well:

> You people have all gathered together here to listen to me speak. Obviously when I say something, you will hear the words. But if at the same time you hear a dog barking outside, even though not one of you came to the temple to hear a dog bark, won't you all hear its *"Woof"*? You had no intention to hear it, to perceive a dog's bark, but the instant it barks, you hear *"Woof."* That is the buddha-nature.

Although with regard to the dog's bark the mind is *Mu,* sheer nothingness, when the dog barks, the mind hears *"Woof"* —not so much as a whisker separates the two. The mind that does not exist yet functions with total freedom is our original nature.

Zen Master Lin-chi, the founder of Rinzai Zen, explains this point admirably:

> There's nothing at all difficult around here. . . . I tell peo-
> ple to see what comes to their eyes, to hear what comes to
> their ears, to smell what comes to their nose, to talk with
> their mouth, to hold things with their hands, to move
> their feet when they walk.

Lin-chi, using his typically spirited language, says that from his vantage point, there is no difference at all between Shakyamuni Buddha and anyone else. Everyone sees with their eyes, hears with their ears, speaks with their mouths, grasps things with their hands, and walks moving their feet. Even if Shakyamuni were to reappear on earth right now, he would see willows as green, flowers as red. Other people would see them that way too. Could there be any difference in the way they see them? Shakyamuni would hear a sparrow chirp, a crow caw, just like everyone else. There wouldn't be the slightest difference in the way they hear those sounds.

Both Shakyamuni and Bodhidharma became buddhas by re-alizing that the mind does not exist. If we, too, can grasp that the mind does not exist, we will forthwith become buddhas. Our own nothingness and the nothingness of Shakyamuni and Bodhidharma are the same. The nothingness is universal, extending throughout the three periods of past, present, and future and the ten directions of the universe. Because it extends throughout the ten directions, we function with complete, unhindered freedom, hearing "*Woof!*" when a dog barks and "*Moo!*" when a cow cries out, smiling when we are happy and crying when we are sad. Shidō Munan expresses this in a well-known verse: *Be a dead man while alive, thoroughly dead, do as you will, and all will be fine.*

We laugh and we cry, but there is nothing at all; there is nothing at all, yet we continue to live and function as we please. The mind moving freely like this is called wisdom. The Buddha's words, "Living beings all possess the virtues of the Tathagata's wisdom," mean that everyone is possessed of this same wisdom. What follows—"They fail to realize it only because of their delusions and attachments"—means that the unenlightened mind cannot achieve this freely functioning mind because it is always caught up in some matter or other and attaching to various things. Moreover, since the wisdom described here is perfectly clear like a mirror, beyond birth-and-death, free from all suffering and pleasure and transcending all good and evil, to grasp such wisdom means to attain the prajna paramita, to pass over to the other shore of wisdom.

37

THIS VERY MIND
IS BUDDHA

I N THE *Sutra of Meditation on the Buddha of Immeasurable Life*
(*Kanmuryōju-kyō*; also known as the *Meditation Sutra*), one
of the three principal sutras of the Pure Land tradition, are
the words "When you contemplate a buddha, your mind itself takes the form of his thirty-two physical characteristics and
eighty secondary marks. At that time, this very mind is Buddha—mind itself is Buddha." Is it not extremely interesting to
find that these precious words so often used in the Zen tradition, "This very mind is Buddha—mind itself is Buddha," derive from a Pure Land sutra? I believe that both the believing
mind (*shinjin*, the mind of faith; the believing mind) of Pure
Land Buddhism and the satori of the Zen school ultimately
boil down to one and the same mind. In the realm of the believing mind, there is in fact no self-power or other-power. The
Zen verse "Inscribed in the Believing Mind" (*Shinjin-mei*) has

Belief and mind are the nondual reality, / Nondual reality is the believing mind.

Shōma of Sanuki Province, who practiced Nembutsu on the island of Shikoku, was a true *myōkōnin*, literally "wondrous, excellent person," a designation given to lay followers of the Pure Land school who are distinguished by especially deep and pure faith. Someone once asked Shōma, "Isn't it worrisome how popular Christianity is becoming these days? Before long, the Buddha's teachings may disappear." "Yes," replied Shōma, "but there isn't any teaching that surpasses an ordinary person becoming a buddha."

Isn't Shōma a wonderful example of what the Pure Land schools call a person of firmly established faith? Even though we speak of the *tariki*, or "other-power" teaching, insofar as it is the Buddha Dharma, the ineffable experience of attaining the believing mind cannot exist apart from the unenlightened person feeling the joy of being a buddha.

Shinran sings of this in his *Wasan*:

It is taught that a person who takes delight
In shinjin is no different from the Tathagata;
A mind of great faith is the buddha-nature,
The buddha-nature is itself the Tathagata.

He says that people who experience the joy of firmly establishing themselves in the believing mind, with their afflicting passions and evil karma undiminished, exist in a mental state not one bit different from the Buddha. In fact, their deep belief is, in itself, Buddha. The final lines, *A mind of great faith is the buddha-nature / The buddha-nature is itself the Tathagata*, from the *Nirvana Sutra*, mean that achieving an unshakable faith is no different from grasping the innate buddha-nature, the essential mind we have when we are born into the world.

On reaching this point, the truth of the "believing mind" of the Pure Land schools has the same flavor that is savored in the *anjin* (or "settled mind") of Zen, which Hakuin portrays in *Song of Zazen* as *All beings are from the first buddhas, / Their kinship is like water and ice.* Hence Shinran's verse:

Your karmic obstacles become a body of merit,
Existing in a relation like that of ice and water;
Where there's much ice, there is also much water,
When obstacles are many, virtues abound as well.
—*Kōsō Wasan* (*Hymns of High Priests*)

The relentless and intense self-reflection Shinran undertook is rare even in the history of world religion. He lamented that no one was as sinful or burdened by so many evil passions as he was, declaring that he was "submerged in a vast ocean of desire, straying waywardly through towering mountains of fame and profit." But in truth, Shinran was inherently possessed of a truly noble mind, and for this reason his profound self-reflection and contrition could arise. A truly noble, mirrorlike mind that engages in such deep self-scrutiny—that is the buddha-nature.

In Shinran's *Tannishō* (*Deploring Deviations of Faith*) we read, "The ordinary person weighed down with evil passions, the world as impermanent as a burning house, and everything else as well—these are all words devoid of meaning . . . utterances bereft of truth. The Nembutsu alone is true."

There is no doubt whatever that the world is as ephemeral as a burning house. A family sits down together for the evening meal and an hour later the house is washed away in a flood. A family lies sleeping peacefully in the same room and by morning they and the whole village lie buried under a mudslide, only one young daughter left alive. These are not events that took place hundreds of years ago; they happened only last year. This world is truly a burning house. There is nothing at all in which we can place our trust.

The fourteenth-century Japanese historical epic *Chronicle of Great Peace* (*Taiheiki*) narrates stories of the period of war between the Northern Court in Kyoto and the Southern Court of Emperor Go-Daigo (1288–1339), situated in the mountains of Yoshino. In one passage, the emperor is described living forlornly in his remote mountain retreat, deeply lamenting the truth of a passage he came upon in a Buddhist sutra: "Although you have a wife and child, property and wealth, even though you occupy the throne as an emperor, when you die, nothing you own can you take with you."

The words are all too true. This being the case, you are obliged to reflect deeply on the reality that you are an unenlightened being encumbered by all the afflicting passions, a being that can place no trust in a totally untrustworthy self, a self that might, given the chance, perpetrate misdeeds of the most abhorrent kind.

The Sutra of the Buddha's Bequeathed Teaching speaks of the mind as "more terrible than venomous snakes, ferocious beasts, or bloodthirsty bandits." The only reason people do not commit horrific offenses or crimes is because they have been fortunate enough to not have been placed in circumstances that would cause them to commit such acts. Human beings are in any case truly frightening creatures. Who knows what they might do at any given time? Their very life is unsure. They cannot rely on their spouse, children, or family, on property or wealth or social position, or on society, the nation, and the natural world in which they live. Nor can they rely on themselves. Where, then, can they place their trust? How are they to live? The task of grasping that final refuge, somewhere you can truly depend on, is the concern of religion. Using other words, we could also say that religion is grasping the eternal, the infinite.

On this point, Shinran's words not about Buddha or the Pure Land being true but about Nembutsu alone being true, assume great profundity and significance. They are words to be very deeply savored.

Nembutsu means keeping Amida Buddha in mind, which is to say, keeping the infinite in mind. If we keep the Buddha in mind, then this very mind is Buddha. If we keep the infinite in mind, this mind is infinite.

Infinity is a place where ordinary people and buddhas are

no different, where subjectivity and objectivity have become one, where it is meaningless to reason about self-power or other-power. The Buddha, the infinite realized in your own mind, is the true mind, a mind that will fill you with such joy and delight as to make you tread the very air in exultation.

Shin Buddhism uses the term *kenshin*, "seeing the truth," to express this experience; Zen calls it kenshō, "seeing the self-nature." Shin Buddhism's shinjin, the believing mind, is none other than the self-awakened buddha-nature. Or as I like to think of it, zazen is reciting the Nembutsu with your body, and Nembutsu is doing zazen with your mouth.

38

A MIRROR OF PURE
LAPIS LAZULI

I T IS SAID that the invention of tools and writing and the use
of mirrors set human beings apart from the other animals.
The discovery of the use of tools, which has led to today's sci-
ence-based civilization and technology, started with extremely
simple stone axes and primitive earthenware pottery. From these
beginnings human technology has developed atomic and hydrogen bombs. While the invention of writing was instrumental in
the evolution of the human brain and human culture generally,
I believe the use of mirrors played an important role in opening
up the world of religion.

Human beings gain no benefit from seeing themselves in a
mirror. In the material world, mirrors are of no help in producing things; they may even be said to hinder such production.
People clamor about religion being an opiate, of no possible
benefit to human beings. Despite that, I think human beings'

inability to stop looking into mirrors is a strong indication that they will not be able to cast religion aside. Is there not found in this strong inclination the deeply rooted tenacity of their religious feelings?

I think we can say that our purpose in looking into a mirror is self-examination. It allows us to criticize the good and bad, the beauty and ugliness in ourselves. Animals are said to live their entire lives without any consciousness of their own faces. They are unaware and totally unreflecting as regards their own behavior. When human beings go before a mirror, they immediately recognize their face. They do everything they can to make it appear in a better light. And they will try, by reflecting on their own behavior, to create a better life for themselves. Herein lies the nobility of human beings.

Science has advanced to the point where human beings can produce atomic and hydrogen weapons, but the question of whether it is good or bad to use them is a matter that will require human self-reflection. At no time in history has there been a greater need for this self-reflection, which means there has never been a time with a more urgent need for religion. If science alone continues to progress without accompanying self-reflection, there is no way to avoid human life vanishing from the earth.

I mentioned in a previous essay that while scholars explain the Shintō term *kami* (deity) in various ways—holding that it means "upper" (as opposed to lower), that it is a corruption of the word *kabi* (mold), or of the word *kakuri-mi* (hidden body)—the most plausible theory is that it is a shortened form of the word *kagami*, or "mirror." That was the conclusion drawn by, among others, Hakuin's disciple Tōrei, who was the son of a Shinto priest and a keen student of Shintō.

The mind of the Shintō kami is said to be as pure and undefiled as a mirror, perfectly impartial and selfless, a mind that has penetrated to the infinite. In Buddhism this is called the Great and Perfect Mirror Wisdom (*Daien-kyōchi*). A mirror is the best symbol for the Shintō kami and for the buddha-mind. In Shintō shrines, a mirror is usually set out before the altar. In Emma, the Lord of Hell's Court of Judgment, through which all dead souls must pass, a mirror of pure lapis lazuli (*jōruri kagami*) is set out that reflects unerringly all the actions of their lives, good and bad, omitting nothing. It moves like a revolving lantern, revealing everything and causing the dead, in spite of themselves, to look back over their lives and evince the desire to seek expiation for their sins.

But once you have died and are hauled before Emma's court, it is too late. You must examine yourself daily while you are still alive and reflect on how you can live a better life. This is what Buddhism calls *sange*, the repentance of past evils. I don't think there is any religion that does not preach self-reflection and repentance. Shintō calls this *o-harai*, "purification"; Christianity, repenting of one's sins; Buddhism, *zangi sange*, feeling shame for one's sins and repenting of them.

Acceptance of the Buddha's precepts has long been a part of Zen training. It is a solemn ceremony in which initiates receive the Buddhist precepts as a full-fledged disciple of Buddha. They pray to all the buddhas in the trichiliocosmic universe, repeating their names. They perform bows stating that they are ashamed of their sins and repent of them, and that they have created karmic hindrances with their six sense organs and vow to extinguish them and their evil passions. The ceremony continues for a week, during which time the initiates' minds, like dirty robes that have been given a thorough washing, are totally purified. Purified and free of defilement, their minds are now ready to receive the Buddha's precepts.

It is stated in the sutras that "living beings who receive the Buddha's precepts enter immediately into the ranks of the buddhas, with a great awakening that is no different from theirs." As members of the Buddhist order standing on the same level as the august and noble buddhas themselves, they now carry on their practice together with all the buddhas of the three worlds.

People feel the need to repent in various ways—superficially and profoundly, partially and fully—according to their characters. A person like Shinran, who judged himself to be burdened with evils of the worst kind, or the apostle Paul, who writes in 1 Timothy 1:15, "I am the worst of the sinners," were men who had engaged in a most powerful and profound self-examination.

However, even though someone engages constantly in serious self-examination and experiences intense suffering, that does not necessarily mean that they are religious or that it will lead to their salvation. The reality of salvation only appears when a finite, suffering human being is taken in by the infinite; embraced by the boundless. Only then do they acquire the great peace that comes with a truly settled mind (*anjin*). Hence, repentance does not have meaning just because someone continues to suffer endlessly in the limited world of relativity. They become one with the Buddha and the Shintō kami when they throw themselves straight into the arms of the infinite and are assimilated in the melting pot of the Boundless One. This means that repentance becomes genuine and sins disappear only when the nonduality of the mind of faith (*shinjin*) is attained. Expressed yet another, more direct way, doing zazen and reciting the Nembutsu are true repentance.

The *Samantabhadra Contemplation Sutra* says, "All obstructing karma is produced by delusory thought. If you want to seek repentance from that karma, sit straight and erect and contemplate the true reality of things. All the sins you have accumulated will dissipate under the sun of wisdom as completely as frost or mist." In other words, sitting erect and clarifying the true form of the eternal self, penetrating to see the real self, is the best way to gain repentance for your karmic transgressions.

"No other good is necessary, for there is no good that surpasses the Nembutsu. Neither should you fear evil, for there is no evil that is greater than the Nembutsu, the working of Amida's vow," Shinran confesses powerfully in the *Tannishō*. But whether good or evil, as long as you remain attached to a self that is merely a fleeting appearance reflected in a mirror, you will never be saved. Genuine repentance does not appear in such a reflected self but in a self that *becomes* the reflecting mirror and penetrates to the real form of the true and eternal self.

39

FORGETTING
YOUR FINGERS

A LTHOUGH I HAVE likened these essays on the *Song of Zazen* to a slow local train, somewhere along the line they seem to have left the tracks. I'm an old priest holding forth in the midst of a sightseeing boom, and being unable to make myself sound like the young ladies warbling their information over the station loudspeakers, I have been obliged to press on with my usual classic explanations. My derailment came just as I was going to treat readers to a grand tour of Mount Fuji's five scenic lakes and perhaps take in the hot springs at Hakone. But wearying of these peregrinations for now at least, I somehow or other have managed to find my way back to the main line once again. Even so, I have always felt that occasional interludes or sideshows of this kind are beneficial adjuncts of human life, which otherwise would be a mere humdrum existence shorn of any spontaneity.

Looking back over the sights I've shown the reader so far—

the four lakes of giving, charity, diligence, and prajna wisdom; the landscapes of the six paramitas; the cascade of the six characters of Amida's name; the deep pool of repentance—I sincerely hope they have afforded them a splendid prospect or two, the kind that, in the mere recalling, helps purify the mind.

The next line in Hakuin's *Song of Zazen* promises the appearance of yet more attractions: *And other good acts in countless number.* Certainly there is no lack of equally famous religious sites—the grove of deep awareness, the hillock of divine meditation, the rapids of the sixty thousand practices, the memorial to the cross of Jesus—but unfortunately we have neither time nor space to visit them all. Here, however, are two of them, described in a well-known verse by the Sung poet Su Tung-p'o:

Misty rain on Mount Lu, the tidal surge on the river Che,
When you have not yet been there, your regrets are many,
Going home after seeing them, they weren't so special at all.
Misty rain on Mount Lu, the tidal surge on the river Che.

The sublime grandeur of Mount Lu veiled in rain and mist, the thrilling prospect of the tidal bore moving upstream in the Chien-tang River near Hang-chou—these are two of the greatest spectacles China has to offer. Before seeing these sights, Su Tung-p'o may have felt he hadn't experienced all that he should, but he realized on actually visiting them that they were not so remarkable after all—just the mist and rain over Mount Lu and the Chien-tang tidal bore surging upstream. This is like what people say about climbing Mount Fuji: it is foolish not to do it once, but to do it twice is equally foolish. It would have been foolish for the poet not to view these two magnificent sights, but just as foolish for him to go and view them a second time.

An old senryu poet agrees with him:

Coming and seeing it,
  Not all that grand,
Mount Fuji.

For all the ballyhoo about sites of great scenic beauty, you realize once you have gone and seen them that they are all no more than different combinations of mountains and water. We fuss in the same way about the six paramitas and acts of repentance, though in the end they all boil down to the two Chinese characters that make the word *zenjō* the mental state that is "being free of forms externally, being undisturbed within."

It is the same with giving charity. Giving is not true giving as long as it is offered with any thought of giving; a donation is genuine only when it is given without any notion of self and the very act of donating is forgotten. Zen Master Shidō Munan wrote,

There is no person who
  Donates three sen,
No priest who receives
  A three-sen donation.
You must be able to offer a donation of even tens of thousands

of yen with the same casual and carefree feeling you would have donating a mere three sen. Those receiving the donation also must receive it as though they were receiving three sen. Buddhism calls donating in this way "the three rings" (*sanrin*) of donor, recipient, and donation, stressing that each of the rings must be "empty and serene." Did not Jesus speak of "not letting the left hand know what the right hand is giving"?*

A true donation—genuine giving—can thus take place as a result of zenjō (*dhyana*), the concentrated state of mind where the mind is free of forms externally and undisturbed within. Conversely, the practice of true giving will lead as a matter of course to the realm of zenjō. The same holds for the other paramitas as well—upholding the precepts, forbearance or patience, diligence, and wisdom. If you genuinely uphold the precepts and practice forbearance, diligence, and wisdom, they will all be assimilated into the realm of zenjō. Hakuin's *Song of Zazen* expresses this as *And other good acts in countless number / Are all deep rooted in Zen [zenjō] meditation.* The six paramitas that bodhisattvas nobly practice in this way are all embraced within the one zenjō paramita.

The Zen poem "Song of Realizing the Way" (*Cheng-tao-ke*) says, *Once you have suddenly awakened to the Tathagata's Zen, / you will embody to perfection the six paramitas and all other practices.* In

* The quotation should be "what the right hand does." The author plays on the double meaning of the verb *hodokosu*, which is generally used in the Japanese translation of this biblical passage, but in a Buddhist context means "donating" or "giving."

207

other words, if you can grasp experientially the one paramita of zenjō, the other paramitas, containing all other practices, are included within it as well.

Zen Master Ta-chueh's *Treatise on Zazen* (Ch. *Tso-ch'an I;* Jap. *Zazen-ron*) has "Zazen is the Dharma gate of great liberation. All other Dharmas issue from it, all religious practices are achieved through it." Ta-chueh means that not only the six paramitas but all the many and varied Buddhist teachings, the writings in the Buddhist canon, the thirteen sects and fifty-six schools, greater and smaller vehicles, provisional and true, holy path and the Pure Land path—are all produced from zenjō.

There is an old verse:

Invoking the name
    With no buddha or self,
Namu-Amida-Butsu,
    Namu-Amida-Butsu.

Recitation of the name of Amida Buddha without any hint of self—no self to recite the name and no buddha to recite it to—takes place in the nondualistic realm in which ordinary person and saint, self and other, and all other distinctions and discriminations have fallen away. It is the samadhic realm of zenjō, "free of forms externally, undisturbed within." Nembutsu is itself zenjō. True Nembutsu can be recited only within the realm of zenjō.

Hōnen Shōnin states the same thing in his declaration that

"the reciting of just the six characters of Amida Buddha's name includes all other practices." Since the Nembutsu is itself zenjō, it too contains all other paramitas and practices as well. Seen in this way, Hakuin's *Nembutsu, repentance, ascetic practice / And other good acts in countless number*—indeed, the practice of religious exercises of every kind: offering prayers, fasting, contemplation, serving others—return to the two characters zenjō. Expressing it differently, we could say that they *originate* in those two Chinese characters.

This principle is not limited to religious exercises alone. Zen has long been called the source of the various traditional Japanese ways. Their inner secrets all return to their origin in the two characters *zenjō*. Performers of Japanese dance perform singlemindedly, oblivious of their bodies. Singers or chanters perform with full-hearted devotion, unmindful of their throats. Pianists forget their fingers when they play. Actors perform various roles without thinking of their true ages. Skilled workers devote themselves to their work unrelentingly, with all the strength at their command.

Only someone whose mind is "free of forms externally, undisturbed within" can evince truly wondrous skill in the traditional Japanese arts and in other secular undertakings as well. The flowering of traditional Asian culture as seen in the oneness of tea and Zen, swordsmanship and Zen, haiku and Zen— was and is possible only on the basis of zenjō, not merely in the realms of religion and morality but in every aspect of social life. The *Song of Zazen* thus celebrates the greatness of zenjō: *How great the dhyana of the Mahayana, / No praise could ever exhaust its merits!*

40

SELF-POWER AND OTHER-POWER

IN PRAISING the virtues of the Mahayana zenjō as being immeasurably vast, in calling it the place to which the six paramitas, or perfections, practiced by bodhisattvas all return and from which all the marvelous skills in the arts and traditional ways and the ideal conditions of secular life have their source, I may give the impression that I am beating my own drum, holding up Zen as the only proper method of practice. But I assure you that I am not at all speaking with a sectarian bias. One of the ancients said, "Zen is another name for mind; mind is the body of Zen," meaning that the word *zen* simply gives a name to the truth of our human nature, human nature being a problem that all of us must face. Grasping the truth of human nature and thereby achieving unwavering stability of mind is what the word *zenjō* signifies.

I would like to add my own definition of zenjō, rephrasing

the Sixth Patriarch's "*Zen* is being free of forms externally; *jō* is being undisturbed within" to read "*Zen* is grasping the truth of human nature, *jō* is achieving thereby unwavering stability." What is called the Buddha Dharma is simply a matter of grasping the truth of human nature and awakening to the true self. It is to this that the various divisions of the Buddhist teaching, greater and lesser, provisional and true, and human endeavor of every kind must all return.

Living in society as well, if you carry on in disregard of the true self, everything is false and untrue, dreamlike, illusory, nonsensical, and meaningless. It must be said that social life in the proper sense is not realized until you grasp the unwavering stability that comes upon grasping the truth of human nature. For you to reach the concentrated mental state of zenjō, which is the most important desideratum of human life, the practice of seated meditation is the most appropriate method. Zen is a religion that advocates zazen—seated meditation—and Hakuin, who wrote the *Song of Zazen* in order to make ordinary people everywhere aware of its merits, now lavishes praise on this method of seated meditation. Please, readers, do not mistake the *Song of Zazen* as some kind of sectarian propaganda aimed at glorifying Zen, narrowly defined.

I believe most people seek religion because they experience a sense of impermanence, a feeling of guilt, an awareness of insecurity or anxiety in their lives. Human life abounds in contradictions, failures, impasses; and at those times, everyone may experience anxiety. Human beings, in short, who are bound to a finite world, never cease desiring the freedom of the infinite. I believe the sense of awareness that makes a person desire this freedom is religious in nature.

So upon acquiring religion, if you flap the two wings of freedom and independence on the vast plain of infinity and are able to strike deep into the boundless mother lode that lies buried there, you are, in the paraphrased sense of Christ's "blessed are the poor in spirit, they who mourn, and they who hunger and thirst for righteousness," a truly blessed being. The ones to be pitied are those who spend their lives comfortably in favorable social circumstances without ever experiencing the slightest tinge of humility.

The Japanese search for religion was at its most avid during the Kamakura period (1185–1333), a time of conflict with the rival Heike and Taira clans drawn into a series of great military assaults that turned the country into a battlefield of unimaginable carnage. Members of the same clan were pitted against each other in brutal struggle, ordinary people were in a state of exceeding anxiety, and the entire country was plunged into the depths of despair where nothing whatever—wealth or rank, social position or family, even life itself—was certain or could be relied upon.

It was during the Kamakura period that Hōnen's Pure Land teaching swept through the country like wildfire, providing comfort and sustenance to people's hearts and minds like a beneficent rainfall in time of drought. Hōnen taught that without need of learning or ascetic practice, regardless of the difference between aristocrat and commoner, all a person had to do was to recite the formula *Namu-Amida-Butsu* and they would be assured of rebirth in Amida's Pure Land of Ultimate Bliss. This simple teaching, so easily put into practice, was adopted enthusiastically by people of all classes and ranks of society—from aristocrats and samurai down to the prostitutes in the port towns on the Inland Sea.

It was at this same time that Master Eisai (1141–1215) went to Sung China to study Zen and brought the Zen teachings back to Japan where they prospered, gaining followers from among the courtiers, the samurai, and those in high positions in the government. The Zen school is often said to be the way of self-power; of requiring learning, religious practice, and great perseverance. However *self-power* and *other-power* are terms originally used by the Pure Land tradition in proselytizing its own teachings. Zen never describes itself using the term *self-power*. Zen Master Dōgen wrote, "Learning the Buddha Way is learning the self. Learning the self is forgetting the self." Understanding the Buddha Dharma means understanding the true self, and understanding the true self means forgetting the self.

Far from being a self-power teaching, Zen is instead a matter of casting off the self. It can be said, however—temporarily borrowing the words *self-power* and *other-power*—that in Zen, self-power is self-power until self-power is cast off, and other-power is other-power until other-power is cast off. When people reach the point in Zen practice where the self is forgotten, and the point in the Nembutsu teaching where all schemes and calculations are forgotten, do they not find themselves in the same place? It is a state of no-mind where distinctions between self and other do not exist.

Reading the *Song of Zazen*'s next lines—*The merit you gain from just one sitting / Cancels vast stores of obstructive karma, / Keeps you from entering wrongful paths, / Keeps the Pure Land always close at hand*—we feel how much in common those words have with Hōnen's Pure Land teaching, its "attainment of rebirth in the Pure Land with even ten repetitions of the name." A person who believes that ten repetitions of Amida's name will cancel out all their evil karma and usher them into the Pure Land will have little trouble believing that sitting even one time in zazen will bring them prompt attainment of buddhahood. In fact, I think people in today's modern, scientific-based world would be more likely to agree to the possibility of a single session of zazen bringing them in touch with the reality of human nature than to that of attaining rebirth in the Pure Land through ten repetitions of Amida's name.

The *Contemplation Sutra* teaches in the same vein: "Amida Buddha is not distant from here. . . . The Pure Land is not far." The human nature is Buddha, Amida. If you penetrate to that truth, then Amida Buddha truly "is not distant from here. . . . The Pure Land is not far." If repeating the Nembutsu is keeping this truth of human nature tenaciously in mind, then zazen is pitching you headlong into that truth.

41

HUMAN LIFE . . . LIKE FLECKS OF FOAM

DURING HAKUIN'S LIFETIME, there was a wealthy man named Yamanashi Heishirō living in the hamlet of Ihara, about a league distant from the Okitsu post station in Suruga Province. An influential figure in the village, Heishirō was a fine, vigorous man in the prime of life. He had little interest in religion and never set foot inside a temple. However, when a proposal was voiced to enshrine a stone image of the guardian deity Fudō-myōō beside a waterfall in the neighboring hamlet of Yoshiwara, a village priest was somehow able to persuade Heishirō to donate the funds for the statue.

An auspicious day was chosen for the ceremony to "open the eyes" of the new image, and Heishirō, who had never taken part in such a Buddhist ceremony, was obliged as the donor of the statue to attend. He took his son and a few other acquaintances along with him. After the ceremony ended and Heishirō was seated with his fellow villagers eating his bento and sipping sake, his eyes happened to focus on the base of the waterfall, where he saw foam forming where the water struck the stream at the bottom of the falls.

The bubbles formed and vanished, formed and vanished, over and over. Some of them floated a few feet over the surface and disappeared, some floated for several yards, some kept floating for a longer time before fading away, while yet others vanished almost as soon as they formed. On observing them Heishirō felt how strange it was that though all the bubbles appeared from the base of the same waterfall, they each had different destinies. Suddenly it dawned on him that human life was just the same. Some youths died at the age of ten, some at twenty, some lived to be seventy or eighty, while some died at birth—just like the flecks of foam on the water. In the end, whether they were rich or poor, happy or unhappy, beautiful or ugly, good or evil, all of them perished. Unable to restrain the strong feeling rising within him, he got up and fled the gathering unnoticed, leaving behind his son, acquaintances, and his bento. On the way back home he passed a small temple where the resident priest was reciting a religious text in a loud voice. Normally Heishirō would not have paid this any notice, but on this day his mind was somehow drawn to the sound. He stood outside the temple listening to the priest recite the words: "A strong and resolute person may attain buddhahood in a single instant of thought. An indolent person cannot attain nirvana even with the passage of three kalpas." The words intrigued Heishirō, so he went inside and asked the priest what he was chanting. The priest said that it was a passage from the *Dharma Words of Takusui*.

The words "a strong and resolute person" set him to thinking: "I'm an able-bodied man. There's no reason I can't give my best effort, even at the risk of my life, to attaining nirvana. A method like this one that will enable me to become a buddha right away is my only chance of achieving buddhahood in my lifetime." On returning home, Heishirō sought a secluded place where he would not be bothered by others. He chose a room set aside for guests to take their baths, which was rarely used. Taking a cushion inside, he wedged his staff against the door so it could not be opened, sat down, and began doing zazen.

Heishirō's knowledge of zazen was limited. He knew only that you sat cross-legged. So that is what he did. There was complete silence all around, but Heishirō's mind was busier and more confused than a beehive. Unnecessary thoughts and delusions crowded into his mind one after the other, completely beyond his control. But he was not the kind of person to give up. He bore down diligently, focusing solely on the words "a strong and resolute person may attain buddhahood in a single instant of thought." Finally, sitting there struggling valiantly to overcome the pain in his legs, he lost consciousness.

When he came to his senses, he realized that both his thumbs were throbbing with pain. Outside the window, dawn was lightening the sky. He heard sparrows chittering. He realized that he had continued sitting in zazen throughout the night. On opening the window he noticed that something was strange.

The world he now saw was completely different from the world his eyes had seen up until the previous night. The green of the pine tree, the shape of the rocks, the color of the moss—they all seemed different. He wondered if this could be due to having attained satori or enlightenment. He resolved to sit for one more night, and he ended up sitting for three successive nights. Marveling at the bright clarity of his mind and the beauty of the surrounding world, he felt that he might be experiencing the realm of enlightenment. However, since he was not familiar with such matters, he decided to go to a temple and ask a priest about it. Having heard that an eminent priest named Hakuin resided nearby, he made up his mind to pay him a visit. He had a palanquin made ready and set off for the Hara post station.

When the palanquin carriers stopped to rest at the top of the Satta Pass, Heishirō got out and looked around, surveying the mountains of Izu peninsula across and beyond the port of Tagonoura on Suruga Bay. The panorama below him seemed to him more beautiful than any he had ever seen. He had traversed the Satta Pass countless times, but never had it looked like this. Perhaps he was viewing it in the light of buddha wisdom? He could hardly contain his joy, and with endless tears flowing down his cheeks, he pressed the carriers to hurry so he could reach Hakuin's temple as soon as possible.

Zen Master Hakuin immediately granted Heishirō's request for an interview. He listened carefully to Heishirō, who explained everything he could about his state of mind, and then he asked Hakuin for his help. After testing him with two or three koans, Hakuin confirmed Heijirō's attainment. I think Hakuin himself must have been astonished. He put down a sheet of paper and wrote that he had not seen such a wonderful kenshō in many years. He then brushed in the Buddhist name Ryōtetsu Koji, "Layman Who Has Fully Penetrated," and presented it to Heishirō.

Both Hakuin and his student Tōrei often used this story in teaching ordinary, unlettered laypeople. It is a fine example of how someone can achieve kenshō and buddhahood if they seriously apply themselves to Zen practice.

The merit you gain from just one sitting
Cancels vast stores of obstructive karma,
Keeps you from entering wrongful paths,
Keeps the Pure Land always close at hand.

If you do zazen even a single time and are able to press forward and reach the genuine state of zenjō, all the bad karma you have accumulated from the beginningless past will without a doubt vanish, and in one instant of thought you will attain buddhahood. When that happens, why should you need to worry any longer about the evil destinations of karmic rebirth in the six paths? When you attain the experience of satori and awaken to Amida's presence near at hand, the actual world right where you are is at that very moment the Pure Land—the lotus paradise of enlightened being.

42

CREATING A BETTER FACE

A SERIES OF photo-news articles entitled "Enjoying Summer" has been appearing in the newspaper lately. The stories include the minister of education visiting a small primary school on an island near Hachijōshima and university students who were evacuated there as children during the war now paying visits to the priest in the mountain temple that had taken them in. One article was about the popular young actress Kyō Machiko's visit to worship the famous Nyoirin Kannon enshrined at the Chūgu-ji in Nara Province. Magnanimously admitting defeat, she declared herself no match for the bodhisattva's beauty. Encountering the Kannon's celebrated smile, she marveled at its eyes, like those of a Noh mask; though carved in wood and unmoving, they seemed half watchful, half hidden. She compared their subtle, mysterious charm to the ineffable mystery revealed at the highest reaches of the traditional arts, which she said could "capture her heart and keep it enthralled."

Art critics such as Aizu Yaoichi and Kamei Katsuichirō praised the Chūgu-ji Kannon as being "unmatched in the world," its "eternal smile" a symbol of compassion and wisdom. Why is it that this bodhisattva captivates the minds and hearts of all who see it, Buddhist or non-Buddhist, Japanese or non-Japanese, learned or unlearned? I think it is because its appearance and aura touch something deep in the human soul. The compassion and wisdom it so abundantly manifests are the fundamental essence of our human nature; its eternal smile is our inmost soul. It has the power to make us feel an immense nostalgia for the human spirit.

Zazen is the path by which we self-awaken in various ways to this fundamental essence of our nature. It is the wonderful means of returning us to the true and original form of human being.

Ikkyū has this Chinese verse:

An inch of incense, an inch of buddhahood,
Inch by inch, till a buddha five meters high,
Its thirty-two major and eighty minor marks
Natural endowments of the Original Man.

If you do zazen for the time it takes a stick of incense to burn down one inch, you are for that period of time a buddha. For that time, you manifest the fundamental essence of your human nature and return to the true form you intrinsically possess. When you do that every day for an inch of incense, you naturally acquire in your present human frame the full body of a great buddha five meters high, endowed with all a buddha's characteristic thirty-two major and eighty minor bodily features.

I have heard that one of the exercises people perform to make themselves look attractive to others is to keep the backbone straight and erect, so that they "feel like a doll or puppet hanging by a thread from the ceiling." But that describes the zazen posture perfectly. Doing zazen, maintaining not only this correct bodily posture but also a mind constantly at peace, is the finest beauty regimen you can perform to preserve your looks.

Speaking of good looks, I am reminded of a story told about Abraham Lincoln. One of Lincoln's cabinet officers introduced a friend to the president, praising him as someone who could perform any task he was given. He urged Lincoln to give him a post in the government. Lincoln refused the request, and when the cabinet officer asked why, he replied, "I don't like his face." "He can't help the way he looks," the friend countered. "He got that face from his mother when he was born." "No," said Lincoln, "once a man passes the age of forty, he has to take responsibility for his face."

I believe that the goal of men and women should be to perfect their character; that human life is a workshop in which we all must create a countenance worthy of respect. In that sense, the finest method I know for perfecting the character or personality and for creating an excellent physiognomy is zazen. It returns you to your original state of being and makes your original form function as it should.

Lord Kujō Michiie, who was responsible for establishing the Tōfuku-ji monastery in Kyoto, once said to National Master Shōichi, "The doctrine of your Zen school is exceedingly difficult. It is so unapproachable that it leaves people completely at a loss. What kind of practice should I or any other lay follower undertake? Even if we do engage in Zen practice, there is no assurance we will reach enlightenment. Don't you think it would be a great disappointment for someone to fail to attain awakening after devoting themselves to Zen with the utmost assiduity?"

Shōichi responded, "The Dharma teaching of zazen is a marvelous path that enables a person to break free of karmic suffering. It enables an ordinary person to become a buddha just as they are, even without engaging in difficult ascetic practice. A person who hears this teaching even once and truly accepts it with a thankful heart thereby establishes a strong link to satori. If they not only hear about it but go on to actually engage in zazen practice, they will manifest the buddha-mind in the very act of their sitting.

"Originally there is neither illusion nor enlightenment in the buddha-mind. When you do zazen you are residing serenely at this place where neither illusion nor enlightenment exists.

"The six years of zazen that Shakyamuni performed in the Himalayas was in itself the marvelous practice of satori. The zazen Bodhidharma engaged in for nine years facing a rock cliff at Mount Sung was a manifestation of satori as well. So even if a student does not achieve satori, they should not stop practicing it. If they do zazen for one hour, they are a buddha for one hour. If they sit for one day, they are a buddha for one day. If they continue sitting for their entire life, aren't they a buddha for their entire life? Those who trust in this and proceed to engage in zazen practice are known as 'persons of superior capacity and wisdom,' 'great Dharma vessels.'"

Ikkyū's line, "An inch of incense, an inch of buddhahood," was probably suggested by National Master Shōichi's teaching, "If you sit for one day, you are a buddha for one day. . . . If you sit for a lifetime, you are a buddha for a lifetime." Zazen is a religious teaching that enables us to be saved just as we are, in our ordinary deluded state of mind, burdened with bad karma. Sitting even once in zazen cancels the boundless sins we have accumulated until now and leads us directly to buddhahood. I believe clear evidence of this is seen in a gradual transformation in the facial features of someone who undertakes the practice of zazen.

43

THE MOON OF TRUE SUCHNESS SHINES BRIGHT

RECENTLY I MET for the first time in many years a former general in the Japanese Imperial Army who is now incarcerated as a war criminal in Sugamo Prison. As he shared his thoughts with me during this time, I was moved by the profound self-reflection he has undergone regarding the war and the Japanese defeat and by the deep sense of responsibility he feels. I listened carefully to him talk about the pain and suffering he has gone through in confronting the basic problems of human life. He survived the war. He did not commit suicide. Although he was not among those sentenced to death by the military tribunal, he was condemned to lifelong imprisonment. Although in the past, incarceration would have meant deep disgrace for a samurai, he must now submit to spending the rest of his life inside a prison. After agonizing for a long time over the meaning of human life, he finally reached the conclusion that "the object of human life is to perfect the human character."

He said that although he had often heard others express such commonplace notions, that he himself had uttered them, now when he was earnestly engaged in coming to grips with human life, words that he had previously not thought very deeply about had come to possess a strong and urgent potency.

"It was only when I grasped," he said, "that the object of human life is not to become rich, rise up in the world, or become learned but is rather to work at cultivating and perfecting my character—that is when I attained the stability of a settled mind. This is something anyone can do, without regard for how much money they have, their social standing, or their education. Ever since I realized this was something I could work at wherever I was, I have been employed perfecting my character using this prison as my sole training hall."

Goethe said, "There can be no greater joy for a person than his human character. No matter how much wealth he accumulates in his life, he cannot always have it at his side. But his character is something that is always with him wherever he may be." The question then becomes, "Though we may agree that the object of life is to perfect character, can ordinary people like us achieve that end?"

Ordinary devotees of Pure Land Buddhism might criticize such an idea: "Shinran declared he was an ordinary, ignorant man possessed of all the wrongful passions, deeply sinful and villainous, forsaken by the buddhas of the three worlds and certainly destined for hell, saved only thanks to Amida's original vow, so for us to attempt to perfect our character would from the first be a prideful exercise of self-power." The Zen sect, although often called the school of self-power, never speaks of perfecting human character. Ridding oneself of self-power, casting the self aside—that is the path of Zen. Achieving a state of no-mind, no-thought, awakening to the true self—that is Zen. That is how Zen achieves the perfection of the self with remarkable efficacy; and that is why it declares, *All beings are from the first buddhas.* It is not that you do zazen, engage in ascetic practice, and become a buddha. It is rather that by doing zazen and achieving the state of no-mind, you are made to realize that you are a buddha from the beginning.

Jesus said, "Unless you become as a little child, you cannot enter the kingdom of heaven." Ikkyū wrote,

> How sad a little child
> Its wisdom increasing
>   From the time it is born
> Should move ever more
>   Distant from Buddha.

A baby is truly an angel, a buddha just as it is. No matter what the size of its nose, whether its forehead is prominent or not, all infants are adorable, lovable little buddhas. As the years pass and they grow older and acquire more knowledge, they draw further and further away from their intrinsic buddhahood, and sadly many of them end up as demons, hags, and stingy old misers. You will no doubt find such people in countries everywhere in the world, but you will certainly never come across any stingy young babies. An infant's state of no-mind is in itself the buddha-mind. It is the human character perfected. Therefore to return to this no-mind of our youth—a state someone has compared to an eternal smile—is the object of human life. You don't become a buddha through self-power, or through other-power either. You do it by discarding self-power, discarding all reasoning and discrimination, and returning to the original state of no-mind, the pure mind of the self-nature—*that* is the satori of the Zen school, and *that* is the believing mind (*shinjin*) of the other-power Pure Land schools.

National Master Bankei often gave people teachings like this:

> Man's original nature is like a mirror. It is from the out-set nothing, and because it is nothing it reflects things that come before it, and when the things depart, nothing remains. Even though a person or object is reflected in the mirror, the mirror did not create it, and even though the person or object vanishes, the mirror did not make it perish. This is what Buddhism means by "unborn and undying." Although the mirror reflects a beautiful flower, the mirror does not thereby become beautiful, nor is it defiled because it reflects some dog droppings. This is what is meant by "not defiled, not pure." The mirror does not

increase in weight because something is reflected on the mirror, nor does the mirror decease in weight because it is no longer reflected. This is called "no increasing, no decreasing." In just the same way, the original nature of human beings is unborn and undying, undefiled and unpure, does not increase or decrease. More simply, it is the unborn buddha-mind.

In this way our original nature is unborn and undying, pure and undefiled. Like a mirror not being defiled by reflecting the filthiest of things, the original nature remains undefiled no matter what kind of sin you create. No matter how splendid the deeds you perform, the original nature does not thereby become more splendid. Shinran said, "No other good is necessary, for there is no good that surpasses the Nembutsu. Neither should you fear evil, for there is no evil that is greater than the Nembutsu, the working of Amida's vow."

Grasping the original nature in this way is the satori of the Zen school, the believing mind (*shinjin*) of the other-power Pure Land schools. When you grasp the original nature, you experience "the perishing of the countless sins you have accumulated up until the present." In point of fact, the sins do not actually perish, for there were in the first place no sins to eliminate. There are no longer any evil karmic destinations such as hell, hungry ghosts, or fighting spirits for you to be rid of. Now the eternal moon of true suchness shines bright and clear, and you enjoy daily the pleasures of *Jakkō-do*, the Land of Tranquil Light.

44

THE MISSION
OF BUDDHISM

ACCORDING TO A NEWSPAPER article, Dr. Daisetz Suzuki delivered a lecture recently on Buddhism in the West
at a meeting of various Japanese Buddhist sects held at Eihei-ji,
the Sōtō sect's headquarters temple in Fukui Province. As I did
not attend the meeting, I do not know all the particulars of Dr.
Suzuki's talk, but according to the newspaper account one of the
main points he made was that Buddhism could liberate Westerners from their fear of God.

I have heard many people who travel overseas remark on how
deeply rooted Christianity is in the lives of people in European
countries. One man said, "On Sunday they all go to worship at
the church and listen to the preacher's sermon. Even someone
who is not a churchgoer would angrily refute a person who tried
to deny the existence of God. This is true as well in Eastern So-
viet-bloc countries like Bulgaria and Yugoslavia that maintained

their traditional social order and moral principles even in the immediate postwar turmoil." Another person said, "In Europe, if the schools fail to provide moral guidance, the church can be counted on to furnish children with solid ethical teachings. When Japan discarded Buddhism and Confucianism in the second half of the nineteenth century following the Meiji Restoration, it endeavored to inculcate ethical standards in the public schools instead, but now even that attempt has been abandoned. How can children be expected to acquire a good moral sense?" Yet another challenged Japanese Buddhists to return to their senses, exclaiming, "What can they be thinking of?"

Christianity teaches that God created the world and human beings, that we owe our lives and our daily bread to God's divine favor. The morality that Christians practice stems from God's commandments. God always watches over us, and when we die, we receive God's judgment; the virtuous are summoned to God's side, the evildoers condemned to hell. Christians baptized into the faith at an early age must believe in its teachings, fearing God, obediently following God's command, and observing God's moral teachings. It can be seen from this that for Christians, morality is an extremely serious matter.

It is quite different in Buddhism, which teaches that the world and the people in it are created not by Buddha but through causes and conditions. Ordinary men and women do not receive their daily bread from Buddha; it is the fruit of their own labor. Their morality is contingent on self-awakening. The Buddha does not command them to follow a certain moral code, nor does he watch over them. If a person goes to hell, it is their own doing, not because the Buddha passes judgment on them and sends them there. The role of Emma, the so-called Lord of Hell, is merely to examine their past actions and record them according to their gravity. Emma does not wield any punitive authority.

No carpenter is needed
    To create a wheel of fire;
You make it yourself,
    Then hop on it and ride.

This old verse, which has been attributed to Zen Master Ikkyū implies that you bring retribution on yourself through your own actions. In Buddhism, you are not given orders, you are not supervised, and you need have no fear that the Buddha will render a verdict on you. Buddhism is extremely free. It should be regarded as a religion that pays great respect to human beings. By comparison, while Christians may live highly moral and respectable lives, it strikes me that they do so because they are compelled by a God who is always watching over their lives. This makes me wonder whether a morality so lacking in autonomy, subject to external controls and impositions and based on fear, can be called a genuine morality.

I believe, among those who began promoting Christianity after the war, there may have been some who did so for utilitarian reasons: "I myself can't believe in the existence of God, but I can see nothing wrong with it if it brings people together in the church. And it should bring about a decrease in crime. I think Christianity offers the best way to save Japan, especially in the wake of the catastrophic defeat we have suffered."

Dr. Suzuki, at any rate, seems to have come to the following conclusion:

Members of the Christian church, instead of enjoying God's blessings, are rather deeply fearful of him. Human freedom isn't possible in such a state of affairs. God is the Lord and Master and human beings are his servants, bound to absolute obedience. It is an extremely feudalistic relationship. Buddhism must help Westerners to attain genuine freedom by releasing them from this fear of God's control. In future years this will become an important mission for it.

I agree with Suzuki. Buddhism on this score is indeed completely free and unfettered. A mere ten callings of Amida's name and you can reach the Pure Land paradise. Sitting in zazen one single time cancels out all the karmic obstacles you have created from the timeless beginning; abolishes the realms of hell, hungry ghosts, and beasts; and makes the Pure Land immediately open before you. It is not a subjective Pure Land, either. When the perfected human character self-awakens, the self and the surrounding environment are purified as a matter of course, morality is exalted, and an ideal world immediately manifests.

On being asked, "If evil people are the objects of Amida's original vow, won't evil people increase dramatically and those who perform good acts greatly diminish?" Shinran replied, "The performing of good and evil acts is all the result of causes and conditions; it is not something performed of our own volition. If you told someone they would attain the bliss of paradise if they killed a thousand people, do you think they would go out and kill a thousand people? Unless causes and conditions make them do it, they would not kill a single person, much less a thousand."

I think Shinran's words — *Your karmic obstacles become a body of merit, / Existing in a relation like that of ice and water; / Where there is much ice there is also much water, / Where obstacles are many, virtues also abound.* — contend that even though a person has no intention of attaining a mind of deep faith (*shinjin*) and makes no attempt to achieve it, deep faith, through the virtuous working of the Buddha Way, will come of itself. When the perfected human character awakens in you in the attainment of satori, you become naturally imbued with the radiance of wisdom and compassion as you realize the life of bodhisattva practice. Then even without being instructed to, even though no one observes you doing it, you will conduct yourself just as you wish in a free, untrammeled manner without fear of being judged, and your every action will be in splendid agreement with the virtuous activity of the Buddha Way. Your character will be perfected, and the Pure Land "not distant from this world" will be established. This is the meaning of Hakuin's keeping *the Pure Land always close at hand.*

45

"REPAY INDEBTEDNESS FOR WHAT YOU HAVE RECEIVED WITH A FEELING OF GRATITUDE"

Kanzan Egen, the founder of Myōshin-ji, said, "When I was with my late teacher, I resolved the one great matter. After receiving the transmission of the Dharma robe and bowl from him, I have never forgotten, sleeping or waking, my desire to repay my debt to him, and my aspiration to make the Buddha Dharma prosper." At the beginning of each New Year, I clean off my desk, quietly light some incense, and read the imperial rescript Emperor Hanazono wrote ordering the construction of Myōshin-ji temple. No matter how many times I read it, I am always deeply moved when I come to the four Chinese characters *hōon shatoku*, "Repay indebtedness for what you have received with a feeling of gratitude." It is at one with Master Kanzan's "To all my students and heirs I say: If you were to forget, even on the day of my death, your profound debt to National Masters Daiō and Daitō, consider yourselves no disciples of mine. You must do everything in your power to repay that debt." And I believe we are justified in saying that the four Chinese characters "Repay indebtedness for what you have received with a feeling of gratitude" express a credo by which all Zen followers—better still, all Buddhists—should lead their lives.

Kanzan's "late teacher" is Daitō Kokushi, the founder of Daitoku-ji in Kyoto. The great matter of human life that is the reason we are born, the object of life, is the great truth that all beings possess the buddha-nature from birth and all must become buddhas. When Kanzan resolved this great matter when studying under Daitō many years ago, he was beside himself with joy.

Among the countless Japanese waka that Emperor Hanazono wrote is this one:

More perilous than stepping across
   A bridge of clouds to a high peak
Is the dangerous path that leads
   Through this world of dreams.

At about the same time the emperor composed this, in the latter half of the Kamakura period, Yoshida Kenkō, the author of the *Tsurezuregusa* (*Essays in Idleness*), living at the foot of Narabiga-oka just west of Hanazono, was writing this verse:

Compared to making my way
   Through this world,

I know now the waves and winds
   Of Naruto are as nothing.*

Kenkō Hōshi (1284–1350), from a secular background, was someone who experienced and overcame much suffering in his life, so it is easy to understand such feeling expressed in his verse. But I am truly amazed to find Emperor Hanazono, who must have spent much of his life deep within the inner chambers of the royal palace shielded from the onslaughts of the transient world, articulate such sentiments.

At this time in the early fourteenth century, with the reins of government firmly in the hands of the Kamakura shogunate and the imperial succession alternating between two different lines of descent, the emperor was unable to do as he wished. Even his choice of successor had to undergo the scrutiny of the military government in Kamakura. Political ambition and intrigue, rife within the factions at court, apparently created a situation in which Emperor Hanazono had no one in whom he could place his full trust. I think this accounts for the pathetic tone of his verse, *The dangerous path that leads / Through this world of dreams.* But here, once again, suffering was the mother of faith. It was the hardships the emperor underwent that led him to Buddhism at a relatively early age. After years of assiduous practice, he happened to encounter Daitō Kokushi, resolved

*Famous tidal whirlpools in the Naruto Straits between Shikoku and Awaji Island.

the great matter of human life, and willingly and joyfully entered the priesthood.

In the second year of the Kemmu era (1335), Emperor Hanazono wrote an enlightenment verse:

A man who has undergone twenty years of pain and suffering
Won't change his old wind and mist as he welcomes the spring.
He'll just keep on living his life, wearing his robe, eating rice—
How could even a single mote of dust exist on the great earth?

Adding a postscript, he presented it to his teacher Daitō: "This is the satori your disciple has achieved, Master. How do you size it up?" After reading it, Daitō inscribed a postscript of his own certifying the emperor's enlightenment: "This old bonze reckons it *thus!*" This document with both their transcriptions, now designated a National Treasure, is still preserved today in Daitoku-ji. Daitō is said to have presented the emperor at this same time with the robe and bowl signifying the transmission of the Dharma.

Emperor Hanazono resolved the great matter of human life, freeing himself from all suffering and awakening to the dignified character of his true self—not to mention grasping the profoundest reaches of the Buddha Dharma and receiving the transmission of the Buddha's robe and bowl. How inspired and invigorated he must have been! He had relinquished his position as a monarch exercising the highest authority in the human world and risen to become a Dharma emperor within the realm of the Buddha.

Religion that does not deeply inspirit and inspire is no different from a mummy displayed in a museum case. In today's Japan, the so-called new religions are enjoying great success because the messages they offer have enjoyed remarkable success in inspiring their believers. It may be because an illness was cured or because someone has been helped to succeed in business. But whatever the case, their teachings inspire even the most uncultivated men and women to worship the founders of the new religions as living gods or buddhas and to willingly donate sizable sums to requite their indebtedness to the founders. The reason Buddhism has fallen into such neglect today is, I believe, found in its failure to inspire its followers.

Someone once said to Shōma of Sanuki, a myōkōnin of the Shin sect who lived at the end of the Tokugawa period: "It's worrisome that Christianity is becoming quite popular these days. Before long, the Buddha's teachings may die out." "Yes," Shōma replied, "but there isn't any teaching that surpasses an ordinary person becoming a buddha!" He was a person of fully attained faith. Although in Christianity a believer cannot become God no matter how much they may try, in Buddhism, an ordinary person becomes Buddha just as they are. Where else is such a precious doctrine found? How could such an exceptional teaching die out?

"REPAY INDEBTEDNESS"

In another verse of Emperor Hanazono,

The Dharma path opens widest
    Amid tempestuous fires;
Torrential rain, wind, snow—
    These are as nothing.

46

RESPONDING WITH
TEARS OF JOY

AKUIN'S *SONG OF ZAZEN* seems to be patterned for
the most part on the *Treatise on Zazen*, a short work on the
essentials of zazen practice composed in the Kamakura period
by Chinese Zen Master Tao-lung, the founder of Kenchō-ji;
and on the *Dharma Words of Shōichi Kokushi*, authored by the
founder of the Tōfuku-ji in Kyoto. The former is composed
in Chinese, the latter in Japanese *kana* script. The two works resemble each other quite closely, although it still remains to be
determined which of them appeared first.

In the *Treatise on Zazen* we read,

This Zen teaching is a Dharma gate of the greatest and
subtlest profundity. Once your ears hear it, it forms a
wonderful, long-lasting link to enlightenment. An ancient said, "Even those who hear and do not believe it re-

ceive good fortune greater than any found in the human or heavenly realms; if they practice it, even those who do not attain a good outcome will go on to finally reach the fruit of buddhahood." Our school is the buddha-mind sect. The buddha-mind from the first has no illusion or enlightenment. The practice of the buddha-mind is truly the wondrous practice of the buddhas. Even if you do not achieve enlightenment, if you do zazen for one sitting, you are a buddha for one sitting; if you do zazen for one day you are a buddha for that day; if you do zazen for a lifetime, you are a buddha for a lifetime. Those who accept this as true are called "persons of superior capacity and wisdom."

National Master Shōichi's *Dharma Words* has this:

Because this teaching of the Zen school is a path leading to emancipation beyond comprehension, if a person hears of it just once, it will produce a superior link to enlightenment. If they actually practice the teaching of this school, they will reach the supreme buddha-mind. In the buddha-mind there is originally no illusion or enlightenment. The Zen teaching is without any doubt the wondrous practice the Buddha engaged in for six years in the Himalayas. If having not yet attained the Way you do zazen for one time, you are for that one time a buddha. If you do zazen for one day, you are a buddha for one day.

If you do zazen for a lifetime, you are a buddha for a lifetime. Those who accept this as true are persons of superior capacity and wisdom, great Dharma vessels.

Hakuin, in composing the *Song of Zazen* as a text for chanting, recasts both these texts simply and succinctly:

The merit you gain from just one sitting
Cancels vast stores of obstructive karma,
Keeps you from entering wrongful paths,
Keeps the Pure Land always close at hand.
If you can hear this Dharma even once
and hold it in mind in deep reverence,
Acclaiming it and embracing it with joy,
The blessings you receive will never end.

The path of zazen is one whereby ordinary men and women become buddhas just as they are; a path where all are equally saved; a path in which their greatest worth is actualized, in which all human beings are emancipated and attain genuine freedom, becoming gods and buddhas. If, upon hearing about the path of zazen just one time, a person with a pure heart responds joyfully to this message and honestly accepts its incomparable meaning, that alone is ample merit and good fortune.

The word *zuiki,* "responding with joy," the subject of this essay, is an important term in Buddhism. It articulates well the character or nature of Buddhism. In Japan it has come to be used in everyday secular speech, with meanings such as "I cried joyful tears." But in its original Buddhist context, *zuiki* expresses a religious emotion of overwhelming gratitude that brings tears to the eyes.

The poet Saigyō expressed this feeling in a verse he wrote on worshipping at the hallowed Ise Shrine:

> Though I know not what it is
>> Has deigned be present here,
> With a sense of deep indebtedness
>> The tears begin to fall.

When you associate with a person who has attained satori, you find your mood becoming brighter and even feel you, too, may someday achieve enlightenment. When you converse with a person who has experienced shinjin, the believing mind of Pure Land Buddhism, you feel a sense of peace and restfulness, as though you too have acquired the believing mind.

As you enter this pure realm, your mind is naturally fresh and invigorated and you experience a deep sense of joy, as though you are solemnly worshipping a wonderful Buddhist image and your entrance into the Pure Land has been decided. The Buddhist term *zuiki* describes this joy, which goes even beyond religious joy and includes a mind that joyfully recognizes and unhesitatingly commends the good acts performed by others. It is said that if you see someone offer a donation and think, "Ah, what a fine thing they do," you receive the same merit as the donor himself. *Zuiki* is also used to describe someone who gladly takes part in a religious ceremony sponsored by others. In even broader terms, used in contexts both joyful and sad, it means putting yourself in the other person's shoes and sharing their happiness or their grief.

There is an old verse:

> A beggar at the gate
>   Crying out for alms,
> My heart feels pity,
>   I've nothing to give.

Even if we have nothing to give as alms, we should at any rate possess the kind of mind that feels pity and compassion for all people. That is the buddha-mind "responding with joy." But sometimes one's baser mind appears, does it not? Giving rise to envy on seeing someone else's happiness, or a smug smile at their misfortune, does not this ignoble self sometimes unreasonably criticize another's faults or impugn their good qualities? We must admit that as we lavish praise on someone or express sadness even to tears sympathizing with them, at times our feelings are somewhat more complex. Small, shameful feelings such as these are a far cry from *zuiki*'s true meaning of responding with wholehearted joy.

Once, when Zen Master Bankei was visiting the city of Okayama, he met a blind man who was gifted with remarkable perception. He could tell everything about a person, from their physical constitution to their personality, merely by hearing them speak. After listening to Bankei's talk, his assessment was:

When I hear an ordinary person discussing a joyful matter, I always sense lurking somewhere in their voice a doleful note, and when they speak of something sad, there is a hint of joy invariably present. But when this priest speaks of something good, he speaks directly from the heart; and when he speaks of some sadness, his sadness is genuine. He is a person whose training has reached perfection.

47

TREAD UPON,
IT DOESN'T ANGER

RECENTLY THE KYOTO MUSEUM held an exhibition of works borrowed from the Louvre Museum in Paris. The galleries were so packed it was difficult to find a place to stand from which to view the artworks. I made my tour hurriedly, trying to keep from getting in people's way, and I was only able to glance at the exhibits, but it was enough to see that they were splendid examples of seventeenth-century French court culture. It was truly a treasure house of art in which goodness and beauty, artistry and skill, God, the human heart, and material objects had all reached the highest possible degree of perfection. And yet to a Japanese—or I should say, to this Japanese—they were not objects for which I could feel any great sympathy. They were all too perfect. They were too good and too beautiful. Passing before one splendid object after another, I began to feel the overpowering richness to be almost intolerable. I believe that Japanese prefer an absence of such fullness and perfection, what one might call an imperfect or incomplete beauty.

An exhibition of traditional Japanese art held in America two years ago is said to have created considerable interest. Great appreciation was shown for the simple ink paintings: Soga Shōhaku's sketch of a monkey, Kaō's drawing of the Zen recluses Han-shan and Shih-te. Most admired of all was Miyamoto Musashi's famous painting of a small bird perched on a withered branch—the ultimate in serene tranquility. Murmurs of "Zen, Zen" could be heard from the viewers gathered before it. An official from the Japanese Ministry of Education which cosponsored the exhibition, commented, "People overseas know how to understand this kind of art. We Japanese are going to have to be on our toes."

I think these examples show that cultural interchanges between East and West are quite a good thing. Yet now, at a time when Europeans and Americans yearn with what almost seems a kind of homesickness for things from the Far East, I question the wisdom of those who live here in Japan, who overlook the good qualities of their own countries in their race after things Western. Wouldn't it be wiser as we take in the good points of Western culture for us to fully savor the good points in our own?

Japanese art, both painting and calligraphy, assigns great value to empty space. Profound meaning is imputed to spaces where nothing at all is drawn or depicted. It is a sensibility that takes pleasure in a beauty that somehow is lacking or incomplete. No doubt this has something in common with the religious mind Hōnen speaks of when he says, "Even if you devote yourself with great diligence to what Shakyamuni taught during his lifetime, you should not go around acting like a learned person but should rather repeat the Nembutsu singlemindedly as though you were an illiterate peasant or an ignorant nun." I think in the Far East, our mentality is endowed with a broad-mindedness that easily accepts what others have to say. I think that a mind that always leaves space to accept the needs and opinions of others is a religious mind.

There is a well-known story told about Nan'in Rōshi, a famous Zen teacher of the Meiji period who taught at the Hakusan Training Hall in Tokyo. One day two students came and requested to see the Rōshi to ask him some questions about Zen. Like many people who say they want to ask you about something but in fact are more interested in giving you their own opinion of the matter, these two students started off telling the Rōshi their views of Zen. Nan'in Rōshi gave them some ordinary bancha. "Come, have a cup of tea," he said. But instead of drinking the tea, the students kept on talking, so the Rōshi began pouring more tea into their cups. "It will overflow!" they exclaimed. "Yes, it will," replied the Rōshi. "If you pour tea into a full cup, it's going to overflow. You two fellows are so laden with theories and arguments that even if I told you something, it would immediately flow in and out of your heads. Come see me again after you've emptied your minds."

When you go to a Zen teacher to receive their teaching, you must do so with an attitude of respect that will allow you to receive their words simply and straightforwardly. Sutra recitations always begin with the words "Thus I have heard." This signifies hearing the Buddha's words directly and selflessly, just as he spoke them.

> If your ears listen,
>   Your mind thinks,
> Your body trains,
>   The evening bell
> Will in time peal out
>   Your enlightenment.

To first listen carefully, to consider what you have heard until convinced of it, then to go on and engage in practice—that is the correct order for someone undertaking Buddhist training. These three steps are called the three wisdoms (*sanne*). "There's nothing that can't be resolved by just talking things over" is a remark one commonly hears today. If adversaries are able to talk things over and reach an understanding without recourse to violence or war, all problems can be peaceably resolved. I think that is the way a society of intelligent people should conduct itself. I don't think much can be achieved when each side covers its ears and merely defends its own assertions without listening to what the other has to say. You need the other person to listen to what you have to say, and you must also listen to what they have to say—not talking to each other, in other words, but listening to each other.

Lawyers and representatives from the Court of Domestic Relations say that the problem that comes up most often today is divorce. How can two people who came together in the expectation of a happy married life so readily file for divorce? It is a modern-day tragedy. Some people say Japanese women must stand up for themselves more, assert their egos. I am against that. In my opinion, there is nothing nobler than the Japanese woman. She listens to her husband's troubles, silently complies with her mother-in-law's unreasonable demands, selflessly indulges her children's whims, and becomes the very foundation of the household, a buffer or cushion that preserves the family peace. To my way of thinking, there is no finer being than a Japanese woman or Japanese mother.

Self-awareness is something that should be urged upon her by family or close friends, not by third parties. I think that they appreciate and respect the nobility of her maternal heart and the position she occupies. Feeling deep appreciation and love toward her, they desire to care for her and protect her. And I believe that when all people attain self-awareness of such a generous, benevolent heart, a genuine peace will prevail in the world.

"The great Way!" exclaimed Master Chao-chou. "It doesn't anger even when it's tread upon." People constantly tread the Way, but the Way never becomes vexed in the least. It shoulders all things, silently taking their burden upon itself. Buddhists, in speaking of "a mind that responds with joy" (*zuiki*) to the act of hearing or seeing something good, are referring to a mind as broad and flexible as the great Way itself.

48

HOLDING A MEMORIAL
SERVICE FOR YOURSELF

SELF-REALIZATION of one's own noble and dignified human character and going on to lead all people to the self-realization of their noble and dignified human characters—or to put it differently, leading all people to buddhahood—is the religion we call Buddhism. The Zen school's teaching is singularly simple and straightforward: you are to point directly to the human mind, see the true self, and attain buddhahood. Some means must therefore be devised that will enable us to realize that noble and dignified human character. To me, the best methods are doing zazen and reciting the Nembutsu.

In doing zazen, you assume the same physical posture the Buddha assumed and give yourself body and soul to your practice. In performing the Nembutsu, you recite singlemindedly the sacred name of the Buddha so that Buddha and self become one. I am often asked, "Do you have to do zazen?" or "What do you do when you're sitting there?" I don't think you should be thinking rigidly that "you must do zazen." Whether you do zazen or Nembutsu, it should be something that you take pleasure in doing, that you are unable to stop doing, like a heavy smoker whose mind is distracted when they don't have a cigarette in their hand.

Many years ago, a man named Kodama Ichizō from Osaka visited my late teacher Seki Seisetsu at Tenryū-ji. "People like me are extremely busy every day, so we have no time for zazen," he said. "Isn't there some simpler method that will bring results?" "Take a deep breath," Seisetsu replied. "From now on when some difficult problem comes up at work, or when you attend an important meeting, or when you are tired and your mind is unsettled, just take a deep breath. Gird up your body and exhale deeply—that's all. As you are doing that, cast everything aside, forget everything, just for those few seconds." He told Mr. Kodama that the samadhi of those few seconds would indeed become the motivating force for all his daily activities. Mr. Kodama left in very high spirits. He practiced this breathing technique throughout the rest of his life, always commending its extreme effectiveness and expressing his deep gratitude to Seisetsu Rōshi for having taught him to do it. "Once when I had a difficult problem that I just could not solve, I got in a car and went to Tenryū-ji to see Seisetsu Rōshi. I was pressed for time, and as I was walking from the main gate of the temple to his quarters, I took a long, deep breath. All at once something opened in my mind and I knew immediately the answer to my problem."

Done with earnest singleness of mind, even one breath is fine, but it won't be easy for you to stop at just one breath. I like to suggest doing at least ten deep breaths, using the *susokkan*, or "breath-counting meditation." Put all your heart and mind into drawing in a deep breath, then expelling it. Once, twice, again, again, until you have inhaled and exhaled ten times. You will experience a truly pleasant, agreeable sensation; your body will feel somehow relaxed and your mind extremely clear and fresh.

This is something you can do anywhere, in the time it would take to smoke a cigarette. I don't smoke myself, so I don't know the taste of tobacco, but when I am in a place where the air is fresh and pure and I take a deep breath, I savor the truly wonderful taste of the fresh air. In the same way that people take time out to enjoy a smoke, I'd like for them to set aside some time to assume an upright sitting posture and take a few seconds to enjoy the exquisite flavor of filling their bellies with deeply inhaled breaths. Plants absorb nutrients from the air, and I believe humans may get nourishment from the air as well, like those ancient sages who lived hundreds of years on the mist they imbibed. If you throw yourself into the realm of Buddha and become one with him, said Zen Master Dōgen, the Buddha will come unbidden to inspirit you and invest you with myriad good virtues and merits. Performing even a little bit of zazen by yourself, however imperfect, will be found extremely helpful in your daily life. *The merit you gain from just one sitting / Cancels vast stores of obstructive karma, / Keeps you from entering wrongful paths.* These words make us keenly realize how truly wonderful zazen is. If a person with a pure heart listens to Hakuin's priceless words and goes on to praise and joyfully embrace them, that in itself will open wide the gates of happiness and fortune for them, because such a person will no longer slip from the right view of human life and the world.

Since just sitting on your own for only a short time, or merely praising zazen, brings this great merit, then if you sit properly in zazen under the guidance of a good teacher and are able to realize your true self, you will be like a dragon entering the water, a tiger striking into the mountain fastness. Your human character will be completely transformed, and you will find yourself ushered into a life of utmost freedom, radiance, and creativity. Such is the meaning of Hakuin's *And how much more so if you turn within, / See beyond doubt your own self-nature.*

The Buddhist term *ekō*, transferring the merit you achieve to others, can be a matter of sitting before the Buddha and reciting a sutra or listening to Buddhist priests chanting sutras before the altar. Transference can occur when the mind of the priest who is reciting the sutra, becoming clear and pure, enters a state of samadhi. Offering the merit accruing from all your practice to the Buddha is the meaning of ekō. It has nothing to do with buddhas being pleased at the sound of sutras being chanted. We priests are often criticized for chanting sutras whose meaning no one understands. But I don't see anything wrong with sutras being incomprehensible. On the contrary, it is easier to enter a state of samadhi when you singlemindedly chant a sutra whose meaning is obscure. And since the merit of this concentrated meditative state of samadhi accrues from chanting the sutra, it does not belong to you; you turn it to the Buddha as an offering to him.

It is difficult for most people to understand the meaning of the Buddhist sutras when they hear them chanted, so it becomes tedious for them just to sit there listening silently to the priests intoning the words. How fortunate it would be if we had a sutra like one of the Christian hymns, which people could vigorously chant out together in a chorus. Everyone in the hall would receive splendid merit as they chanted together as one body. Since all that merit would be transferred to Buddha, what a splendid meeting it would be! But infinitely better than this—better than leading a thoughtless, unconsidered life and then having a child or grandchild hold memorial services for you once you're dead—would be for you to hold a memorial service for yourself while you are still living—by attaining buddhahood!

49

HEARING "WOOF"
WHEN A DOG BARKS

Zen Master Dōgen said, "To learn the Buddha Way is to learn the self, to learn the self is to forget the self." Shakyamuni, in his final words to his followers, counseled, "Make a lamp of your self and dwell within it as your fundamental ground. Make your fundamental ground nowhere else."

Buddhism is a religion that has you discover your true self, discover the radiant foundation or ground within that self. An old verse affirms,

Pressing on in search of the Way all night,
Finally coming upon it; in your own mind!

The Buddha's Dharma is, in the end, a religion in which human beings discover truth, discover the gods and buddhas within their own minds. That is the meaning of the Zen axiom "Pointing straight at the mind of man, seeing into the self-nature and attaining buddhahood." The Zen school wants us to attain buddhahood by pointing us directly at our own mind. But what is first and foremost incumbent upon us is to have a mind that ardently desires to become a buddha—to become a person of great character.

Shinran states in his *Kyōgyōshinshō* (*Teaching, Practice, Faith, and Realization*): "The vajra mind is the mind that desires to become Buddha. The mind that desires to become Buddha is the mind that desires to save living beings. The mind that desires to save living beings is the mind that takes in and protects living beings and brings about their rebirth in the Pure Land of Bliss. This is the great mind of Bodhi." Even a follower of the Nembutsu can never attain true belief so long as their goal is to attain prompt rebirth in the Pure Land; happiness for themselves alone. The mind of true belief is as invincible as a diamond or *vajra*—no matter what circumstances it may face, it cannot be impaired or destroyed. The vajra mind is the mind that resolves to become a buddha no matter what. The mind that desires to become a buddha is the mind that desires to save living beings. The mind that desires to save living beings is the mind that gives rise to the universal vow, the solemn pledge that everyone in the world will be reborn in the Pure Land of Bliss. In other words, it is the great Bodhi-mind. As the Bodhi-mind is the buddha-mind, the believing mind of Pure Land Buddhism is in and of itself Buddha.

So long as Nembutsu followers, in the belief they are only ordinary mortals, think, "How gratifying it is that we are fine just as we are with all our afflicting passions," they will never attain rebirth in Amida's Pure Land. They must rouse a mind so determined it will compel them to become buddhas and devote their most ardent efforts to saving living beings. They will, as a result of these efforts, in time experience a feeling of powerlessness, reaching a total impasse followed by a sense of relief upon discovering that they cannot attain buddhahood on their own, that rebirth in the Pure Land is attained solely through the saving power of Amida's original vow. Only then will they truly realize with complete certainty that they are all right just as they are, with all their afflicting passions. So long as they do not rouse the mind that resolves to become a buddha, to perfect their character—what Buddhism calls "arousing the Bodhi-mind"—they will be unable to fulfill the Buddha Way.

To give rise to the Bodhi-mind and then to deepen your self-introspection through hearing the teachings, reading the scriptures, chanting the Nembutsu, doing zazen, is to transfer merit to yourself, not in the sense of gaining merit but of transferring it to the buddha within your own heart and mind. Owing to the merit of that transference, you will grasp the true self. The Pure Land schools call this "receiving [from Amida the firm belief of] a settled mind." Zen calls it awakening to satori or enlightenment.

Shakyamuni attained enlightenment on seeing the morning star shining in the sky above. Hsiang-yen attained enlightenment on hearing a tile fragment strike a bamboo, Lin-yun when he saw a flowering peach tree, Zen Master Hakuin when he heard a temple bell pealing in the early morning. At that instant, all of them grasped their true self.

During his pilgrimage to visit teachers around the country, Lin-chi stopped for a day at Zen Master Huang-po's temple. In taking sanzen with Huang-po, he asked, "What is the great meaning that has been handed down in the Buddha Dharma?" Before he had even finished speaking these words, Huang-po gave him twenty blows with his staff. He asked once again, "What is the great meaning that has been handed down in the Buddha Dharma?" Once again Huang-po gave him twenty blows. But Lin-chi persisted and asked the question a third time. The result was the same—sixty blows in all.

Lin-chi thought that someone of his meager capacity was a hopeless case and could never attain enlightenment, but he decided to give it one more try at another training hall. Leaving the temple with tears in his eyes, he went to visit Huang-po's friend Ta-yu. After explaining to Ta-yu what had transpired at Huang-po's temple, Lin-chi asked Ta-yu where he had gone wrong. Why had Huang-po given him so many blows? Ta-yu issued a sigh of admiration for Huang-po and said, "Huang-po certainly is a kind old priest." The moment Lin-chi heard the words he suddenly experienced enlightenment; the cry "There isn't much to Huang-po's Zen!" burst from his mouth.

Huang-po struck Lin-chi with such deep compassion that it truly brings tears to my eyes. He could do no more than look on and think, "Don't you understand now? Don't you understand now? Does this hurt? Do you feel the pain? That is Buddha! Isn't that the true self?"

Understood in this way, the Buddha Dharma is indeed ridiculously easy. It is merely to feel heat and cold, see red and green, hear *"Bang!"* and *"Gong!"* Apart from our consciousness itself, there is no Buddha, no true self. Lin-chi's exclamation, "There isn't much to Huang-po's Zen!" is a cry of delight at the discovery that the Buddha Dharma is not difficult and that it has not a shred of benevolence—that it is nothing at all.

Zen Master Bankei often used words like these when he spoke to his large audiences:

> Since all of you here have gathered here to hear me speak, you obviously are hearing the words I utter. If a dog barked right now outside the temple walls, even though not a single one of you came here to hear the dog bark, you would still hear the *"Woof."* You had no intention to hear it or to perceive it as a dog's bark. And yet the instant the dog barked, not a hairsbreadth interval would elapse before you heard *"Woof."* That is the buddha-nature.

It is certainly true that the mind is *Mu*—that is, in a state of nothingness as far as the sound of a dog's bark is concerned. It hears the *"Woof"* from a place where there is nothing at all. From this same ground of nothingness it says "Ouch" on feeling pain, cries "Hot" on feeling heat, becomes angry, smiles on seeing a cute baby, delights when it feels happy, weeps when it is sad. Knowing that a human being's fundamental nature is in fact nothing at all, boring through to the truth of Hakuin's *Your own self-nature being no-nature*—is what Zen calls satori.

50

CHAO-CHOU'S *MU*

IN THE HEIAN PERIOD, at the time the Japanese priests Kōbō Daishi and Dengyō Daishi were traveling in T'ang China to study Buddhism, there was a great Zen priest named Chao-chou living there. Born in a village in Ts'ao-chou, in present Shantung Province, he was residing as a *shami*, a novice who had left home to join the Buddhist order but had yet to receive the precepts, at the Jui-hsiang temple. He entered the priesthood at the age of eighteen, and in making the rounds of the temples in search of a teacher, he happened to visit the priest Nan-ch'uan in Chi'ih-chou (in modern Anhwei). When he was shown into Nan-ch'uan's chambers, he saw the master lying down, looking as though he was all tired out. When Chao-chou introduced himself, Nan-ch'uan asked him, "Where did you come from?" "From Jui-hsiang temple in Ts'ao-chou," he replied. "*Ahaaa!* You came from Jui-hsiang, did you?" said Nan-ch'uan. "No doubt you worshipped the august Buddhist figures there."* "No, I didn't worship any of them. I worship a reclining buddha."

Aware now that he'd have to be on his toes with this young fellow, Nan-ch'uan slowly got up and said, "What are you, a shami with a teacher, or a teacherless shami?" "It is the greatest of Dharma joys to find that even amid this frigid midwinter cold, the master's noble body is in such very fine fettle," Chao-chou replied. He then made three deep bows, already having made up his mind to become Nan-ch'uan's student. Nan-ch'uan was greatly taken by the young boy's wit and resources and lavished great care on his subsequent training.

Chao-chou was fifty-seven when Nan-ch'uan passed away. At the age of sixty, after having observed a three-year mourning period, he put on his traveling sandals and set out on a pilgrimage to visit and study under noted priests around the country. Upon embarking on his journey he made a great vow: "If even a lad of seven is superior to me, I will ask him about the Way. If even a graybeard of one hundred years is inferior to me, I will undertake to teach him." Reaching the advanced age of eighty, Chao-chou was for the first time appointed head priest of a temple, the Kuan-yin-yuan in the suburbs of the city of Chao-chou in modern Hopeh. Until his death some forty years later at the age of 120, he continued teaching the monks and laypeople who constantly thronged to his temple from all around.

*Nan-ch'uan plays on *jui-hsiang*, "auspicious figure," a term applied to Buddhist images.

Living twice as long as ordinary people, he endured three times their difficulties, as a result of which he made a truly great contribution to his fellow beings. However else Chao-chou might be described, he was above all a priest of unprecedented greatness. Zen Master Dōgen spoke in glowing praise of Chao-chou as a priest whose Zen style "truly was like the dragons and elephants [great masters] of old, a priest whose virtuous behavior we must deeply cherish."

Once a priest came to Chao-chou and asked, "Does a dog have the buddha-nature or not? Shakyamuni taught that all living beings without exception possess the buddha-nature. If so, what about those dogs and cats we see roaming the temple, do they have the buddha-nature? No, forget about dogs and cats, what about me, does an ignorant person like me have the buddha-nature?" Chao-chou replied, "*Mu!*" His answer became the famous koan known as "Chao-chou's *Mu*," which has vexed so thoroughly generations of Zen disciples.

The Chinese character *Mu* literally means "no" or "nothing." Does Chao-chou's reply indicate that a dog does not have the buddha-nature? If so, it would mean he was stating something counter to the teaching of Shakyamuni Buddha. It would also contradict Lin-chi's words, "Above the mass of red flesh is a true man of no rank." In this case, the word *Mu* does not belong on the ordinary dualistic level of being versus not being, having versus not having, nor is it emptiness where there is nothing at all. Commenting on this koan, the priest Wu-men, the author of the *Gateless Barrier* koan collection, stated that Chao-chou does not say the dog has no buddha-nature but that the buddha-nature exists in a state of nothingness.

As I have often said before, since our fundamental nature, the buddha-nature, is originally formless, it is neither large nor small, neither is it round or square, red or green, heavy or light, male or female, young or old, rich or poor, learned or unlearned, beautiful or unsightly, good or bad, deluded or enlightened. It is absolute, something utterly prior to expression or explanation by verbal means. Chao-chou expresses this with the single Chinese character *Mu*, revealing to the priest the vital, living buddha-nature itself.

Hakuin says of this: *Your own self-nature being no-nature, / Has nothing to do with empty words!* In Buddhism, "empty words" is anything that deals in empty theories and thus is divorced from reality. To grasp Chao-chou's *Mu*, in other words, means to *realize* satori and *see* your true nature, to *understand* that the self-nature is no-nature.

In the *Gateless Barrier* koan collection, Master Wu-men teaches, "A person who passes through here will not only meet Chao-chou in person, they will stride hand in hand with all the generations of Zen patriarchs, linking eyebrows with them, seeing with their same eyes, hearing with the same ears as theirs."

Grasping this character *Mu* is like getting your hands on a permit that ushers you through all the most difficult koan barriers. You will not only encounter Chao-chou face to face but also join hands with all the Zen masters and patriarchs of the past and stroll together with them through the Pure Land, viewing the world with the same eyes as Shakyamuni, Bodhidharma, Nan-ch'uan, Po-chang, Huang-po, and Lin-chi; hearing with the same ears as those great priests. What a wonderful experience it will be! That is why all Zen students make the greatest effort to grasp this single character *Mu* and attain satori.

Grasping *Mu* is grasping the true self and at the same time grasping Buddha. It means entering the same realm as the buddhas of the three worlds and all the Zen teachers who have transmitted the Dharma to the present day. Could there be anything as pleasurable as that, anything happier or more fortunate? For it is here that we experience the extremely great joy of realizing the purpose of human life.

51

WHAT IS YOUR NAME?

"I'M UNABLE to attain peace of mind. Please tell me: What should I do?" This was the earnest plea the monk Hui-k'o, later the Second Zen Patriarch, made to his teacher Bodhidharma. Bodhidharma quietly replied, "That mind of yours that can't find peace, show it to me and I will pacify it."

After some thought, Hui-k'o said, "Show it to you? How can I show it to you? The mind is completely ungraspable. If you try to get hold of it, it's nowhere to be found." With majestic finality Bodhidharma replied, "Nowhere to be found? Then your mind is at peace." At these words Hui-k'o suddenly entered the great serenity of enlightenment.

The *Diamond Sutra* says, "The past mind is unobtainable, the present mind is unobtainable, the future mind is unobtainable." The past mind, because it is no longer here; the future mind, because it does not yet exist; and the present mind, because the instant you say "present mind," it is already far away. The Sixth Patriarch Hui-neng taught that a mind in which "not a single thing exists" is the Zen the First Patriarch Bodhidharma transmitted to his successors.

As the Japanese proverb says, however, *Mune ni ichimotsu, senaka ni nimotsu*, "Having one thing in your heart means having a burden of two things on your back." Owning property, having status or position, having a self—anything you have, the very having of it becomes a heavy burden. From this having stems all our distress and suffering. Yet people cannot conceive of living without possessing things. If you tell them that all things are *Mu*, they will not feel relieved; they will probably feel anxious.

If told there is no past or future or present, they might well be led in desperation to believe that nothing matters. Yet even then, the reality that everything returns to *Mu* remains unchanged. It is thus necessary to discover within this *Mu* a new, perfectly free heaven and earth. You must release your grip from the edge of a precipice; you must take one more step beyond the tip of a hundred-foot pole. It is there and there alone that peace of mind is found.

In the Pure Land's other-power teaching, peace of mind is a matter of casting aside the existing heaven and earth—"The ordinary person weighed down with evil passions, the world as impermanent as a burning house, and everything else as well— these words are all devoid of meaning . . . utterances bereft of truth"—and living at peace in a new heaven and earth where "Nembutsu alone is true." This leap of faith is essential to religion—being born anew in the attainment of faith, a self-awakening that completely transforms your life.

The nun known as Nyodai (1223–1298), secular name Chiyono, was a disciple of National Master Bukkō (Wu-hsueh Tsu-yuan) in Kamakura. One day she was out carrying a bucket of water on her head and the bottom of the bucket suddenly fell through. She was drenched. And she attained sudden enlightenment:

> A pail on Chiyono's head
>   Has burst its bottom,
> No water can be held,
>   No moon reflected.

When the bottom fell out of beingness, Chiyono realized the original shape of *Mu* itself. Grasping that you have no self does not mean everything suddenly vanishes; it means you awaken to the self that is not the self—a new and greater self; it is a self-awakening to life itself. An old verse alludes to the thrilling experience this sublime realization engenders:

> Oh, to live at home
>   In the empty void,
> No floating clouds
>   To shroud the mind.

This new self is provisionally given the name "Buddha," and from it arises the wisdom that grasps the entire universe as the self as well as the great compassion that cannot help but love all things as one's own children.

This is the mental state of Shakyamuni's "Now this three-fold world is all my domain, and the living beings in it are all my children" (*Lotus Sutra*). It is what Zen Master Wu-men describes when he says, "You will stride hand in hand with all the generations of Zen patriarchs, linking eyebrows with them, seeing with their same eyes, hearing with the same ears as theirs. How delightful it will be!"

From long in the past, Zen priests have expressed the buddha-nature by drawing an *ensō*, or circle. Being round in shape, it is also called zero. An ancient teacher said, "The circle is like the great void, lacking nothing, with nothing left over." A person doesn't become convex because they are a buddha or concave because they are an ordinary unenlightened person. Buddhas and ordinary persons are both perfectly round. Zero is not large or small, beautiful or ugly, good or bad, wise or foolish. Only by grasping that the true self is zero can you enter the ranks of the buddhas.

No matter how many zeros you add to it, zero remains zero. It is zero no matter how many zeros you subtract from it. It remains zero however much you divide it. In the *Heart Sutra*, zero is *unborn and undying, undefiled and unpure, does not increase or decrease.*

Zen Master Yang-shan Hui-chi once asked Zen Master San-sheng Hui-jan, "What is your name?" San-sheng replied, "My name is Hui-chi." "Hui-chi is my name," said Yang-shan. "Then I am Hui-jan," said San-sheng. Yang-shan, delighted to come upon such a fine young opponent, burst into laughter.

Even if you weren't a Zen master like Yang-shan, how wonderful it would be to attain a realm like this where you are me and I am you! Is it not desirable to have a full, rich life, free of opposition, where oneself and others, oneself and society, are not in a constant state of competition, struggling desperately over rights of one kind or another? A life where the husband appreciates the standpoint of the wife, the wife puts herself in the husband's shoes, the parents duly consider the feelings of the children, the children understand the parents, the company president takes the employees' feelings into account, the employees doing likewise, so that there is mutual understanding, each one showing sympathy for and getting along happily with the other. This can occur only when you have understood that self-nature does not exist, that *Mu* is absolutely universal and impartial.

I can do no better at this point than quote two verses of Zen Master Shidō Munan. They should be read over, not once but multiple times.

> There is no jeweled lotus seat
>   In Buddha's Land of Bliss
> Apart from knowing you have
>   No self or body while alive.

> Become a dead man
>   While you're living,
> Do as you please,
>   And all is right.

52

WHO AM "I"?

ZEN MASTER Yang-shan Hui-chi (807–883), one of the founders with his teacher Kuei-shan of the Kuei-yang branch of Chinese Zen, once dreamed that he traveled to the training halls of Maitreya Bodhisattva in the Tushita Heaven and that when he arrived, he was invited to take the second seat in the hall. When he had taken the seat, a dignified old priest appeared. Beating a clapper, he announced, "Today it is the monk in the second seat's turn to preach."

Now obliged to say something, Yang-shan rose from his seat, beat the clapper, and greatly advanced the Zen teaching style by stating simply, "The Mahayana Dharma is beyond the four propositions and transcends the hundred negations. Listen! Listen!" A hundred people were in the assembly. They may or may not have understood Yang-shan's meaning, but in any case, they got up one by one and left the hall. Yang-shan often made prophecies and predictions, resembling in some ways, it seems, the founders of the new religions of modern Japan.

The Mahayana Dharma, to use the words Shakyamuni uttered when he passed his transmission to his disciple Mahakashapa, is "the repository of the true Dharma eye, the wondrous mind of nirvana." We may also call it the buddha-nature, indicating the true and authentic self. The four propositions and hundred negations are logical principles or alternatives in ancient Indian philosophy that begin with the four basic propositions: being, nonbeing, being and nonbeing, neither being nor nonbeing. A further multiplication of these four, involving multifold negations, leads eventually to the hundred negations.

There is a complex logic behind these propositions and negations, but Yang-shan's "the Mahayana Dharma is beyond the four propositions and transcends the hundred negations" means that the true mind is inexpressible no matter what words we use. Whatever you say, it can never quite hit the mark. It transcends logic.

To repeat what I have said before, our true self is neither male nor female, young nor old, learned nor unlearned, wealthy nor poor, good nor evil, beautiful nor ugly, aristocrat nor commoner, buddha nor devil, being nor nonbeing, life nor death, difficult nor easy, round nor square, red nor white, big nor small, heavy nor light, parent nor child, elder brother nor younger brother, friend nor foe, grocer nor fishmonger, chauffeur nor chauffeured. It is in fact nothing at all, yet it will respond "Yes" without a hairsbreadth interval when someone calls out to it. Then who in the world am "I"?

There is no way you can express the real self, since no words you can possibly use will make the grade. Hence Yang-shan's "The Mahayana Dharma is beyond the four propositions and transcends the hundred negations. Listen! Listen!" Zen Master Hakuin has *Your own self-nature being no-nature, / Has nothing to do with empty words!*

"Empty words" (*geron*) is chopping logic, raising arguments that serve no useful purpose. Shakyamuni warned against this in his final instructions to his followers: "You Buddhist monks, if you engage in various kinds of sophisticated argument and debate, it will disturb and distress your mind; and even though you have left your homes, you will never reach salvation. Because of this, you should immediately discard any idea of engaging in foolish argument. If you wish to obtain the bliss of nirvana, all you need do is rid yourself of this malady of foolish, trivial talk" (*Sutra of the Buddha's Bequeathed Teaching*).

The mind-nature totally free from any foolish talk is our self-nature; to understand this is to understand Buddha. It is to understand that we are buddhas just the way we are, that we are saved just as we are. This is the meaning of the Zen school's "seeing the self-nature and becoming Buddha," and the Pure Land school's "rebirth in the Pure Land in this present life."

There may be nothing wrong for a person to suffer constantly because self-reflection tells them that they are more sinful, more ignorant and uglier, or more plagued by evil passions than anyone else. To be sure, the sentiments themselves are not ignoble ones. But getting caught up in ideas such as sin, evil passions, ignorance, and ugliness is an example of what Hakuin calls "empty words." And it becomes the cause for our overlooking the true self. For instance, however hard you may struggle to sweep away the darkness in order to see the radiant light that emerges after it, such is a useless undertaking. If you make a lamp of your self, the darkness will disappear as a matter of course. To engage in religious practice to rid yourself of evil passions and become a buddha is both an impossible and a fruitless task. But if you light the radiant lamp of satori, kindle the light of the deep-believing mind (*shinjin*), the darkness of the afflicting passions will vanish on its own. That it does not presently vanish is simply because the light radiating from your lamp of satori is not strong enough.

Shunning all foolish talk and frivolous discourse, Mahayana Buddhism makes the bright, clear lamp of satori first and foremost. In forsaking all human designs and speculations, it kindles the genuine radiance of the believing mind. It penetrates the innermost depths where the true self is known to be beyond the four propositions and transcend the hundred negations, and it grasps that the self-nature is no-nature. It remains forever like the dewdrop's pure and immaculate light that keeps shining as it moves and rolls this way and that on the lotus leaf, never adhering or being inhibited in any way.

53

THE STRENGTH TO LIVE
YOUR WAY THROUGH

The following talk was given at memorial services held during the week of Higan ("other shore"), and telecast live in the main hall of the Myōshin-ji headquarters temple in Kyoto on September 24 last year [late 1950s].

LET ME WELCOME everyone who has come here on this mid-autumn day. It is a fine season indeed, neither too hot nor too cold, and we expect this refreshing autumn weather to continue for a while. Heartwarming reports are coming in of a bountiful harvest throughout the country this year, so we can look forward to a bright and cheerful autumn the likes of which we have not experienced for more than a decade. The mind of satori, the mind that attains the other shore, is just such a bright and cheerful state of mind.

The *Dhammapada* says,

Those who are victorious are resented,
The defeated undergo sleepless nights.
Those detached from victory and defeat
Are untroubled both asleep and awake.

This realm transcending victory and defeat, struggle, resentment and hate, and birth-and-death is one that can never be overwhelmed by either suffering or pleasure. Buddhists call such a perfectly bright and clear mental state the mind of enlightenment, the mind of the other shore.

This past week has been designated "Be Kind to Animals Week." Someone in the West has written that a love for animals not only sustains them but also renews the sense of kindness in the human heart. A mind that cherishes the lives of all living beings is one of the most beautiful assets any person can possess.

When you think about it, the individual has probably never been more highly regarded than he is today. I don't suppose there has ever been a time when human life and basic human rights have been so deeply respected. In spite of that, I believe it is also true that there has never been a time when human life has been so easily and unthinkingly taken. The daily newspaper is filled with such bloodcurdling stories of murder and mayhem that you want to avert your eyes from the page.

We must all begin by realizing how precious our own lives are, for only someone who has understood the value of their own life can appreciate how precious others' lives are and finally grasp that all life is precious in the extreme. Human life is irreplaceable.

It does not come again and cannot be relived. It is so precious that no matter how deeply and seriously one considers it, one can never consider it too seriously or give it too much concern.

The poet Masaoka Shiki (1867–1902), who struggled with tuberculosis throughout the later part of his life, wrote an essay titled "The Six-Foot Bed" about his illness. "I was wrong to think that Zen's satori is a matter of being able to die calmly in any possible circumstance," he wrote. "Satori is a matter of *living* peacefully and quietly in all possible circumstances." The strength to endure and to live through pain and suffering—that is Zen. At the same time, taking the true path of human life without becoming attached to or immersed in pleasure or enjoyment of any kind—that also is Zen.

A world that transcends pleasure and suffering; a world that rises above victory and defeat, strife and hatred, life and death; a mind as lovely as a bright autumn day—that is human life's eternal "other shore" (*higan*). It would be even better, however, not to limit the other shore to the realm of the human mind but to proceed on and establish an ideal other shore in the actual world in which we live. When that happens, calls for peace will no longer be mere strategies blazoned by contending political groups. Even the utopian visions of religious leaders would disappear. Thinking people would all realize the stupidity of war, and those who did not desire peace would disappear. If the world's scientists, thinkers, religious leaders, mothers, and youths would join hands and hearts together in wishing for peace, and if atomic energy was limited to peaceful purposes alone, the entire world would take on the richness and abundance that we in Japan are experiencing this autumn, and it would not be long before the bright, ineffably lovely world of the other shore would be a reality.

The realm of oneness or nonduality that exists within opposition yet transcends every opposition is the paradise of the other shore. When Shakyamuni awakened to perfect right enlightenment beneath the Bodhi tree, he is said to have cried out, "One buddha has attained the Way; and all the plants, grasses, and land have attained buddhahood." In keeping with the oneness of cause and effect, at the same time Shakyamuni achieved satori, all living beings that were engaged in practice on their way to satori attained buddhahood as well.

The *Flower Garland Sutra* says, "When aspiration for buddhahood first arises in the mind, in that very instant full awakening is achieved." In other words, the moment we give rise to the Bodhi-mind for the sake of our fellow beings and society, that moment is itself the realization of enlightenment, of becoming a buddha. To board an airplane for the United States is no different from having arrived there. Indeed, if all people in the world wish for peace, it is the same as achieving a peaceful world. What is of paramount importance in the path to buddhahood is to begin by arousing a mind that strongly desires enlightenment. And the reason we are able to arouse such a mind is because we are originally, from the first, buddhas. The effect is already present in the cause, the cause already present in the effect. Hakuin sings that when we grasp this wondrous principle, *the gates of nondual cause and effect open.*

The *Lotus Sutra* is a central text in the Buddhist canon. Said to contain the essence of the Mahayana teaching, it has been acclaimed the "king" of sutras. The lotus flower—a metaphor for the wondrous, unsurpassed Buddhist Dharma—is prized in both India and China. Its seeds are already formed when the flower blossoms; blossom and seed appear simultaneously. Moreover, the lotus does not flower if placed in clear pure water; it only blossoms in muddy water. The Mahayana teaches that the flower of enlightenment blossoms without ridding itself of the mire and mud of the evil passions, that the flower of nirvana opens without discarding the defilements of samsaric existence. This realm of the oneness of cause and effect, of *not two or three,* is the other shore to which we must all aspire.

54

TOYOTOMI HIDEYOSHI'S ASPIRATION

WHEN THE GREAT Toyotomi Hideyoshi (1537–1598), who rose from the humblest origins to become the de facto ruler of Japan, assumed the title of *taikō* (retired imperial regent)* in the final decade of his life, someone asked him, "Since you have risen in the world so remarkably, reaching the pinnacle of success and power, your aspiration from an early age must have been different from that of other people. What was it that enabled you to achieve such a high position? Surely your subjects would find any words you might have useful in their own lives."

"I never had any intention of becoming head of state," Hideyoshi replied, "When I was serving as a foot soldier, I gladly

---

* Hideyoshi assumed this title in the final decade of his life although he continued to maintain supreme power.

performed my duty as a foot soldier with singleness of purpose.
I kept at it, and I somehow became a regular soldier. As before, I
gladly focused solely on performing my role as a samurai. When
in time I became a *daimyo*, I made even greater effort to carry out
the duties of such an exalted position. Finally I gained control
over the country and assumed the title of taikō. But as I said,
from the beginning I never once had any aspiration to assume
that position."

This, it seems to me, is an extremely edifying story. We generally concern ourselves solely with achieving future results,
neglecting to see what is right under our feet, tending to be inat-
tentive to the duties we should be attending to right now—but
therein lies the cause of our failure. If we work steadily at something day by day, whatever it is, our future success is assured—it
will come of itself. It will be there waiting for us.

In Hideyoshi's devotion to his role as a foot soldier, the
buds had already formed that would bear fruit in elevating him
to samurai status, and his diligence in carrying out his duty as
a samurai produced the buds that bore fruit in his becoming a
daimyo. The promise of the further glory he achieved in subduing the entire country and becoming taikō was already present
when he served as a daimyo. There is an old proverb, "Unsowed
seeds never sprout." Without a cause, an effect does not appear.
The effect is always present in the cause; the cause can always be
seen in the effect. Buddhism speaks of this as *inga ichinyo*, "the
oneness of cause and effect."

"If you want to know the future result," the sutras tell us,

284

"look to the present cause. If you want to know the past cause, look to the present result." A future result is included within a present cause; a past cause appears clearly in a present result.

> If you continue forward without faltering,
>   You see for a thousand leagues ahead,
> Even if you lumber on at a leisurely pace,
>   Trudging your way like a water buffalo.

Moving forward smartly and steadily day by day is the only way to open the path to a bright future. At the end of the haiku poet Bashō's life, when his followers asked him to compose a death verse, he replied, "The verse I made yesterday is today's death verse. The verse I made today is tomorrow's death verse. Every haiku I have written has been my death verse." Are his words not ones to prize and cherish? If you live each and every day as though it is your last, when death does come you will have no regrets.

> Not knowing if this autumn
>   Will bring rains or storms,
> I continue my work weeding
>   The fields day by day.

Is not such a life, singlemindedly dedicated to working without thoughts of profit or loss, pleasure or pain, something to cherish dearly? It is dedication of this order that informs the well-known phrase *ichigo ichie*—"one time, one meeting,"—that is, treasure each meeting; it will never come again—often used at tea gatherings. It signifies a full, rich way of life that has reached through to the eternal. Hakuin's line *The gates of nondual cause and effect open* is expressive of just such an existence.

In Zen Master Ta-chueh's *Treatise on Zazen*, which I have mentioned before as one of the sources for Hakuin's *Song of Zazen*, the words "oneness of cause and effect" appear in the ninth of a series of questions someone poses to Ta-chueh:

Question: If we do not accumulate merit and perform good deeds, how can we attain buddhahood and be fully endowed with all possible virtues?

Answer: A person who accumulates merit and performs good deeds may indeed become a buddha after the passage of three immeasurably long kalpas. But if they practice the oneness of cause and effect, they can attain buddhahood in their present lifetime. In clarifying their own mind and grasping their self-nature, a person realizes that from the first they are a buddha—from the time they are born, that it is not something they attain now for the first time.

The questioner gives voice to the common notion that the Zen school preaches nothing but seeing the self-nature and attaining buddhahood, and it does not encourage students to accumulate merit through the performance of good deeds. The master's reply is that if you think accumulating merits, doing good deeds, engaging in one practice after another will lead to fully endowed buddhahood, inasmuch as good deeds are countless and evil passions infinite, you may perhaps become a buddha if you are born and reborn over and over and practice religious exercises for an infinite length of time. But when such an attainment might occur is quite beyond human comprehension. If, on the other hand, you grasp the Dharma of the oneness of cause and effect, you can become a buddha in your own lifetime. Isn't that a wonderful teaching? To achieve kenshō—seeing your true self-nature, knowing your true self—is to confirm that you have been a buddha from the time you were born. You don't do zazen because it is a religious practice whose merit enables you to become a buddha. Zazen is above all else a matter of understanding that you are *already* a buddha, that you don't suddenly become a buddha now for the first time.

People of the Pure Land tradition often say that the Zen school is based on self-power: a student must achieve buddhahood by performing difficult ascetic practice. But such an understanding is grossly mistaken. Zen itself certainly does not make ascetic practice its goal. It does not even rely on good works or the accumulation of merit. Zazen is a Dharma teaching that enables you to realize that you are a buddha already, without engaging in difficult ascetic practice.

The line *All beings are from the first buddhas* quoted earlier from the *Song of Zazen* appears in this same question in the *Treatise on Zazen*. The line *The gates of nondual cause and effect open* is also based on a passage in the *Treatise*: "If they practice the oneness of cause and effect, they can attain buddhahood in their present lifetime."

A single husk of rice is the result of untold billions of previous rice husks, and it is the cause of untold billions of future rice husks as well. Our Bodhi-mind is the result of the Bodhi-minds of untold billions of past buddhas and at the same time the cause of the Bodhi-minds of untold billions of future buddhas. They are all really the same buddha of the oneness of cause and effect; every buddha is the result of all other buddhas and the cause of them all as well.

55

THE GREAT
WHITE OXCART

I WOULD NOW like to the return to the parable of the great white oxcart, which I cited in a previous essay. There was once a very rich man in ancient India who lived on a great estate surrounded by high walls. It contained many different buildings—the main living quarters, detached living quarters, guesthouses, pavilions, teahouses, a house for retirement, quarters for his many children and his servants, and storehouses and sheds of different sizes. As this great and extensive estate had been in his family for many hundreds of years, among its countless structures were some that had been neglected and in need of repair. Others, also in a ruinous state, had become the lairs of foxes, badgers, and other creatures, including great snakes, and were on the verge of toppling to the ground.

One day the rich man spotted a fire burning fiercely in one of the buildings. It was spreading quickly, and there was one building about to collapse. He rushed outside the gate in a panic but then remembered that many of his children were still inside the compound. He turned back to rescue them, crying out, "Fire! Fire! Come out! Get out of the house as quick as you can!" The children, knowing nothing of the dangers of fire and not understanding why they had to leave their home, remained deeply engrossed in the games they were playing.

Although at his wit's end, the rich man suddenly devised an expedient means to convince his children to leave. "Everyone hurry outside, I have some splendid carts for you!" he cried to the children. "A goat-cart, a deer-cart, and an oxcart too. They are all waiting for you to ride them. Hurry on out! The first one out will get the best cart!" With that, the children all rushed outside the house.

Children are fond of vehicles like carts that they can ride on. Today's children, if asked what they want as a present, would probably tell you they want a toy train, automobile, or streetcar; and children in the past were no doubt just as fond of such vehicles. So when the rich man's children heard carts were waiting outside, they dashed out to see them and thus avoided being caught in the conflagration rapidly engulfing the estate. Of course when the children got outside, they found no goat-carts, deer-carts, or oxcarts waiting for them. But there was nothing whatever to reproach in the rich man's deception, since he resorted to it only to save his children's lives.

He did not have the carts he had promised to give them. Instead, he gave them a vehicle he himself used, a large and priceless white oxcart. He told them they could regard it as their own and enjoy themselves riding in it whenever they desired. Hinduism regards the sacred white ox that pulls a great cart to be a messenger of the gods; he is as important as the deities themselves. This is similar to the white snake and white fox in Shintō, which believes the two are messengers of the deities Benten and Inari. In India, a pure white bull was kept in an ornate enclosure; it did nothing, had no duties, was fed delicacies, and its urine was ingested as medicine. The rich man's cart was pulled by one of these immense, immaculately white oxen, so we may imagine that the vehicle he ended up giving his children was a truly magnificent one, an oxcart such as only the very wealthiest householder could afford.

In this parable from the *Lotus Sutra*, our world is likened to the rich man's old house being consumed by fire, putting millions upon millions of Buddha's beautiful children in peril. The children play with little toys—their various desires, pleasures, and divertissements—oblivious of the world's transience and life's impermanence. Seeing this and feeling great compassion for them, Shakyamuni said, "There is no ease or comfort anywhere in the three worlds of unenlightened beings. . . . I alone can save them." He proceeded to devote his life to the work of rescuing living beings from the suffering of the burning house.

First of all, he made known the vehicle of the sravaka, or "hearer," setting forth the teaching of the Four Noble Truths: suffering, the origin of suffering, the cessation of suffering, and the path to its cessation. Next, he announced the vehicle of the pratyekabuddha, or "private" buddha, and taught the truth of the Twelve Causations, which explains the condition of birth-and-death to which all living beings are subject. Finally he propounded the bodhisattva vehicle and revealed the practice of the six paramitas, or perfections. Since his followers all possessed different natures and dispositions, they were able to be saved from the burning house that is the threefold world of unenlightened being by learning those among the three teachings most suited to them.

However, Buddha's promulgation of the three teachings of hearer, pratyekabuddha, and bodhisattva, adapting them to a diversity of human natures, is an example of the use of expedient means (*upaya*); it does not convey his true intent. Just as the rich man was lying when he told his children about three carts pulled by three different animals, the Buddha's true purpose, what he really wanted to expound, was the one vehicle, the single path. It is mistaken to try to create two or three different levels in human beings' true natures. They are all equal, they all possess the same buddha-nature, and they all can become Buddha.

The *Lotus Sutra* teaches, "There is only one vehicle, not two, not three." The *Song of Zazen* has *One way, not two or three, runs straight ahead.* The hearer and the pratyekabuddha, which we call the two vehicles, become three vehicles when the bodhisattva vehicle is added. But the *Lotus Sutra* teaches that the true Buddha Dharma is neither two vehicles, nor three, nor four; that there is only one single Dharma teaching—that of the Mahayana, or Great Vehicle.

In the doctrinal classification formulated by later Buddhist scholars, Shakyamuni's preachings are arranged into five periods: the first period of the *Flower Garland Sutra*, the second of the Agama sutras, the third of the Correct and Equal sutras, the fourth of the Prajna or Wisdom sutras, and the fifth period of the *Lotus* and *Nirvana* sutras. It was said that from the time the Buddha first preached the Agama sutras until he preached the Prajna sutras, his teaching employed the expedient means (*upaya*) of the two vehicles and the three vehicles and that finally, in the last eight years of his life, he preached the *Lotus Sutra* on Holy Eagle Peak at Rajagriha. This is the old, traditionally accepted belief, though I doubt if you would find many people today who accept this classification. I think, however, that few would dispute the fact that the Mahayana thought set forth by Shakyamuni in the *Lotus Sutra* represents his true teaching.

The Mahayana, the Great Vehicle, is the great white oxcart, the vehicle for buddhas and other great human beings who have consummated their training. Shakyamuni's ultimate aim was to provide this beautifully fitted-out vehicle of buddhahood to each and every one of us, enabling everyone to open their minds to a view of human life no different from their own, the view he himself had set forth—to realize in satori the proper view of human life that he had expounded and to follow that path steadfastly in our own lives.

56

HOLDING UP A FLOWER, AN UNDERSTANDING SMILE

HOLY EAGLE PEAK, also known as Vulture Peak, a small mountain located northeast of Rajagriha, the capital of Magada, was Shakyamuni's favorite retreat and the scene of many of his discourses. One of the teachings he delivered there was the *Lotus Sutra*, containing his deepest aspirations, those for which he originally appeared in the world. I believe that when Shakyamuni preached the *Lotus Sutra*, his thought and personal attainment were at their peak. He no doubt sensed that his life as a human being was nearing an end, and I think we may also assume he had given long and careful thought to the survival of the Buddhist order after his death.

One day the Lord of the Brahma Heaven held out a yellow *kompira* flower to the buddha and requested that he deliver a sermon. Shakyamuni ascended to the teaching platform. He stood wordlessly holding up the flower. His eyes, blinking from time to time, were as beautiful as rolled lotus leaves. The assembled audience waited for him to speak. But he uttered no words; he just stood there silently like a dumb or deaf man, blinking his eyes. Mahakashapa, one of the Buddha's ten chief disciples, acclaimed as superior to all others for his religious practice, was among those in the assembly. Mahakashapa responded to Shakyamuni with a smile. He alone had understood the meaning of holding up the flower. Shakyamuni then spoke for the first time:

> I have the true Dharma eye, the exquisite mind of nirvana, the true form of formlessness, the marvelously subtle Dharma gate that does not depend on words and phrases and is a separate transmission outside the scriptures. This I entrust to you, Mahakashapa.

These famous words, which first appeared in a Chinese text of the Sung dynasty, are quite difficult in the original, but since for the Zen sect they are the most important of all the utterances made during Shakyamuni's lifetime, I would like to say a few words to explain their meaning.

Here is a simple paraphrase of what I believe the words mean: *I possess a great treasure of genuine wisdom that will enable you to see that you yourself are the world in its entirety. There is a marvelous and ineffable mind that is apart from the entire world and yet is constantly working together with the world. It is beyond doubt that this is true, yet since this mind has no color or form, there is no possible way to express it. We may call it a "wondrously subtle existence" or a "marvelously subtle function," but you can't really describe it in words or phrases or teach it through verbal means. This incomprehensible mind I entrust to you, Mahakashapa. I ask you to guard it carefully and transmit it so that it will never disappear from the earth.*

This incomprehensible mind, which the Buddha called the treasure of the true Dharma eye, the exquisite mind of nirvana, is also called Zen. It is sometimes referred to as *Anuttara-samyak-sambodhi*, "the highest, most perfect enlightenment." Using still different words, we might describe it as self-awakening to the absolute oneness of the world and the self, which is possible to all. It means grasping the Buddha's mind when he said, "Now this threefold world is all my domain, and the living beings in it are all my children" (*Lotus Sutra*).

Mahakashapa smiled, and the Buddha confirmed his understanding, awarding him his *inka*, or Dharma seal, and saying, "You have understood the Buddha's mind. Its innermost secrets have been imparted to you. Do not allow them to disappear; they must live on forever."

In this way, Mahakashapa received the transmission of Shakyamuni's Dharma, becoming the first in what would become a long line of patriarchal Zen teachers. From Mahakashapa the Dharma passed to Ananda, from Ananda to Sanavasa. Bodhidharma, the twenty-eighth patriarch in the transmission, established Shakyamuni's Dharma in China. Among the Japanese priests who transmitted it later to Japan was Daiō Kokushi. Daiō passed it to Daitō Kokushi, Daitō transmitted it to Kanzan Egen, and in time it reached Zen Master Hakuin. This person-to-person transmission of the Buddha's mind is said to be like water transferred from one vessel to another. The Zen school is for this reason also called the buddha-mind sect.

The Japanese Zen school recognizes twenty-four different Dharma lineages that were transmitted from China down through the centuries. However, in today's Rinzai school the vital Dharma teaching is found in the lineage of Master Kanzan alone, the so-called Ōtōkan school (the elements that make up the word *Ōtōkan* are taken from the names *Daiō*, *Daitō*, and *Kanzan*). We consider it a truly great honor to belong to this teaching line, and we have a responsibility, equally great, to ensure that the Dharma lamp is kept burning and transmitted to future generations. It is my firm belief that followers of Zen, clerics and laypeople alike, must strive together as one and stake their very lives on protecting this precious Dharma. We at the Myōshin-ji feel an even deeper indebtedness, because the full name of our Myōshin-ji monastery, Shōbō-zan Myōshin-ji, the "Temple of the Exquisite Mind," the "Mountain of the True Dharma," was taken from the very words Shakyamuni spoke on Holy Eagle Peak.

Daitō Kokushi chose the name Myōshin-ji for our temple. When Daitō was approaching death, Emperor Hanazono dispatched an emissary to inform him that he wished to turn his detached palace at Hanazono into a Buddhist temple. He asked Daitō to give the temple a name and suggest a possible abbot. In his reply, Daitō likens Emperor Hanazono to the great god of the Brahma Heaven, he himself to Shakyamuni, and his student Kanzan Egen to Mahakashapa. I believe the name Daitō chose for the temple can be traced to his devout wish for the genuine Buddhist Dharma to be transmitted long into the future.

The name Myōshin-ji and the names of subsequent head priests and various buildings within the monastery compound all derive from or allude to words that occur in the story of Shakyamuni's "Flower Sermon." Allusions appear in the temple's "mountain name," Shōbō-zan, "Mountain of the True Dharma"; and temple name Myōshin-ji, "Temple of the Exquisite Mind"; and in the first abbot Kanzan Egen's posthumous title of Musō Daishi, "Great Master of Formlessness"; and in the second abbot Juō Sōhitsu's posthumous title of Mimyō Daishi, "Great Master Wondrous and Exquisite"; in Nenge-shitsu, "Holding Up the Flower Chambers," the name given Emperor Hanazono's living quarters in the Gyokuhō-in sub-temple; in the name Bishō-tō, "Tower of the Faint Smile," Kanzan's mausoleum; and in the name of an artificial hill behind the temple, Keisoku-zan, Japanese for Kukkutapāda, the mountain in India where Mahakashapa died.

In the mid-sixteenth century, on the occasion of Zen Master Kanzan's three-hundredth death anniversary, the eminent priest Gudō Tōshoku (1577–1661), head abbot of Myōshin-ji, offered incense and read out a verse in honor of his great predecessor. Even today we cannot help being deeply moved by the clear-sighted awareness in Master Gudō's heart:

HOLDING UP A FLOWER

We had twenty-four lineages in Japanese Zen,
Regrettably most of them are no longer around.
    Good thing the descendants of Kanzan have been
    Transmitting the torch these three hundred years.

57

"THE WORLD IS A BURNING HOUSE"— AN OLD WOMAN'S STORY

[AN OLD WOMAN related the following story:]

Toward the end of last year, a fire broke out near our house. It kept raging closer and closer, creeping right up to our door and threatening to engulf us in flames. Thankfully it was contained, and we were saved from harm. But things like that happen from time to time, and you never know when some disaster will strike at you personally. It makes you realize how utterly unpredictable your life is. Our family had the good fortune to escape, but this year we were visited by a calamity of another kind that caused my son-in-law untold suffering.

After becoming the guarantor for a loan, he was forced to repay it himself when the borrower defaulted. Now any of my neighbors will tell you that there is no finer person than my son. He is like a buddha—if someone comes asking for his help, he is unable to refuse. The amount of the debt may not seem large to some people, but for us it is a considerable sum. The interest on the debt keeps accumulating, and there is no telling when we'll be able to pay it all back. But if we don't, it will cause great distress for others, so our family has come together and resolved to see it through somehow.

I turned over to him the pocket money I'd been saving up every month. I told him I didn't need it. I had devoted myself wholeheartedly to my faith, worshipping regularly at temple and shrines, although I had neglected that practice for some time. We were burned out of house and home during the war and have only recently been able to acquire a place of our own. It makes me sad to reflect on how unexpectedly arduous things turn out in this world.

I became a widow at the age of forty-two. My husband was forty when he died. We had no children of our own. Three years before he died, we took in one of his nieces as our daughter. My present son was adopted into the family as her husband. That was fine. My son is now forty-nine, my daughter forty-two — just the age I was when my husband passed away. So everything worked out pretty well after all. I put it all down to karmic destiny. There's nothing I can do to change it. It was fated to happen. After all, there is no way to avoid hardship or adversity. Our family has now become resigned to our situation. And who knows, we could easily have been visited by an even worse calamity.

Anyway, the man who was the cause of all our problems has moved into a small house, and he lives most frugally. I sincerely hope he will be able to get back on his feet. After all, he is a relative of mine! I can't tell you how ashamed I was, having my son come and apologize to me every day: "Thank you so much for your help. Please bear with it a little longer." Now, ever since I was a young girl I have experienced more than my share of trouble, yet I don't think I have ever done anything that would cause any great distress to others. At my age, however, having someone apologizing to me like that every day is hard to bear.

My own mother-in-law was not like me. She was a very strong woman of the old school. She had had a terribly difficult life. I had hoped, after she breathed her last, to be able to tell my husband about all the suffering and anguish, the terrible times I went through in her final years when I was caring for her. But he passed away before she did, and for three years after that my mother-in-law remained bedridden. It is hard to express how difficult those years were for me, a widow, managing a home business, caring for a sick person, and with a little child to escort to school.

My thorough disgust with human society was what led me to religion. I didn't know whether there was a hell after death or a heaven, but of one thing I was certain: I had no desire to be reborn as a human being again. If there was any teaching that would assure me I would not be reborn in the human world, I was eager to know it. It was about that time that I began to feel a desire to draw closer to the Way of Buddha.

But I still had an elderly invalid to look after, and a small daughter to take care of, and I was struggling to run a shop as a single woman. I didn't have time to go and ask about such things. Now I can only remember how truly difficult life was for me then.

The world is a burning house. But unless an ordinary person like me, someone heavily burdened with karma, undergoes suffering of this kind, the aspiration to leave the burning house does not arise in their mind. My karma would have continued to cause me suffering until the day I died. Still, I tried through all those difficult years, even on the hardest days, to at least make our house warm and comfortable. This was something I felt strongly about, being yet a young woman. Even while undergoing a life of suffering I had been fortunate to adopt a fine son, and he too was able to achieve a deep religious faith (*shinjin*). My foster daughter has always been very kind to me as well. Our household life has been maintained in as agreeable a manner as I could hope for.

I had long sought a chance to talk to someone about the Buddha's teachings. Then one day a person who was promoting a religious teaching of some sort came to the door and asked me to buy a magazine he was selling. I told him, "I have yearned to seek the Way but have always been held back because, when priests held meetings or gave religious talks, I was unable to leave the house. I would like very much to read about such matters in my home." So I subscribed to the magazine and became a member of his group.

For the next two or three years, whenever this man came by, I listened to his teaching. Customers who happened to be in my shop at the time listened as well. Gradually, however, I came to doubt the truth of what he was saying. Perhaps even someone like me can, little by little, attain some manner of understanding. I wrote him a letter telling him not to come again. It was from about that time that delusions of various kinds began rising in my mind, and the anguish and distress of trying to achieve a mind of true faith (*shinjin*) gnawed at me. Thankfully, however, at that point I encountered a good and true teacher and heard a teaching that was fitted just right for my needs. Nothing could have caused me more happiness!

58

ASSUMING SHAPES
OF CLAY

THERE IS AN old verse about the clay figurines known as *Fushimi ningyō* that are produced and sold by the roadside in the Fushimi district in southern Kyoto:

Saigyō Hōshi and cats
    Hotei and everything else
Given shape through clay
    All along the Inari Road.

Pilgrims and others who visit the large Inari Shrine in Fushimi, south of Kyoto, pass by the many shops lining the road that sell these *Fushimi ningyō*. There are figurines depicting the poet Saigyō, beautiful ladies, cats, the corpulent "Laughing Buddha" Hotei, and many others as well. Since all of them are made of clay, Saigyō is not really Saigyō and Hotei not really Hotei;

they have merely been transformed into those shapes. From the perspective of the clay, they are only clay and essentially without form; but from the standpoint of the shapes, the clay has merely been shaped into those various forms. Although essentially formless, they have assumed these provisional forms. This is the point Hakuin addresses in his words, *Your form is now the form of no-form.*

At the atomic level, mountains are atoms, rivers are atoms, grasses are atoms, trees are atoms, and birds and flower are atoms. All things are just accumulations of atoms; they are shapeless, merely and entirely formless flows of energy. But in the natural world, various forms are manifested. We see mountains, rivers, trees and grasses, birds and flowers—in the Buddhist phrase, "ten thousand forms in complete array"—with all their forms now assuming the form of no-form.

As human beings are also accumulations of atoms, there are no men or women, good people or bad. Everyone is absolutely equal, not a bit of difference between them. From this mass of human beings, undifferentiated in their sameness, may for a brief time appear a head of state, a police officer, a thief, a chauffeur, a customer—people manifesting different shapes and forms, each with its own standpoint and its own walk of life.

I am reminded of a stimulating old Zen saying: "He leaves with his flask to buy wine at the village shop; returning, he puts on a robe and acts as master of the house." Dangling his old sake flask, the man looks just like a servant out to buy some cheap *doburoku* sake, but when he returns home and dons a formal robe with a short coat over it, he is a gentleman of great dignity. At home, a gentleman may work like a servant stoking the bath fire, though out in society he is an exemplary company president. At times, a person sweeps the garden like an apprentice monk; at times dons a scarlet robe and become the *kanchō*, or chief abbot. Herein is the unique flavor of human life, the freedom of human beings. There can be no certain or established form or shape that human beings must conform to, for the form of no-form is their authentic mode of existence.

We can view human life as a kind of play or performance. One actor can act the roles of both a daimyo and a menial servant, can become a samurai and an ordinary citizen, can be the one who wields the sword and the poor soul who is cut down. Although they can play any role, assume any character, on returning to the dressing room, they revert to being a member of the company of players. Then they no longer have the swagger of a feudal lord or the deferential manner of a servant; although they take part in swordplay on the stage, cutting down opponents or being cut down themselves, back in the dressing room they are neither the domineering lord nor the fawning lackey. It is enough that they wholeheartedly enact their role. Once they leave the stage, they have no reason to display those same emotions. I find this most interesting and think that human life altogether would benefit from such a dressing room. Knowing the free, unfettered realm liberated from all forms whatever is a life in which *your form is now the form of no-form.*

Years ago, my teacher commissioned me to build a temple

in Tokyo on the site of the mansion where the celebrated Layman Yamaoka Tesshū had lived. I was obliged to reside for several years in the area of Nakano in the northwest part of the city. One evening I had been invited to have a few cups of sake and was walking home in good spirits. As I passed through the Shinjuku area, I saw a palm reader sitting out beside a glowing lantern in the frigid winter night, looking very cold. I was in fine spirits, as I said, so I let him read my palm and scrutinize my face. Slowly he brought out a book and, pointing to one of the images, said, "This is your physiognomy. You have the face of an aristocrat. You can expect to have good fortune. Within three years you will be appointed the kanchō (chief priest) of a large temple." He was pulling out all the stops to flatter me.

As I had little interest in becoming the priest of an important temple, his words had little impact, but I was in high spirits, so I gave him a double fee of one yen and left. Three years, five years, ten years passed. No one came asking me to become the kanchō of a large temple. Perhaps the fortune teller had put one over on me. Or perhaps in the meantime my physiognomy had greatly deteriorated. After all, the lineaments of one's face and the palms of one's hands are constantly changing. Or maybe I needed more frequent visits to the fortune teller.

Every day we laugh or cry or get angry, grimacing like a turkey. But our real face—which one is that? Our face when we laugh? When we weep? When we are angry? Or is our real self the one with the prim, composed countenance we assume when sitting for a group photograph at a wedding?

Could there be what can be called a "definitive edition" of one's face? Inasmuch as it is always shifting and changing in various ways, I doubt there is any one face you could point to as the real one. Still, your face at each and every moment must be said to be your real face at that moment. Having no fixed appearance or configuration, it continually manifests different shapes, living *the form of no-form* day by day.

On a spiritual plane, the self-nature that is no-nature and the true self have no shape or form or face. Yet in spite of this, to take my own case, there is the face of the head priest of Rei-un-in subtemple, the face of the president of Hanazono University, and the face of the rōshi at the Shōfuku-ji training hall as well. A woeful situation, being obliged to traipse around, in a shameful sweat, showing these various sorry faces. Yet being unable simply to exist in a state of unconcerned formlessness is one of the many hardships intrinsic to this transient world of pain and suffering. Perhaps, as the saying goes, it's a case of someone with an inherent buddha-nature doing something they know is wrong.

59

"DON'T SPEAK WITH YOUR MOUTH"

To return once again to the Fushimi figurines, from the standpoint of the clay, the figures of the poet Saigyō, the cats, and Hotei are all the same clay and can only be deemed formless. Viewed from the standpoint of form, however, the figures must be clearly distinguished: the cat is a cat; the beautiful woman, a beautiful woman; Hotei is Hotei. That being said, the clay and the cat are not different. As the *Heart Sutra* teaches, *Form is no different from emptiness, emptiness no different from form, form is emptiness, emptiness is form.* If we say that the formless clay is emptiness and the shaped cat is form, it follows that "the cat is no different from the clay, the clay no different from the cat; the cat *is* the clay, the clay *is* the cat."

Our fundamental nature is originally no-nature, and it is formless; neither male nor female, rich nor poor, learned nor unlearned, young nor old. It is at the same time true, beyond any possible doubt, that males and females, rich and poor, salaried workers and merchants, young and old do exist, living out their lives in various ways every day. The true reality is formless; there is nothing whatever, and yet within that reality these various provisional forms must appear and live out their lives. But that does not mean there is a true form apart from a provisional one or a provisional form apart from a true one. If you understand that the provisional form is itself the true form and the true form is itself the provisional form, there will not be a single form in the world you will look down on or belittle.

A saying appeared during Hakuin's lifetime parodying his famous "sound of one hand" koan:

Instead of hearing the sound of Hakuin's one hand,
Let's clap our hands together and do some business.*

Human life only comes once and can never be relived. I firmly urge people to live seriously, dedicating themselves constantly to leading the most genuine and honest life they can.

Nothing in the voice
    Of the cicada intimates
How soon it will die.

---

*Shopkeepers drummed up business by standing outside their shops clapping their hands.

When the cicada emerges into the world after being buried in the earth for seven years, it fully possesses the freedom to move its wings, make shrill cries, and flit about at will. It lives for only a week, a truly fleeting existence, clinging to the bark of a tree and making loud noises by rubbing its wings and legs together. A cicada is the perfect example of a totally earnest life. Seeing the cicada striving so resolutely, it is hard to believe its life will soon come to an end. It doesn't lament the seven years of hardship it had to endure underground or the shortness of its life. It doesn't fear its imminent death. It just continues producing its song with all the strength it possesses. Although some might say this is merely a case of instinctive behavior, I still believe we have much to learn from the dauntless resolution the cicada displays.

We feel an equally deep respect for Bashō's penetrating insight and marvelous power of observation in creating such a verse. Indeed, this was the person who told his followers when they asked him for a death verse, "The verse I made yesterday is today's death verse. The verse I made today is tomorrow's death verse. Every haiku I have written has been my death verse." Bashō devoted himself singlemindedly to the way of haiku, pouring his body and soul into every haiku he wrote. Is it not here, in Bashō's total earnestness, that we discover the meaning and joy of human life? I think the line *Your form is now the form of no-form* also conveys this same sense of thoroughly living out a genuine human life.

The *rakugo* storyteller Sanyūtei Enchō (1839–1900) was once invited to Yamaoka Tesshū's training hall. Tesshū, a prominent samurai and swordsman, was also a well-regarded lay Zen teacher. Tesshū told Enchō, "When I was a little child, every night before I went to bed my mother would tell me the story of Momotaro. It always held my interest, no matter how many times I heard it. Tell the Momotaro story."

Enchō felt uncertain and confused. Telling stories was his profession and he was good at it, but being asked to talk about Momotaro in front of a group of rough and rowdy-looking young martial artists threw him for a loop. Obliged to do the best he could, however, he told the Momotaro story as requested. When he finished, Tesshū said, "That wasn't very entertaining. My mother told it much better. To start with, don't speak with your mouth." Enchō left and returned home, these curious words running through his mind.

Unable to get Tesshū's comment out of his mind, the next time he visited him he said, "Last time I was here you said not to talk with my mouth. How can I do that?" "That's just the point," replied Tesshū. "Until you understand how to do it, you'll never become a first-rate rakugo artist. If you want to learn how to do it, try some zazen." So Enchō, backed into a corner, began to practice zazen.

Singleminded devotion is a wonderful thing. Three years later, Enchō passed the koan barrier Tesshū had given him, achieving kenshō, or enlightenment. But then Tesshū again threw him for a loop: "You've got your satori. Now tell me the story of Momotaro." This time, Enchō told the story with great panache. "Good, good," said Tesshū, clapping his hands. "Today your story was very entertaining."

Later, when Tekisui Rōshi of Tenryū-ji traveled to Tokyo and met with Tesshū, they discussed the matter and agreed to award Enchō the layman's name Muzetsu Koji, "Tongueless Layman." In front of Tesshū's gravesite at the Zenshō-an at Yanaka in Tokyo is a smaller stone engraved with the name Sanyūtei Enchō Muzetsu Koji, imparting the feeling that Enchō is there still performing his Momotaro story before Layman Tesshū.

Because Enchō spoke with a tongueless tongue, he became a legendary rakugo storyteller. A marathon runner wins laurels by running unmindful of their body, a pianist performs music that enraptures the audience by striking the piano keys with fingerless fingers, an actor gains praise for their virtuosity by transcending their age in their portrayals of younger people. The business of your form assuming the form of no-form is no doubt the inmost secret that enriches to the utmost these performers in the drama of human life, filling them to overflowing with a sense of happiness and well-being.

60

ARE YOU PREPARED?

I AM AT present taking a group of twenty-eight Zen monks on a trip to Hokkaidō, where we will engage in a begging tour of the island. I am intrinsically a carefree, optimistic sort of person, not easily troubled. I have never felt burdened by any stiff or formal notions of responsibility. In theory, I have heavy responsibilities as head priest of the Reiun-in subtemple of Myōshin-ji and as president of Hanazono University. My positions as head abbot of the Myōshin-ji monastery and teacher at the Shōfuku-ji training hall might be said to make that responsibility an even heavier one.

Even so, my neglect of such duties continues unabated. I tell people, "I didn't take on those positions because I wanted them. It was only because everyone got together and compelled me to. I am fully aware how unqualified I am to hold them, so any time I make a great hash of things, I will just tie on my straw sandals and become a regular monk (*unsui*) as before."

Nonetheless, I must say that on this trip I do feel a certain sense of responsibility. My physical constitution has never been what could be called hardy. Leading two concentrated training sessions (*sesshin*), the regular one at the monastery and another one at the university, has tired me out. And there was a mountain of business that had piled up and had to be taken care of before setting out.

This Hokkaidō trip will continue for two months. Events are scheduled every single day. Any free time will no doubt be spent meeting people and scribbling calligraphy for them with my clumsy brush. Moreover, Hokkaidō is experiencing a period of unseasonable weather, and I am concerned whether my body will be able to bear up for the two months we will be trouping from place to place.

What if I break down halfway and am obliged to cancel the rest of the trip? How about the considerable funds that have been spent? What trouble it will cause the temples and laypeople we are scheduled to visit, not to mention the twenty unsui here with me who will be left completely in the lurch in the midst of their journey. As this trip began, such worrisome thoughts brought home to me what a serious obligation I had undertaken. At any rate, this time I was obliged to consider my social responsibilities very keenly.

With the trip underway, I became uncharacteristically meek and acquiescent. It was an extravagance, but I allowed a bed to be booked for me in one of the sleeping cars. I slept for thirty-six hours, almost the entire way from Osaka Station to Tōyoura in Hokkaidō, and repaid an outstanding sleep debt that I had been piling up.

What about my mental readiness for the trip? How well I could understand the resolution of those Japanese climbers who made the first ascent of Mount Manaslu in Nepal in 1956, and the explorers who brave the Antarctic continent. Our own expedition was not a perilous one, yet I believed I could sympathize with the feelings of the young men who had set out as novices with me on the heavy seas of human life and social interaction. Embarking on this great journey, putting our lives on the line, how should we be prepared mentally? What determination and resolution should we possess?

As to how one should go about this preparation, many different ideas might be offered: "Education is important," "You've got to understand the art of socializing in friendly gatherings," "Diligence is of the essence, and utter sincerity"; or perhaps "No, you must first of all learn how to get on in the world and earn money," "No, because if you lack religious sensibility . . .", "None of those are really necessary, what you must do is adapt to the new world in which we live"; or "You should just devote yourself to the life you have chosen for yourself."

But by now I realized, perhaps belatedly, that the most important and fundamental mental preparation is zazen. The Sixth Patriarch said, "*Sitting (za) means not giving rise to thoughts in the face of any and all external realms, good or bad. Zen means remaining undisturbed internally as you see the self-nature.*"

"Not giving rise to thoughts in the face of any and all external realms, good or bad" means that the mind remains unmoved and unperturbed by anything whatever in the outer world. If my mind remains unconcerned, thoughts such as "Hokkaidō is remote," "The weather is bad," "Too many events have been scheduled," and "My body is frail" will not arise. I should just remain detached and continue walking forward with confidence, thinking of nothing at all.

From the train window, an endless variety of landscapes and phenomena appear before the eyes, one after another. But the window itself does not move; it merely receives their images. Because of this, it never tires out. Human life requires an awareness of this kind as well. If I thought, "We're coming into Kanazawa now," "We'll be arriving at Akita," "We'll be in Aomori soon," continually reflecting on what an extremely long journey we were making, I would feel tired. If, on the other hand, when the ocean or a mountain or a river appears, I realize they are images entering the window of my mind yet leaving the mind itself completely unmoved, my mind will remain composed. Recalling this brought home to me that the secret of avoiding the fatigue of travel is mental composure.

If I started thinking about how intolerably busy I am—the begging rounds, Zen lectures, sanzen, memorial services, talks, and so on—I would feel exhausted. When people bring various problems to me, my mind must remain completely steady and undisturbed. And just as two landscapes do not come through the window at once, if I can just deal with these problems calmly, one by one, then no matter how busy I am, nothing could be more untroubled or carefree.

Such a mental state is like sitting in a theater gazing at one of those wide Cinerama screens they are using these days. You don't move at all; the movement out there all comes to you. You see beautiful leafy lanes in Bali, Swiss mountains, pastoral American landscapes, all while sitting in your cushioned seat. You can tour the entire world that way. You must be careful, though, and not become deluded into imagining that it is you who is doing the moving. You must stay on guard against that!

"Practice that confirms things by taking the self to them is illusion; things coming forward to practice and confirm the self is satori," said Master Dōgen. How true those words are. Bankei said, "Because Shakyamuni was completely free and unhindered wherever he went, he became master of the world." Knowing that wherever you are in the world is your home, never feeling you have arrived at a new or unknown place, always acting freely and spontaneously—isn't that a pleasant way to undertake the journey of human life?

The window of the mind is originally empty—there is nothing in it at all. From this nothingness no movement arises. All that happens is the outside world comes in, so wherever you go, anywhere in the world, no matter what event arises, if you know that it is only a landscape reflected in the window of the mind, you have no reason to feel tense or constrained. Hakuin's *Song of Zazen* says,

> *Your form is now the form of no-form,*
> *Coming or going, you never leave home.*

61

THE ORDEAL OF THE OATS

I WOULD NOW like to retell a story about Shakyamuni's disciple Purna that I cited earlier in connection with the forbearance paramita (see chapter 33). Purna paid him a visit before departing on a trip to spread the teachings in the hinterlands of central Asia. Buddha said to him, "Purna, the people in that land are savage and lacking in refinement. When they see you, they may revile you and insult you in various ways. Are you prepared for that?"

"World-Honored One," Purna replied, "if they insult me or revile me, I will think, 'These people are kind and courteous. They would not strike me with stones and shards.'"

"And if they did throw stones at you and beat you with sticks?" asked the Buddha.

"I would think that they are kind and courteous and would not kill me."

"What if they became more violent and tried to kill you?"

"I would consider my body to be an accumulation of evil passions and sins, and desire to be free of its constraining shackles as soon as possible. I would think with gratitude of those kind and courteous people who were liberating me from pain and suffering."

"Splendid," replied Shakyamuni, pleased with Purna's replies. He gave sanction for the trip, saying, "You should go and spread the teaching in the western lands." For Purna to go into such uncivilized lands and preach the Dharma meant that he possessed a state of mind that would not shrink at laying down his life if necessary.

The privation and suffering of the first pioneers who went and began farming in the northern island of Hokkaidō at the beginning of the Meiji period, and the hardships of the fine Zen teachers who went and built new temples there, were of no common order. This year marks forty years since the building of Gokoku-ji in Muroran, fifty years since the building of Denchū-ji in Takasu, and sixty years since the establishment of Enmyō-ji in Toma. Each of those temples held large-scale commemorative memorial services this year. In view of the difficulties those priests incurred in the past half century, one cannot help but be deeply impressed at what they accomplished.

Shakyamuni is said to have suffered through nine great ordeals. One them was "the ordeal of the oats," when he led five hundred monks to pass the ninety-day summer retreat in the village of Vairanja in Kosala state. The headman of the village, a

Brahmin named Agnidatta, had promised to provide for Shakya-muni and the monks during the retreat, but he was later persuaded by a heretic to renege on the promise, and they received no alms from him. As it was a famine year, even though the monks went out begging, no one had anything to give them.

Shakyamuni and the five hundred disciples were on the verge of starvation when a passing horse merchant saw them and felt compassion for their plight; he offered them a portion of the inferior oats he used as horse fodder. Eating this poor fare, the men grew thinner and weaker by the day. Finally the Venerable Maudgalyāyana said, "I would like to muster all my supernatural powers and comb the entire world to find some food for us." But Shakyamuni would not agree. "Indeed you have great supernatural powers, so what you say may be possible," he said. "But what about the helpless monks without your powers who find themselves in extreme distress in the latter day of the Dharma?"

The Venerable Ananda then came forward and said, "Let me dispatch someone to Kapila and ask my relatives in my native place to send us food as alms." But again Shakyamuni would not agree, saying, "It may be possible for someone like you who has wealthy relatives, but what about those who have no such relatives owing to bad karma in the latter day of the Dharma?" Ananda then said, "If we ask King Bimbisara of Magadha, or King Prasenajit of Shravasti, or the wealthy Mr. Suddata, I'm sure they would provide us with help." But Shakyamuni would not agree to this either, saying, "That might be possible at a time when such wealthy patrons exist, but what about those monks of meager virtue who live in the time of the latter-day Dharma?"

So Shakyamuni and his five hundred monk disciples ended up eating horse fodder for the entire ninety days of the summer retreat. Given Shakyamuni's stature at the time, he could surely have obtained offerings of food from any number of sources, whether the protective god Indra, the state of Kapila, or the wealthy donor Suddata. Yet in his deliberate refusal to do so, in his decision to patiently accept and endure the poverty apportioned him and his disciples, we encounter the deep nobility of Shakyamuni's mind. For those who live in the latter day of the Dharma, when Buddha's teachings lose their power to lead people to enlightenment, he was demonstrating the proper conduct for a religious leader using his own life as example.

The Japanese Shingon priest Jiun Sonja wrote, "Making this day sufficient unto itself, this present place sufficient unto itself—the ancients can be said to have made this the basic principle of their lives." Remaining settled, self-reliant, and at peace at every place and at every time while not impinging on others' territory—this is the life of the Zen person, for whom *form is now the form of no-form, / Coming or going, you never leave home.* This is affirmed in the old verse:

Knocked over,
Popping right back up,
A Daruma doll.

In Hokkaidō we will form a row of twenty-three men and begin walking along the road on a begging expedition that will last
over a month. We will have a warm reception wherever we go,
never encountering anyone like the uncivilized tribes the Venerable Purna had to visit. Members of the lay community will
cheerfully greet us and provide for our needs, so we will never
experience any of the ordeals Shakyamuni faced. What a welcome experience it will be!

And truly we owe it all to the great virtue of National Master Kanzan, the founder of Myōshin-ji, and to the great virtue
of all the enlightened ones of the Zen school; and also, I believe, to the generosity and human kindness of those who live on
this unique island of Hokkaidō. May I add that I do not think
the simplicity, warmth, and generosity shown by the people of
Hokkaidō can be found anywhere else in the country.

My meager life soon will end,
    Doubting we will ever meet again,
My old eyes fill with tears.

62

CH'IEN SEPARATES FROM HER SPIRIT

URING THE T'ang dynasty there lived in the city of
Hang-yang a man named Chang Kien. He had a young
daughter of great beauty named Ch'ien and a very handsome
nephew named Wang Chao. As children, the two often played
together, and watching them Chang Kien would jokingly say,
"When you grow up and get married, you will make a beautiful bride and groom—just like a pair of ornamental dolls."
But when they came of age, Chang Kien arranged for Ch'ien to
marry a gentleman who was in high repute in the community.
He refused to listen when Ch'ien revealed her reluctance to accept the match. He paid no heed to repeated entreaties from
Wang Chao, who reminded him of the words he had formerly
spoken about them. Finally Wang Chao, in great anguish, hired
a boat and left Hang-yang, resolving to make a life for himself
in a distant land.

Four or five days up the Yangtze River, as the boat was ty-ing up at the riverside for the night, Wang Chao noticed some-one running toward the boat on the levee road. It was Ch'ien. She had defied her father and run away from home. Reunited, the two young lovers proceeded hand in hand to the Shu capi-tal. Five years later, their family having increased by two, Ch'ien began longing to see her parents and felt homesick for her na-tive Hang-yang. So one day Wang Chao and the whole family boarded a boat and sailed downstream to Ch'ien's former home.

On arriving at Hang-yang, Wang Chao left his wife on board the boat and went to pay his respects to her father. He was delighted to find that Ch'ien's parents were both in good health, and after expressing his sincerest apologies to them for the elopement, he told them about their two young children and begged them to recognize their marriage.

"What are you talking about?" replied Chang Kien, staring incredulously at him. "Ch'ien became so despondent after you left that she took to her room and has been bedridden ever since. If the matter weren't so serious, I'd laugh to hear such nonsense. We've been at our wit's end. We have done everything we can think of to save our daughter from this mysterious illness!"

"But that's not possible," protested Wang Chao. "Ch'ien is perfectly healthy. She has thought of nothing but seeing you once again. She came here to Hang-yang with me and is right now at the boat landing with our children, waiting for me to call her."

Although he was certain that Wang Chao was mistaken, Chang Kien dispatched a servant to the boat landing. He returned with the news that Ch'ien and the two children were waiting there just as Wang Chao had said. Chang Kien's bedridden daughter Ch'ien was a complete invalid and had not uttered a word for years. But when she was told what had happened, she immediately broke into a smile. Chang Kien took her down to the boat landing, and there the two Ch'iens met. They smiled at each other, then suddenly transformed into one person.

This fanciful tale is told in a number of old Chinese works such as *Li-hun chi* (*A Record of Losing a Soul*) and the Ming collection *Chien-teng Hsin-hua* (*New Stories Written While Trimming the Wick*). On reading it, a Chinese writer of former times is said to have quibbled that if the story were true, the two Ch'iens would have been wearing two different robes as well, and he posed the question: When the two Ch'iens became one, which robe was the real Ch'ien wearing? The ancients had an eagle eye. Very little got past them. But in any event, the Zen school took this old supernatural story and gave it a profoundly religious twist. It is included as a koan in the *Gateless Barrier* collection.

People who live in society have homes and children, and they work hard at jobs. They have diverse interests and pleasures interspersed with suffering and hardships. But do they not feel some uneasiness or anxiety in all this, a sense of lack, a sadness or self-questioning: "Am I really satisfied with my life?" Is there not some feeling of restiveness, as though they had a spiritual home somewhere they were unable to forget, a place where their parents are waiting expectantly for them to return as soon as possible?

Yearnings from which such concerns appear give rise to the religious mind. Since when all is said and done, everything in life is imperfect, insufficient, unsatisfactory, and limited, I think every person has a hankering to seek their native home, a place that is eternal, perfect, certain, and absolute. And what they discover when they finally return to this spiritual home is that it is the buddha-nature, the true self, or as I sometimes say, the eminently ennobled Person.

The true self has long been sleeping away in some back room of the mind. When the apparent or temporal self sees that it has returned to its native place—the time when two people become one and break into a smile—only then is our religious mind truly satisfied and our life fulfilled. If we call this true self "Zen" or "Nembutsu," then our life becomes one with Zen or Nembutsu, and for the first time we discover the royal path of truth, the way that is *not two or three*, and your each and every step becomes a training hall. You are living your life in Zen; Zen is living within you. You are living your life in the Nembutsu; the Nembutsu is living within you. Then for the first time your life has the unshakable support of an utterly stable ground, the unwavering backing that enables you to lead your everyday life in the eternal even as you remain just as you are in your provisional self. Whether you proceed to the state of Shu, make your way to Kuangtung, or go anywhere else in this world, that place itself, and nowhere else, is your true spiritual home. This is Hakuin's meaning, *Your form is now the form of no-form, / Coming or going, you never leave home.* Lin-chi speaks of it as "being on the road and never away from your home."

Musō Kokushi, the founder of Tenryū-ji in Kyoto, was a highly celebrated priest whom seven successive Japanese emperors respected and regarded as their teacher. Musō is known to have constantly moved around the country during his career. He changed his residence frequently from the time he was an ordinary monk in training, and this pattern continued even after he had become a famous priest. His biography shows him on the road almost constantly, walking from one place to another. We read of him being in Kamakura, then in Hitachi or Shimotsuke in northern Japan, then in Kai Province near Mount Fuji, then back in Kyoto in western Japan, then off to distant Tosa on the island of Shikoku.

One of his students once asked him, "I used to find it hard to understand why such an eminent priest, a National Master, changes his place of residence so often. Then I remembered the edict the Buddha issued about 'sleeping under the trees at night wherever you happen to be.' Is my assumption correct?" "No," answered Musō, "it is not. I regard this whole world as my home, so wherever I go I never feel I'm changing my place of residence. It's like a person being in their home and not away from their home when they are in the living room or kitchen." Musō had attained a state of mind where the whole world was his home, and he never had the impression, wherever he went on all his many travels, that he had come to a new or unfamiliar place.

63

VARIOUS OUTLOOKS
ON HUMAN LIFE

FOLLOWING ONE of my recent monthly talks at my temple, a college student came to my chambers. He had something on his mind. "To tell the honest truth," he said, "I thought life would be an opportunity for me to firmly secure my own happiness. I was surprised today to hear you say that we should set our own happiness aside and work for others."

He was not speaking idly or arguing for argument's sake. What I said seems to have genuinely surprised him. I later heard from his teacher, his parents, and others that from the time the student was a young child, he had actively engaged in helping others.

When I heard what he said, I myself was genuinely surprised. I thought, "Is this what today's students are thinking as they engage in their studies?" Adopting a longer view of the matter and taking into account my own experiences as a young man, I reflected on how greatly young students' ways of thinking have changed. In the Meiji era, students' notions were pretty much focused on rising in the world, succeeding in life. When a boy shouldered his travel satchel and left the family home—perhaps reciting the well-known lines, "Once the aspiration arises in a boy and he leaves his home, if he doesn't succeed in his studies he cannot return home till he dies"—it was with a strong determination to make his mark in the world and achieve great things. He would endure any difficulties he might encounter as he strenuously pursued his goal of becoming a government minister, a general, or perhaps a successful businessman. Moreover, his quest was not necessarily a self-centered one. He burned with a resolve to be of use to his country and his fellow men and might be heard to express grossly overconfident sentiments: "If I do not succeed, how can anyone?" "If I do not become a minister of state, who will save Japan?"

During the following Taishō period, the Russian Revolution occurred and everyone and their brother fell under the spell of Marxism. Unless you had read at least one proscribed book, your fellow students—young men who would debate with fierce intensity whenever they gathered together—would not accept you.

Then came the Shōwa period and the Pacific War, when young men sixteen or seventeen years old would volunteer for suicide missions, writing out sacred oaths in their own blood declaring their loyalty, patriotism, and selfless devotion. It was an astonishingly radical change in young men's thinking.

The end of the war brought another dramatic change. It was defeat one morning, hardship the next. American individualism came streaming in waving the banner of democracy. After a period of great contention and confusion, human life gradually came to be seen as a matter of each person seizing their own happiness.

Admittedly these observations are broadly sketched, but the basic point I wish to make is that young people's thinking is always changing. While it would be difficult to determine precisely when the mental attitude of young Japanese was on its soundest footing, that is to say at its most wholesome, it is my belief that in the present generation it has sunk to its lowest ebb, its most deplorable level. It happened, I think, because today's youth have no great dreams or lofty ideals; they are solely concerned with the pursuit of immediate pleasure.

Everyone who is engaged in society, not just young people, has a view of human life, and no one can compel anyone else to accept their personal view as the correct one. Even when notions of human life expounded by great thinkers or artists have gained general acceptance, moreover, this does not make their ideas categorically true.

Does that mean that no view of human life can be absolutely and undeniably correct? I am firmly convinced that such a true view indeed exists. Rooted in human nature, it is a perspective that everyone can acknowledge and accept, an outlook that anyone, anywhere, at any time will find convincing. I speak of the view of life that was held by Shakyamuni Buddha.

The *Kannon Sutra* praises Kannon Bodhisattva, his life, and his outlook on things, calling him "one who views the world truly, views it purely, views it with all-encompassing wisdom, views it with mercy and compassion; one who is always to be worshipped and revered." The true view of human life is just such an outlook—so pure that egoism cannot defile it, an all-encompassing wisdom founded on mercy and compassion and filled to overflowing with love; a view that others will always worship and revere. I think the most important and basic of these attributes is purity. To see things purely is to view them from the standpoint of emptiness. It is the genuine way of seeing human life unstained by the kinds of self-centered notions that might arise based on one's own very limited personal experience and knowledge or that reflect ideas and recollections gained from others. To put it in other words, it is a view of life that has realized (made real) the very essence of the humanity, the pure mind of the self-nature, from which alone true intuitive knowledge can emerge. Here there is neither a self to be concerned about nor a one-sided happiness aimed at gratifying only the ego-self.

Seeing a flower, the flower is you; seeing the moon, the moon is you; hearing an autumn cricket, the autumn cricket is you. Vast wisdom emanates from understanding that the entire world is as such you yourself. You are then seeing with the all-encompassing wisdom of Kannon Bodhisattva. Understanding that the world is yourself, the world and yourself are not two different things, generates unreserved and unconditional love.

Such is the merciful seeing, the compassionate seeing, of the Mahayana bodhisattva.

The words *hi* (mercy) and *ji* (compassion) are often used together as a composite term in which both their meanings of mercy and compassion are included. They also appear in the context of eliminating suffering and conferring peace as *dai-hi dai-ji*, "great mercy and great compassion." An example of viewing things with the eye of mercy and compassion is the Hibo Kannon, or Merciful Mother Kannon, a form of the bodhisattva that epitomizes the love of a mother for her child. This maternal love of a mother feeling her child's sufferings and troubles as her own and doing everything in her power to eliminate them, is explained as her "great mercy" (*dai-hi*) that eliminates pain and suffering. "Great compassion" (*dai-ji*) is explained as paternal love, a father doing everything in his power to ensure that his child will have the greatest peace and happiness, always focusing on the child's welfare and education—finding the child a job or making certain that they have a family of their own, and so on.

A true outlook on life is thus based on our awakening to the pure, egoless, undefiled human nature itself, grasping the original nondualistic oneness of the world and self, society and self, and from there perceiving the humanity innate within us, experiencing a love of humanity that leads us to devote our life to benefiting other human beings and society as a whole. This, it seems to me, is a true and timeless outlook on life that all people can accept and cherish.

64

THE DAUGHTER-IN-LAW
ISN'T HATEFUL

THE COLLOQUIAL Japanese word *tamoguso* refers to the lint that gathers unnoticed inside the sleeves of a kimono; it is of course found in the pockets and lining of Western-style clothing as well. In the year-end housecleaning, as soon as you start shifting chests and bookshelves about, this cottony ash-colored dust begins to appear. It is surprising how such minute particles, almost invisible to the eye, can grow and accumulate over time.

Although generally I adhere to a policy of not acquiring new things, six months into the year I invariably find my desk buried under newspapers, magazines, books, and other articles that people have sent me. While meaning to glance through them all, I never seem to find time to do it, and the clutter keeps accumulating. At the year-end it will probably all end up in the closets, which are filled up with other odds and ends as well.

I am extremely fond of giving people things. But I have so many things, many of which I can't find a suitable recipient for and some I wouldn't feel right about giving anyone. To make matters worse, I am one of those thrifty types who never throws anything out. I even keep the wooden containers for the cakes and sweets that people bring me. Because these articles keep piling up, I make an attempt at least to keep them in some kind of order, when what I would really like to do is use them as kindling for the bath furnace.

I also have stacks of old manuscripts and calligraphy I will never be able to dispose of. If I pass away before I have done something about them, I will be leaving an onerous burden for others to sort out. To keep from leaving these unsightly remains behind me, I would like to consign the whole kit and caboodle to the flames. My visible universe is undoubtedly covered over with dust, but what about the invisible world, inside the mind? I wonder if matters are not the same there. Or perhaps even worse.

Buddhism sometimes refers to the mind as the *alaya* consciousness, from the Sanskrit word *alaya*, meaning "storehouse." Himalaya, the name for the great mountain range of northern India, means "the storehouse of snow (*hima*)," a place where snow remains throughout the year. The alaya consciousness is a bottomless repository in the mind that stores all our experiences and knowledge as memories. The working of memory is something modern-day physiologists have difficulty explaining, though they believe memories are stored somewhere in our brain cells. Whatever the case, the inner mind is a truly mysterious storehouse of unlimited capacity.

The well-known naturalist and ethnologist Minakata Kumagusu (1867–1941) possessed a truly phenomenal memory. He once wrote out at one sitting a diary in which he noted down everything that had happened over the previous forty-three days, including changes in the weather and the names of all his visitors. He remembered everything. It is said that in his youth, he completely memorized several vast collections of Buddhist scriptures after reading them through three times. When queried about a passage in the sutras, he could immediately give the volume and page number where it occurred, the chapter and verse in the old woodblock-printed Ōbaku edition of the Tripitaka, and the page number for the modern edition published in the Taishō period. Where in the world does the human mind store such vast quantities of knowledge?

Most of us have rather poor memories. We tend to forget things, although with some effort we are usually able to recollect them. No doubt they have merely been shelved away somewhere back in the mind. When we are dealing with experiences or knowledge acquired after we were born, that may suffice, but the so-called subconscious, which stores up all the experiences of our parents and even ancestors who lived before we were born, is a truly formidable thing. Psychologists say that if schoolchildren visit a zoo, one in ten or twenty thousand will faint on seeing a lion for the first time. This occurs, they say, because the terrifying memory suddenly emerges of the time our far-off ancestors, be they rabbits or badgers, were attacked by lions. They also say that a dream of falling from a high place and stopping before you reach the ground is traceable to the memory of our immediate progenitors, the monkeys and apes, who would sometimes fall from trees and save themselves by catching a tree branch.

You might think that empty sky should be devoid of color, but when we look up, the sky appears blue. This phenomenon is said to result from the cumulative effect of infinite dust particles in the atmosphere. In just the same way, an endless accumulation of myriad specks of experience, knowledge, and memory is heaped together within our minds, congregating within a darkness so intense that nothing whatever is visible.

Buddhism calls this avidya, or primal ignorance, a state in which afflicting passions and delusions ferment as though they were a kind of methane gas. We assume that within this concoction of mental states our self exists. What we call the self, in other words, is an accumulation of memories and experiences, nothing less than an enormous mass of primal ignorance. The frictions and troubles that arise in human society do so because the assortments of memories found in the egos of its various members are each different. "Can't you understand what I'm saying!" we bluster at someone. What we are actually saying is "Why can't you understand my collection of memories!" Thus Prince Shōtoku wrote, "What they think is right, we think to be wrong; and what we think is right, they think to be wrong. Neither of us is a sage; neither of us is a fool. We are all ordinary human beings, so who is to decide what is right and what is wrong?"

I think this is also the reason why the ideas of the young and old are often in conflict. Ultimately it is not the clash of two individuals but the clash of two separate sets of memories. What makes the matter much more doubtful and uncertain is the altogether limited and imperfect nature of the experiences the two groups possess.

Zen Master Bankei offers this interesting observation. "You often hear people talking about a hateful daughter-in-law or a hateful mother-in-law. But daughters-in-law aren't hateful; neither are mothers-in-law. 'My mother-in-law said such and such. She spoke so harshly. She was so nasty that even the memory of it is distasteful to me,' says the daughter-in-law. But if you just rid yourself of those memories, the mother-in-law or the daughter-in-law would no longer be hateful."

The New Year draws near once again. Everyone is no doubt engaged in their year-end housecleaning, sweeping out the closets and cupboards. But I am sure you will want to sweep out the excessive dust flying through your minds as well. Then you can welcome in the New Year with your mind in its originally clear and uncluttered state. Best wishes to you all. Please have a splendid New Year.

65

TREATING THE REED
WITH KINDNESS

ITHINK PASCAL'S WORDS about man being a "thinking reed" are wonderfully true. A person's genuine worth lies in their thought. Thought opened the door to civilization and the flowering of culture. The power of thought gave birth to science and philosophy. Shakyamuni achieved his splendid enlightenment after acquiring and closely scrutinizing all the available knowledge of his day. The "eighty-four-thousand gates," or ways to salvation, he left behind as precious Dharma treasures were formulated after he had given the deepest consideration to the varying capacities of living beings and thereby devised specific means for each that they could easily understand. Without thought we would have no chopsticks or teabowls, we would not be weaving cloth for garments, and we would probably never have begun tilling the soil. Life as we know it arose from human thought.

While I was in Hokkaidō, I heard reports of farmers amusing themselves by holding obstacle races for their draft horses each spring. I have seen films of similar races in the United States. Farmers assemble at a fair where their prize draft horses pull carts loaded with heavy sandbags through a hilly course in which various obstacles have been set up. Horses that pull the heaviest load in the fastest time are awarded prizes. Farmers gather from far around to enjoy the daylong competition.

But the human beings alone enjoy this competition. The horses get no pleasure from it at all. They don't canter back to the village sporting victory wreaths and boast of their victory. For the horses there is nothing but misery and suffering, repeated whipping and thrashing. Why? It is because horses do not think in the human sense. They may, in their lack of thought, experience suffering, but they cannot think about their achievement and draw pleasure from it.

As there are a great number of horses and cows in Hokkaidō, there are also a lot of veterinarians. When I asked one of these men about the illnesses prevalent among the animals, he told me that they suffered mostly from digestive problems. But as it seemed to me that since horses and cows eat only what their owners provide them, they shouldn't overeat or overdrink like human beings do, I inquired into the reason for their digestive complaints. The doctor said it was due to the ignorance of the farmers who owned them.

During the busy farming season, the horses must be made to work very hard. The farmers, feeling sympathy for them, treat them as though they were human and give them large quantities of fodder all at once. Since the capacity of their stomachs is limited, this overeating causes considerable damage to their digestive organs. The veterinarian said he warns the farmers not to feed the animals in this way. He tells them that they should focus on gradually building up their stamina day by day, with small amounts of food. But the farmers do not heed his warnings.

It may work on humans, but when you give food to horses and cows, they do not show any gratitude no matter how much you give them. They don't think, "I've really got to bear down in my work now that I've been fed so much delicious fodder." The point to bear in mind here is that animals do not engage in thought. Only humans do.

Buddhist teachers are always telling people such things as "Don't think! Don't discriminate! Rid yourself of all designs and intentions! Become like an utter fool!" They aren't suggesting you revert to an animal-like state, to act like a horse or a deer; rather, you should keep unnecessary thoughts from entering your head. Don't waste your time on them. That is the time-honored teaching: don't go thirsting after illusions.

In recent years I have had people brought to me who are helplessly sick. If the person is a student, they will say, "I bought my schoolbooks. I have them on my desk, but I can't seem to get down to any real study. I've stopped going to class altogether. In the daytime I just stay in bed under the covers. At night I'm always wide awake. I hate meeting people, and when I do, I can't talk to them." Although you might wonder if the student is just lazy, the ones I meet are generally kindhearted, if quite timid as well. A medical doctor can find nothing wrong with them. So they are sent here to me, along with the suggestion that if I talk to them and have them do zazen, they might improve. But there is usually nothing I can really do to help them.

Full-grown adults come to me with similar problems. Company presidents, members of the board of directors, people of the highest social ranks display the same symptoms as the students. They are favored with wealth and social standing; they are well educated and have successful family lives and fine children. They would seem to lack nothing whatever. When you ask them about their problems, they will say they just feel uneasy all the time. They can't keep still. They can't sleep at night. They don't like meeting people. Their doctor says they can find nothing wrong with them and suggests they talk to a priest.

What is the reason for this mystifying condition? Why are so many people suffering from such maladies these days? It appears to me that the answer to these questions is found in the waste of spiritual energy, psychological stress, and excessive thinking.

As thinking reeds, we humans must engage in thought. In the present day, there are so many problems to be resolved—scientific problems, problems of human life, business and managerial problems, and so on—that even if we are commanded not to think about them, we are unable to keep them out of our mind; we have no choice but to consider them. Moreover, by using our brain unnecessarily to indulge in dreams and idle fantasies, we accomplish nothing but a dissipation of our mind and spirit; we bring no resolution to our problems. It is a like a labyrinth without any satisfactory way out. Once we have fallen into this terrible maze, we even lose the courage to raise ourselves up again.

A human being is a thinking reed, a truly frail stalk of grass, buffeted by wind and rain, unable to withstand mist or frost. He is a pitiful reed, often buckling and collapsing from the effects of too much thought.

I think we must rectify this waste of our spiritual resources in line with Christian teachings such as "Take no thought for the morrow; sufficient unto the day is the evil thereof" and "Take no thought for your life, what ye shall eat, or what ye shall drink; nor yet for your body, what ye shall put on," and induce the mind to give rise to good sound thoughts. I am further convinced that the true antidote that can bring your thinking into proper order is zazen, seated meditation.

66

"YOU MUST BECOME AS A LITTLE CHILD"

A MONK ONCE asked the T'ang Zen master Chao-chou, "What is the meaning of the First Patriarch coming from the West?" "The cypress tree in the garden" replied Chao-chou. As an answer to a question about the great Indian teacher Bodhidharma's intention in coming to China, it seems totally absurd.

A Western writer has remarked that to suffer anguish is to "split" human consciousness. If Bodhidharma had dithered, or if he had tormented himself about going, saying "I wouldn't be happy leaving my native India," "I think there are lots of deluded people in China and I have to save them," "I worry about going to a country with such a different climate at my age," "I wonder how I'll pay for the trip"—that is, if his consciousness had been divided—he would not have been a Zen patriarch. He would have been someone unable to save even himself.

345

But he would hardly have undertaken a difficult journey all the way to China unless an earnest resolve had made him do it. The point of the monk's question to Chao-chou was whether Bodhidharma's coming to China was based on an act of conscious will. If any conscious will were involved, it would have to have been what Zen calls the thought of no-thought, or perhaps the will of no-will. The grasses, plants, and trees—reeds of all kinds that are found in the natural world and do not engage in thinking—resolve subtle reasoning of this kind without the least contradiction.

I am writing this essay in a mountain temple in Mino Province. Outside in the garden, the plum flowers are in full bloom. Does the cypress tree in the garden, or a plum tree, possess a will? Of course the plum tree does not have feelings or consciousness like humans do, so from that standpoint we would have to reply that it has no will. Yet if it has no will or purpose at all, why does it produce flowers of such immaculate purity? Why do they emit such an exquisite scent? Is not some hidden will or purpose perhaps conceivable in this? Inorganic minerals would seem to have even less will or purpose than plants, yet why do each of them crystallize in its own special way and possess properties unique to it? Is it not conceivable that there is some sort of profound, innate will at work within rocks as well?

Does the great universe itself have a will? Of course here too there is no question of personality or perception in the human sense, yet somehow I can't help sensing an unseen presence of some great will at work, moving through all eternity.

And what is the meaning of the evolution of living organisms? Can we ascribe it merely to chance or natural processes? Where or what is evolution's ultimate goal? To my way of thinking, it is like an immense journey, in which living things have only recently evolved to the level of human beings and will in time reach their perfection in buddhahood.

In other words, may we not say that existence as a whole operates for the purpose of attaining buddhahood, that the universe itself moves with the goal of all things realizing their self-nature? Isn't it conceivable that the universe itself is already Buddha; that Buddha's will is inherent in all living things; that all human beings within it are able to attain Buddha's Dharma Body, attain his Reward Body, even attain his Manifested Body?

All that we see and hear is the Buddha's exquisite shape and voice:

> The willow is charged with Kannon Bodhisattva's forms
> and shapes;
> The voice of the pine tree soughs his teaching that
> liberates all beings.
> The roar of the valley torrent is the long broad tongue of
> Buddha;
> Are not the mountain colors his undefiled, flawlessly pure
> body?

It is in this sense that the evil passions are themselves enlightenment, that this body itself is Buddha: "None of the acts or

347

activities of everyday life in society is at odds with the ultimate and absolute truth" (*Lotus Sutra*). However, our discriminating mind and the endless notions and unnecessary thoughts it generates in such profusion make it extremely difficult for us to penetrate to this truth. It is only by severing ourselves from these thoughts and attachments and surrendering utterly to the great natural flow that we enter the realm of Zen.

One is thus closer to Buddha as a youth than in the prime of life, closer in childhood than in youth, in infancy than in childhood. The many words adults have devoted to praising the wisdom of young children bear this out. So does Jesus when he says, "Unless you become as little children, you shall not enter the kingdom of heaven."

"What is the meaning of Bodhidharma's coming from the West?" Chao-chou said, "The cypress tree in the garden." The realm Bodhidharma had attained was cut off from all illusory thought and discrimination and in perfect oneness with the great universe itself. He was like a wooden statue deeply inhaling and exhaling, sharing the same pulse as the cypress tree in the garden.

Kanzan Egen, the founder of Myōshin-ji, is known for his saying, "The koan 'the cypress in the garden' works like a bandit." You can only understand Bodhidharma's intention in coming to the West when your delusions and discriminations are taken from you, stripped away so that not a single particle of them remains. After Bodhidharma's unsuccessful meeting with the emperor of Liang, he crossed the Yangtze into the Wei state and engaged in a period of continuous zazen at Mount Sung that lasted nine years. He was the spitting image of an old pine tree in the mountains or a cypress tree in the garden.

During those nine years Bodhidharma did not translate books or give talks. He just sat silently doing zazen. In so doing, he left a legacy that surpasses that of any other figure in the history of Chinese Buddhism, one that has brought spiritual liberation to countless living beings and that continues to work vitally and powerfully to this day. It is nothing less than miraculous.

It was possible because Bodhidharma's reason or intent was a "reason of no-reason"; because he lived together in oneness with the great universal life; because through long and continuous practice he had completely emptied his mind of discrimination. Something similar can be said of outstanding artists and performers who demonstrate skill of unparalleled genius. Shedding will and ambition in the continual polishing and refining of their art, they are able to acquire a marvelous technique that is perfectly artless and natural. At this stage of attainment, passions such as hate and love, regret and desire are affirmed as the buddha-mind just as they are.

All our everyday behavior, every movement of our arms and legs, our singing and dancing is then clearly perceived to be the comportment of a buddha. Hakuin speaks of this behavior when he says,

Your every thought is a thought of no-thought,
Your singing and dancing the Dharma's voice.

349

67

"THAT'S HARDER THAN
ONE OF YOUR
FATHER'S KOANS!"

T HE SINO-JAPANESE characters for the term *sanmai* are
a transliteration of the Sanskrit *samadhi*, a state of concentrated meditation. In translating its meaning into Sino-
Japanese, words such as *zenjō* and *shōju* are also used. The word
shōju is made up of two Chinese characters signifying "correct
receiving" or "correct perception," the receiving of sensation or
perception being one of the five *skandhas* ("aggregates") of form,
perception, conception, volition, and consciousness—component elements of all living beings. "Perceiving" refers here to
the ability of the eyes to see colors and shapes, the ears to hear
sounds, the nose to smell, the tongue to taste, the body to feel
cold and heat and objects in the external world, and the mind
to know pain and pleasure. "Perception" in the term *shōju* (correct perception) means perceiving the world of the "six objects"
(*rokkyō*; also called the "six dusts," *rokujin*)—form, sound, odor,

taste, texture, and mental objects—through the working of the "six roots"—the eyes, ears, nose, tongue, touch, and the faculty of mind.

Although the terms "six objects" and "six dusts" both refer to the external or objective world, "six dusts" is generally used in a strongly pejorative sense—that is, the world as litter or debris that pollutes the mind. This does not imply that the external world is to blame for this state of affairs; we ourselves are the true culprits. Once we receive a sense impression and fall under its sway, traces of it always remain with us, never disappearing; hence it becomes waste or rubbish. What is wanted is a mind that reflects things the way a mirror reflects objects that come before it, not retaining them or attaching to them in any way. Sensing or perceiving things in this way, tranquilly and effortlessly—which is, of course, the proper way of perceiving them—is what the word *shōju* signifies. A related Buddhism term, *rokkon-shōjō*, "purification of the six sense organs," signifies the mind becoming as undefiled and unclouded as a bright mirror.

As I sit at my desk listening to the clock go *tick tock, tick tock,* I may open a book and begin reading, and then I no longer hear the ticking. Actually I probably do hear it, but I am not conscious of it. I think this manner of physical perception is the proper one for someone reading a book. If I happen to recall last Sunday's picnic or start to think about the movie I saw the night before, the words in the book are no longer seen. Although I may be looking at the page, the words do not register.

This is not the right way to read a book and certainly cannot be called a "reading samadhi," being totally absorbed in your reading. What is most important, whatever we do and wherever we are, is to have our mind focused unwaveringly on one thing. Only then can we develop skill in the task at hand and bring it to a satisfactory conclusion.

We sometimes see someone playing chess and say they are in a "chess samadhi," or we may speak of a "fishing samadhi," a "poetry samadhi," and so on, which is to say someone's mind or consciousness is concentrated singlemindedly on their activity. Buddhism also calls this state of mind *zenjō* (*dhyana*). I cannot repeat too often the Sixth Patriarch Hui-neng's admirable definition of *zenjō*: "*Zen* is being free of forms externally, *jō* is being undisturbed within." Becoming one with something and forgetting you are one with it is "being free of forms externally." Focusing the mind on something in this way while keeping it perfectly unruffled is "being undisturbed within."

In actual fact, the mind is in a constant state of agitation and confusion, filled with a bewildering swirl of delusions and wayward notions, recollections, experiences, discriminations, schemes, joys and anger, disappointments and delights. That is the reason why students of *kyūdō*, the Way of archery, are taught to think when they loose an arrow, "It is the last arrow in my quiver." Masters of the tea ceremony teach their following the words *ichigo ichie*, "one time, one meeting"—in other words, treasure each meeting; it will not come again. Both phrases are prescriptions for concentrating the mind. And many in the traditional performing arts, after devoting themselves most earnestly to mastering the innermost secrets of their various disciplines, finally end up engaging in the practice of zazen.

Layman Yamaoka Tesshū, a master swordsman of the first half of the nineteenth century who practiced zazen assiduously from the time he was a young man, was a strong believer in the oneness of Zen and swordsmanship. One day, however, when he was dueling against Asai Matajirō Yoshiaki (1822–1894), an expert swordsman of the Ittō-ryū, or "One Sword" school, he found that he was unable to defeat Yoshiaki no matter how hard he tried. Yoshiaki's mere presence overwhelmed him and rendered him helpless. Despite his best efforts, trying everything he could think of, Tesshū found himself impotent in the face of his opponent. Finally he realized that the problem was something apart from skill or technique. An intense religious resolve kindled within Tesshū. He went to study under Tekisui Rōshi at Tenryū-ji in Kyoto, where he threw himself in a spirit of desperation into the practice of zazen. The koan Tekisui gave him is said to have been some lines from Tung-shan's verses on the Five Ranks: *Two blades cross—no need for either to draw back. / Experts here are rarer than a lotus blossoming in fire.*

When he went for interviews, Master Tekisui struck him mercilessly. Murakami Masagorō, one of Tesshū's closest disciples, was incensed to hear of his teacher being treated in such a way. "Striking my teacher like that! I'll kill that outrageous bonze!" he vowed. Masagorō is said to have followed Tekisui for several nights, but in the end he was unable to strike him.

When Tesshū learned of this he laughed: "You think he's the kind of priest your sword could cut down?"

When Tesshū awoke in the night he would immediately get up and do zazen, holding his long *kiseru* pipe like a sword pointed directly between his eyes. His wife, worried at her husband's behavior, went to Master Tekisui. "Please tell my husband to stop doing zazen," she pleaded. "He will lose his mind!"

Layman Tesshū kept up this practice for three years. At dawn on the thirty-first day of the third month, in the thirteenth year of Meiji (1880), he finally broke through, experiencing the intense joy of great enlightenment. Not even waiting for daylight, he hired a two-man rickshaw and had the runners race full tilt to the Rinshō-in in Yushima in Tokyo where Tekisui Rōshi was staying. When the two men saw each other, even before a word was spoken, they both began laughing out loud. Saying there was no time to boil water for tea, Tekisui poured Tesshū a glass of wine instead. Tesshū downed the glass and left. He proceeded directly to Asai Yoshiaki's residence and issued a challenge to a duel. This time he fought with the totally untrammeled freedom he had achieved, his mind emptied of any hint of Asai's presence. Asai threw down his sword, saying, "I am no longer any match for you." Asai is said to have proceeded to transmit the secrets of the One Sword school to Tesshū. Praising Tesshū's outstanding ability, Tekisui Rōshi awarded him his inka, or Dharma seal, and allowed him to train his own disciples as a master of both swordsmanship and Zen.

After Layman Tesshū's death, his daughter Matsuko continued living in a detached residence at Zenjō-an temple in Taninaka until the end of the war. I sometimes met with her, then an elderly lady, when visiting the temple and listened to her tell the story of how as a child she was carried over the Hakone Barrier on the shoulders of the redoubtable Shimizu no Jirōchō.* She said that when they came to the glorious autumn foliage along the hillsides of precipitous Hakone trail, she pleaded with Jirōchō, "Oh, get me some of those leaves." To this Jirōchō replied, "To do that, my young lady, would be harder than one of your father's koans!" Apparently, judging from this, even a former yakuza boss like Jirōchō had studied under Tesshū and been severely tested by his koans.

---

* Shimizu no Jirōchō (1820–1893). A yakuza boss who effectively controlled the eastern part of the Tōkaidō Road in the final years of the Edo period, Jirōchō was regarded by many as a Robin Hood–like figure, protecting the weak against the rich and powerful. After the Meiji Restoration, he worked for the new government, one of his tasks being to help create the modern port of Shimizu in Shizuoka prefecture.

68

OPEN YOUR EYES

THE VENERABLE ANANDA, one of the Buddha's ten principal disciples, is said to have attended more of the Buddha's sermons than anyone else. He had a prodigious memory and remembered everything he heard. Ananda, a first cousin to Shakyamuni, was of royal blood, his father being the brother of Shakyamuni's father, King Suddhodana. It is said he was given the name Ananda—"one who honors the attainment of the Way"—because he was born on the day Shakyamuni attained enlightenment. Ch'ing-hsi, one of the Chinese translations of Ananda's name, may be rendered as "one who experiences joy at another's attainment." Eight years after his enlightenment, Shakyamuni returned to his former home to visit his father the king at the Kapila Palace, and many young boys in the royal entourage there became his disciples. Ananda was among them.

Ananda was never away from the Buddha's side for even a day over a period of twenty-five years, from the time Shakyamuni was twenty-five up until his entrance into nirvana. Ananda was Shakyamuni's personal attendant, caring for his personal needs, accompanying him wherever he went, and listening to all the teachings he preached. Owing to his phenomenal memory, when the Buddha's teachings were compiled after his death at the First Buddhist Council held in Pippali Cave, Ananda was able to stand before five hundred disciples and recite all the teachings he had heard the Buddha preach, beginning each sermon with the now well-known words, "Thus I have heard."

Ananda is said to have had a commanding presence. His manner of teaching was so impressive that it reminded people of Shakyamuni himself. People wondered whether Shakyamuni had returned to the world or whether a new buddha had appeared or perhaps Ananda himself had attained buddhahood. It was said that all the Dharma teachings the Tathagata preached were transmitted to Ananda and radiated through his body. Even the venerable Kaundinya, the first of Buddha's followers to attain arhatship, was compelled by his respect for Ananda to always make a full prostration in obeisance to him each time he chanted a sutra.

One time, Ananda was listening attentively to the Buddha's preaching while experiencing agonizing pain from a carbuncle on his back. Feeling pity for him, Shakyamuni asked his personal physician, the great Jivaka, to treat him. Waiting to perform the operation until Ananda was totally engrossed in what the Buddha was teaching, Jivaka went behind him and lanced the carbuncle, draining the pus and blood from it. Ananda later said that he felt no pain at all, that he was unaware Jivaka was performing the surgery.

On learning of the procedure after the Buddha had finished speaking, Ananda said, "When I listen to you preach the Dharma, World-Honored One, even were all the oil to be pressed from my body, even were my body to be crushed to powder, I wouldn't feel the slightest pain." Ananda had entered what we may describe as a "listening to the Dharma samadhi." A similar story is told of the Sōtō Zen master Morita Goyū (1838–1915), who when suffering from a painful carbuncle had it lanced and drained while he was doing zazen.

A learned Japanese physician recently published an article titled "Medical Research on Seated Meditation," which I thought was extremely well done. I did take issue, however, with one point he made. He wrote, "From long in the past, the Zen school has encouraged a person doing zazen to keep their eyes half open and fixed on a point about three feet in front of them. But I think it is better to close the eyes. A person always closes their eyes when kissing someone because it is easier to concentrate the mind with them closed." Now it cannot be denied that a certain kind of rapture is experienced when two people kiss, and it is true enough that kissing may be a kind of samadhi. Yet it is simply wrong to equate this with the samadhi of the zazen transmitted by the buddhas and patriarchs. Kissing should rather be termed a *bonnō zammai,* a "samadhi of afflicting passions," or a *mumyō zammai*, a "samadhi of primal ignorance"; it is a samadhi that pitches the mind into the total darkness of the so-called cave of ghosts where there is no light and no self-realization whatever. It is certainly not the clear bright samadhi portrayed by Hakuin's *How boundless the cloudless sky of samadhi!*

We should achieve samadhi while keeping the eyes, the windows of the five senses, wide open. Even were we to agree that it is permissible to sit with the eyes shut, how can you shut your ears or your nose? It is not true that we are unable to enter samadhi with our eyes open or to enter samadhi because we are hearing sounds. Looking at something yet not seeing it, listening to something yet not hearing it, smelling something yet not smelling it—those are genuine samadhis. This explains National Master Daitō's verse,

> Doing zazen, comers and goers
> On the Shijō and Gojō bridges
> Like the trees in a mountain forest.

The Rinzai sect's *Zazen-gi* (*Principles of Zazen*), which provides much detailed advice on Zen practice, also cautions against this:

> The eyes should be kept slightly open to avoid drowsiness. If you practice in this way and enter samadhi, you will gain unsurpassed meditative strength. In ancient times there were eminent priests who always sat with their eyes open while doing zazen. In more recent times, Zen

Master Fa-yun of the Yuan-t'ung monastery condemned those who meditated with closed eyes as "ghosts practicing in a cave on Black Mountain." The deep meaning of Fa-yun's words will be known to you when your practice attains maturity.

Gasan Oshō of Tenryū-ji (1853–1900) is said to have told students, "Keep your eyes open wide! *Have 'em goggling out like acorns!*" Paintings and statues of Bodhidharma never show him with his eyes shut; his bulging eyes are always staring directly out at you. The authentic zazen our Dharma ancestors transmitted is described as *ryōryō jōchi,* "constant awareness, perfect clarity," and I think that it is vital within this state of pristine awareness to have a very clear self-realization. This is the mental state Zen terms "the consciousness of unconsciousness," "the thought of no-thought," and "the realization of non-realization"; again, however, I believe that within that consciousness and realization, absolute and totally unobstructed clarity is imperative.

As Master Wu-men explains in the *Gateless Barrier* koan collection, if after a long struggle your practice matures and you achieve a perfect oneness of what is within and what is without, you will be like a deaf mute seeing a dream; it is something untransmittable to others that only you can understand. In that same way, you must achieve the self-realization that you and heaven and earth are one, you and the mountain are one, you and the river are one, you and your work are one. Hakuin writes,

How boundless the cloudless sky of samadhi! Zen Master Dōgen calls this the "King of Samadhis Samadhi." Boundless wisdom wells up within this samadhi, and for this reason Hakuin goes on to say, *How radiant and full the four wisdoms' moon!*

Before preaching the *Flower Garland Sutra,* Shakyamuni first entered the "Ocean Seal Samadhi"; on preaching the *Great Wisdom Sutra* he entered the "Equanimous King of Samadhis"; on preaching the *Lotus Sutra* he entered the "Origin of Boundless Meanings Samadhi"; and on preaching the *Nirvana Sutra* he entered the "Unwavering Samadhi." Even the wisdom of Shakyamuni, with his incomparable enlightenment, would not have been possible apart from samadhi.

69

WORK AND
SELF-REFLECTION

T HE GERMAN socialist philosopher Friedrich Engels
wrote, "If you ask the difference between a tribe of apes
and human society, the answer is labor." A Chinese Zen master
said, "A day without working is a day without eating." Animals
live by relying solely on such resources as they find in nature.
If no such resources are to be found where they are, their only
recourse is to move elsewhere or to perish from hunger. Human beings invented tools and learned how to produce their
own food. By storing it, they were able to survive through the
long winters and overcome the curse of starvation. If work is indeed what sets humans apart from other animals, can we not say
that people who devote themselves assiduously to their work are
most human, and those who contrive to eat without working
still retain a good measure of their animal nature?

Of course, even among members of the animal kingdom

there are some—insects such as bees and ants, for example—
that know instinctively how to work, so when it is merely a
matter of doing work, I don't suppose much difference exists
among animals. The worth of human beings lie in their ability
to self-reflect on the reason why they work. Their answer will
probably be "I work in order to live." They must then reflect
on why they are living. They might say, "Because I was born."
Now they need to self-reflect on why they were born. They
might answer that they do not live for themselves alone but to
help others live their lives; in the desire to be of service to human beings, they are now expressing their gratitude to them.
Such an answer would imply deep self-reflection of a highly
religious nature. Even then, however, it is necessary for them
to reflect on how they can be of help to other human beings.
What are the best and proper means to achieve that end? And
if they reply that they work to bring happiness to their fellow
human beings, they must then reflect on the meaning of the
word *happiness*.

I have mentioned before the trip that I made last summer to
Hokkaidō with twenty young monks. We continued our practice there for two months, visiting various parts of the island
and enjoying many new and unusual experiences. In Furano in
central Hokkaidō, an area known for its large-scale farms, we
were invited to the residence of a farmer who had many square
miles of cropland and rice paddies under cultivation. He told
me about an obstacle race for draft horses that the local farmers
hold every year.

363

The competing horses pull carts loaded with heavy bales of earth over a hilly course along which various obstacles have been set up. The horses that come in first and second are awarded prizes and victory banners. The farmers look forward to this event all year. My initial thought on hearing about the race was that however much the farmers may enjoy such a competition, the horses certainly couldn't get much pleasure from it. Even if they win the race and have a banner draped over them, they won't be returning to the farm and boasting about their exploits. All they get for their efforts are a lot of painful blows on the hindquarters.

I think the difference between animals and human beings turns on the question of whether animals self-reflect, if they have any self-awareness of what they are doing. Hence work is of course important, but the importance of reflecting on the value and meaning of work must be said to be of even greater consequence. In my opinion, the self-reflection Shakyamuni underwent had a depth that has never been equaled. Jesus, too, is said to have left his community of followers from time to time to pray and meditate. Shakyamuni's contemplation extended over a period of six long years. What was he reflecting on? I think he was reflecting on the meaning of all that exists in the universe and the purpose of human life.

Although he ultimately resolved the great questions of the universe and human life within the universe, he achieved this only by digging deep into the core of his human nature. Shakyamuni, in other words, discovered the true meaning of the universe and human life and the circumstances through which they are consummated within his own mind. For Shakyamuni, enlightenment was the rapturous joy of realizing that the self and the world are essentially one and that they are both already perfectly consummated just as they are.

The meaning of human life is thus not found in merely working to live but in awakening to the essence of human nature, in guiding others to self-awakening, and in experiencing the joy of sharing this awakening with them, benefiting oneself by benefiting others. This is a peaceful, harmonious existence in which nothing is lacking.

To achieve that kind of existence we do zazen, because zazen is the one straight and direct path to self-awakening. As Zen Master Dōgen wrote, "Learning the Buddha Way is learning the self. Learning the self is forgetting the self. Forgetting the self is being confirmed by all things. Being confirmed by all things is making your body and the bodies of others drop away." Buddhism is thus a matter of self-awakening to the nondual realm of self and other and relishing life in the joyous, totally untrammeled activity of what is called *yuge zammai*, a "sportive" or "playful" samadhi.

An article titled "Doctor Turner and Zen" by Fujiyoshi Jikai appeared in a recent issue (1957) of the magazine *Hanazono*, published by Myōshin-ji. Ralph Turner is an American cultural historian and professor at Yale University who has an interest in Zen Buddhism. Recently he engaged in a dialogue with the lay Zen teacher Hisamatsu Shin'ichi.* I will conclude this essay with a response to Professor Fujiyoshi's fine article:

It is commendable to concentrate on doing temple work. It is commendable to concentrate on doing zazen. It is commendable to engage in "prayerful work" too. Whatever you do, I think the Zen life is a confident, creative life grounded firmly in the joy of a perfectly clear self-awakening. Science has made extraordinary advances on the side of production, including even the development of atomic and hydrogen weapons. But the current state of affairs, in which scientists have no time for anything but the work before them and show no signs of reflecting on their past errors, has plunged human beings into a most critical and horrific critical plight. I think the anxiety evident throughout the modern world stems from this lack of self-reflection into our human nature, particularly regarding the issue of whether or not to use those weapons. The tragedy for human beings today is their lack of faith in themselves. I am convinced, however, that the King of Samadhis Samadhi,† which the buddhas and patriarchs have handed down to us, is perfectly capable of grasping the truth of human nature and restoring us to our faith in humanity. There is nothing that surpasses the practice of zazen, seated meditation.

---

*The dialogue with Ralph Turner (1893–1964), a professor at Yale University from 1944 to 1961, is found in Hisamatsu Shin'ichi's *Collected Works*, vol. 8 (in Japanese).

†A term used, most prominently by Dōgen, to describe cross-legged sitting in zazen.

70

THE FIRST BUDDHA
WISDOM

BUDDHISM CALLS the immaculately pure, mirrorlike mind that is prior to all experience and knowing the Great and Perfect Mirror Wisdom, the first of the Four Buddha Wisdoms. Of course, that is a metaphorical description; it doesn't mean that the mind is really round and shiny like a mirror. The mind is, from the first, utterly formless. In *Verses on the Believing Mind*, the Third Zen Patriarch Seng-ts'an describes it as "round and perfect as the vast sky above, nothing wanting, nothing in excess."

Human beings are all born with this intrinsic mind, as formless as the great void. Each of us has it in full and equal measure. It is not exceptionally large in a great person or small and shrunken in a foolish one. The myriad differences in experience and knowledge we share appear after we are born, but at birth the mind is exactly the same in us all. Hence we can say that the human character is equal in all cases; it has the same sublimity and nobility in each and every person, exactly the same in men and women, old and young, rich and poor, prime ministers and beggars, judges and criminals.

Zen Master Bankei emphasizes this point when he says,

A human being's fundamental nature is like a bright mirror. There is at first nothing in it, but anyone who comes before the mirror is reflected, and when they leave, the reflection vanishes. And that is the whole story. Because something is reflected in the mirror does not mean it actually exists there, and because it is no longer reflected does not mean it has perished. The *Heart Sutra* calls this *unborn and undying*. The mirror does not get dirty because it reflects a filthy object, nor become beautiful because it reflects a lovely one. The *Heart Sutra* calls this *unstained, unpure*. The mirror does not increase because of the objects reflected in it or diminish because the reflection disappears. This is what the *Heart Sutra* calls *not increasing, not decreasing*. Although the sutra's words "unborn, undying, unstained, unpure, not increasing, not decreasing" all point directly to our fundamental mind, there is no reason for the description to be so long. It is enough simply to say "the unborn mind."

Our mind is truly as pure and undefiled as a mirror. What is more, it is something that transcends birth-and-death. In the same way a mirror is not tarnished by reflecting a pile of dog feces, the fundamental mind is not defiled even by sins of the deepest dye. "You should not fear evil," wrote Shinran, "for there is no evil that can obstruct Amida's original vow." A mirror does not become beautiful by reflecting a flower of the greatest beauty; it simply reflects the flower. In the same way, no matter what admirable deeds you may perform, they do nothing to enhance the fundamental mind. "No other form of good is necessary, for there is no good that surpasses the Nembutsu," wrote Shinran. No greater good exists in the world than awakening to the pristine mind you were born with and living your life within it.

Zen Master Seng-ts'an is said to have suffered from leprosy. The first time he encountered his future teacher, the Second Patriarch Hui-k'o, he said, "I am suffering from illness as the result of past karma. Please purify my sins." "Produce these sins of yours for me," replied the Second Patriarch, "and I will purify them." Seng-ts'an pondered for a moment and then answered, "I've looked for the sins, but they are nowhere to be found." "Then all your sins are purified, are they not?" replied Hui-k'o. On hearing these words Seng-ts'an achieved sudden enlightenment; in time he was also cured of his illness.

Because all sins, however heinous, are so pure that they are beyond defilement, the human character or personality is said to be noble and sublime. Zen Master Lin-chi taught, "The non-discriminating light of a single thought rising in your mind is the Reward Body of the Buddha within your own home." Our fundamental mind, pure and undefiled, is itself the Buddha's Dharma Body, which is the source of the universe.

The fundamental mind might be called "god" as well. I have dwelt before on the various etymologies put forward for the Japanese word *kami* (god): that it derives from the homophone *kami*, meaning "high" (as opposed to low); that it comes from the word *kabi*, "mold," the fundamental source of all life; or that it is a contracted form of the word *kagami*, a mirror that reflects the face. A mirror is placed before the kami in the sacred altar of a Shintō shrine, representing the kami's pristine mind, impartial and selfless as a mirror. As mentioned previously, Buddhism calls this mind *Daien-kyōchi*, the Great and Perfect Mirror Wisdom, which is a buddha's original or primary wisdom and our own essential mind as well. And what we finally discover when we probe deep down into our self is consciousness itself, life itself, absolute truth itself, which alone of all things cannot be objectified. We also give this the name Dharma.

Shakyamuni alludes to this fundamental self when he says, "Make a lamp of your self and dwell within it as your fundamental ground." It is also the Dharma teaching he refers to when he continues, "Make a lamp of the Dharma I have preached and establish it as the abiding foundation of your lives. Make your fundamental ground nowhere else." In other words, the self is the Dharma, and the Dharma is the self. This is also what Shakyamuni means when he says, "One who sees the Dharma is seeing oneself; one who sees themselves is seeing the Dharma." By discovering this Dharma squarely within ourselves, we are able to self-awaken to the true and eternal self, and in so doing achieve the chief object of human life. When a Buddhist follower undergoes the rite of initiation, they are taught and recite "The Three Refuges" (*san-kie*), vowing to "take refuge" in (believe in and uphold) the Three Treasures of Buddha, Dharma, and Sangha. The second of these, "taking refuge in the Dharma," is in fact a matter of taking refuge in the Dharma truth lying deep within the fundamental self while continuing to maintain right thought.

In a youthful verse, the philosopher Nishida Kitarō alluded to the profundity of this fundamental self:

I believe my mind
Has depths no joy
Or waves of sorrow
Can ever reach.

And because this mind is the true reality of the universe, the law that produces and pervades all things, Nishida added an inscription to the verse: "Mindfulness or right thought is like a mathematical axiom, something that must be obeyed absolutely." Buddhism, calling this mind the true self-nature and the Great and Perfect Mirror Wisdom, is in fact a religion bent on bringing about our self-awakening to this law of the mind. Hakuin writes of this first and most essential of the four wisdoms that a buddha acquires on attaining buddhahood: *How radiant and full the four wisdoms' moon!*

71

THE SECOND
BUDDHA WISDOM

ONE FINDS UNIQUE religious thought set forth in the
economist Kawakami Hajime's *Unnecessary Jottings from
Prison*. Kawakami was a warmhearted man with deep compassion for others. We see this in an incident he relates from his
student days. He was attending a lecture meeting being held
at the Kanda YMCA in Tokyo on the environmental damage
caused by pollution from the Ashio copper mines in Tochigi
prefecture. After hearing the speakers give their accounts of the
widespread distress suffered by those who lived downstream of
the mines, he immediately went home, packed all his clothes in a
basket, and gave the basket to a rickshaw man with instructions
to proceed to the disaster area and distribute the clothes anony-
mously to people in need.

On another occasion, when Kawakami was attending a sermon by the Protestant teacher Uchimura Kanzō, he was deeply

impressed by the saying of Jesus, "Whosoever shall strike you on the right cheek, turn to him the other also. And if any man will sue you and take away your coat, let him have your cloak as well. And whosoever shall compel you to go a mile, go with him two miles. Such is the best path for human beings to follow." This inspired Kawakami to read and study the Christian Bible. And when Itō Shōshin, a Shin Buddhist, formed what he called the selfless love movement, Kawakami immediately joined. "That's it!" he thought. "A path that a human being can really follow! Not Buddhism, not Christianity, but selfless love!" However, as he began devoting his efforts to the selfless love movement, he came to discover that as impressive as the concept of selfless love sounded in theory, the people championing it were not selfless in the least. They seemed to prefer sleeping late, eating good food, and going out on the town to enjoy themselves. Kawakami left the organization and, renting an empty hall in the Hongō district of Tokyo, began to organize his own selfless love movement.

After doing this for a time, however, he began to sense an inherent contradiction in the work, which finally ended in a kind of spiritual impasse. "It is true," he later said, "that giving someone one of my two kimonos and a third of my rice seemed like acts of selfless love, but it would have been even better if I gave all my food to others. It was not possible for me, or anyone else, to do that, though. I was thus convinced of the impossibility of knowing where to draw the line between providing for oneself and giving to others."

Kawakami also wrote, "Zen monks do zazen as they try to resolve a koan. My problem was also a koan, no different from theirs. Sleeping or awake, I could think of nothing else." One time while he was writing an article, the contradiction rang out in his mind, and with pen in hand he suddenly forgot himself completely. Body and mind both disappeared. The world vanished. He said that for a long time of indefinite duration he remembered nothing at all. When he finally came to himself and looked out at the garden, he noticed the stones were different from how he had seen them before. Everything seemed fresh and bright. It was as though he was seeing the plants and trees for the first time. At the same time, as he experienced this freshness, he encountered his consciousness in a different way. He had penetrated suddenly to his true self. This was Kawakami's religious truth, his satori. "Unfortunately at the time I didn't know any Zen priest I could visit and study under, but if any one of them later reads this account, perhaps he may award me his Dharma seal (*inka*) and confirm that I had achieved kenshō."

I find the religious viewpoints Kawakami expresses in *Unnecessary Jottings* to be clearly stated and very cogent. The following, for example, seems to have been written with exceptionally strong feeling:

Human consciousness always moves in the direction of the external world. The truth it discovers there is scientific truth. At times a desire to know the self arises in consciousness—the self itself feeling a desire to examine the way in which it works. In doing this, consciousness focuses exclusively on introspective exploration, and the truth it uncovers there is a religious truth. Most scientists do not really understand religion, just as most religious people do not know much about science. But I feel an immense happiness at having grasped both scientific truth and religious truth during my sixty years on earth.

Exploring in this way the inner working of the self, the religious truth we discover there is the Great and Perfect Mirror Wisdom itself, the pure and undefiled mirrorlike mind, the self prior to all knowledge and experience. It is the true essence of the Buddha's Dharma Body. When the pure mind of self-nature engages something in the external world, it breaks through the wall of the Dharma Body and a pure consciousness, flapping its wings freely, soars up into the infinity of the great universe. Here, without any separation between inner and outer, the self self-awakens into bright and vibrant life. Kawakami refers to this as "consciousness being conscious of itself."

Soaring freely through the ten directions of the universe, human consciousness creates mountains, rivers, flowers, birds, stars, and moons, performing the truly marvelous and sacred work of bringing a world into existence. When this takes place, mountains are the self, rivers are the self, stars and moons are the self, flowers and birds are the self; there is nothing in the world that is *not* the self. Dōgen says it all in his famous words, "Learning the Buddha Way is learning the self. Learning the self is forgetting the self. Forgetting the self is being confirmed by all things." All limits or barriers between the Buddha's pure undefiled Dharma Body and the things in the universe fall away so that no separation between them remains. You understand, in other words, that three pounds of hemp is the Buddha, that a stick of dried shit is the Buddha, that there is nothing that is *not* the Buddha. You see the sameness and equality of all things, with no difference whatever between your own body and the bodies of others.

Kawakami's concern was how much to allot to himself and how much to others, but at this point that worry, indeed the problem itself, vanishes.

Wisdom, equally a glittering golden buddha and a lump of dried shit, the lofty wisdom that enables you to see your own body and mind and the bodies and minds of others as equal, is the Wisdom of Nondiscrimination, *byōdo-shōchi*, the second of the Buddha's four wisdoms.

Zen Master Lin-chi taught, "The nondiscriminating light of a single thought rising in your mind is the Reward Body of the Buddha within your own home." That impartial nondifferentiating wisdom, the Buddha's Reward Body that does not separate good from evil, that accepts all living beings and leads them to salvation, is the wisdom of Amida Buddha. It is here that the state of ultimate emancipation Dōgen described as "being confirmed by all things, making one's body and mind and the bodies and minds of others drop away" is understood with perfect clarity.

72

THE THIRD AND FOURTH
BUDDHA WISDOMS

"THE WAY I see it," declared Zen Master Lin-chi, "None of you monks is any different from Shakyamuni Buddha. . . . In the eye, it's called seeing; in the ear, hearing; in the nose, smelling; in the mouth, talking; in the hands, grasping; in the feet, walking." He then demanded to know if any of his monks were deficient in any of those functions. After asserting the essential oneness of ordinary people and buddhas, he asked them, "If your eyes can see, your ears can hear, your nose can smell, your mouth can speak, your hands can grasp, and your feet take you along, what on earth do you want?"

It is just as the Third Patriarch said: "Round and perfect like the vast sky above, nothing wanting, nothing in excess." When it comes to the buddha-nature, all of us are on a perfectly equal footing with Shakyamuni Buddha. In being unenlightened, it is not that we lack something, or on becoming a buddha that we acquire some special power. Through the influence of the buddha-nature, the five senses function with flawless perfection in us just as they do in Shakyamuni Buddha.

The five sense organs—hearing, seeing, smelling, and so on—begin operating in everyone at birth and, illness aside, all five function equally well. You do not learn the wisdom of their operation in school or from your parents, nor do you acquire it through religious practice. It is yours at birth. And what a precious, marvelous, mysterious thing it is! And it is not limited to seeing and hearing and the other sense organs alone. You know when you are born, without being taught, how to suck milk from your mother's breast. You know how to breathe, and you soon learn how to feed yourself. When you chew your food, the necessary saliva is naturally secreted. When the food is swallowed, it is digested in your stomach and nutrients are absorbed in your intestines; they absorb what is needed, evacuating the rest. Moreover, the liquid and solid wastes move along different courses and are expelled from different orifices. The movement is not linear but follows a twisting, spiraling path, the entire process taking place as though perfectly automated.

Your hands have ten fingers that can move freely and grasp whatever they please. Your feet move and carry your body where you want to go. Your body is furnished with impeccable endowments that leave nothing to be desired. What do you lack that would cause you to write yourself off as an ordinary, unenlightened man or woman? Zen attributes this flawless functioning of the five senses to the Wisdom of Perfect Practice (*jōshosa-chi*), the fourth of the Buddha's four wisdoms. Mentally perceiving the working of the five senses and making decisions based on those perceptions is the function of the sixth, or thought-consciousness, a faculty that sees plum flowers and senses that they are red, sees willow leaves and senses that they are green. Here again we are no different from Shakyamuni Buddha. He would see red plum flowers and green willow branches, just as we do. If Shakyamuni heard a sparrow twitter or a crow caw, he would hear them just the same as we do.

This is a point Bankei often makes:

Today all of you have gathered here to hear me say something, so the words I speak obviously will enter your ears. A dog barked outside just now. I don't think any of you came here today to hear the dog bark. You made no effort to hear it. Yet when the dog barked, all of you heard "*Woof!*" right away, without even a hairsbreadth interval. Even if someone tried to convince you that you heard a cat, you would say, "No, what I heard was a dog barking, there's no doubt about it." That mind that has been working in this same way from the time you were born is the unborn buddha-mind.

This same motif appears in many of Bankei's talks, and his conclusion is invariably the same: everything in human life, without our having to discriminate or think about it, "is perfectly well taken care of just as it is in the unborn."

But there is a problem here. Although Bankei says that when a dog barks you hear a dog and won't be deceived if someone tries to tell you it was a cat, surely recognizing a dog's bark is not a wisdom you are born with. You recognize it because you already know the sound of a dog's bark. You have experienced that sound in the past. You are engaging in an unconscious discrimination. I believe that Dr. Daisetz Suzuki, who has done so much to create the deep interest in Bankei's teachings that exists today, is perhaps overgenerous when he interprets this as being "the discrimination of nondiscrimination."

The truth is that in living our lives, we cannot forgo discrimination. We cannot exist apart from knowledge and experience. Even were we to resolve not to discriminate, we would still discriminate unconsciously. When Bankei talks about living without discrimination, he is telling us we should not engage in mistaken or excessive discrimination. We should refrain from being attached to delusive thoughts.

Professor Einstein has said, "Among the world's eternal mysteries, the greatest mystery is its incomprehensibility . . . the fact that it is comprehensible is a miracle." We are endowed with the precious gift of human intellect, which has enabled us, through experience and reasoning, to press forward and unlock the endless mysteries of the natural world.

Owing to this intelligence, it is possible for us to unravel scientifically, philosophically, and ethically all the great problems of the universe. In addition, with regard to our ethical or social intelligence—to the self knowing what appropriate conduct is—that is something we all acquire at birth.

Can anything be as precious to human beings as their intellect? It is owing to their intellect that buddhas and bodhisattvas are able to lead living beings to salvation. Scrutinizing the sentiments and circumstances of those they are teaching, they assess the best way to reach out a helping hand to them. This intelligence is called *myōkan-zatchi*, the Wisdom of Wondrous Insight. It is the third of the Four Buddha Wisdoms.

If the Great and Perfect Mirror Wisdom is the Buddha's essential Dharma Body and Nondiscriminating Wisdom is his Reward Body, then these vital Wisdoms of Wondrous Insight and Perfect Practice are functions of the Buddha's Transformation Body (*keshin-butsu*) and Manifested Body (*ōjin-butsu*), respectively.

73

MY MIND IS LIKE
THE AUTUMN MOON

CHRISTMAS HUMPHREYS, the founder of the London
Buddhist Society, wrote something recently that I think
is worth reflecting on: "Buddhism is a name the West gave in
modern times to the doctrines of Shakyamuni Buddha; in the
East, it is called the Buddha Dharma." The English word *Buddhism* is rendered in Japanese as *Bukkyō*, literally "Buddhist
teaching" or "Buddha's teaching." This term was not altogether
unknown in the East, appearing, for example, in the famous
"Verse on the Precepts Shared by the Seven Buddhas":

Not doing anything evil,
Doing everything good,
Keeping thoughts pure,
Is what Buddha taught.

When Japanese use the word *Bukkyō*, it is generally in the context of other religions, often Christianity or Islam. It thus seems to have a heavily ethical connotation. I think that when a Japanese talks about "understanding Christianity," they are referring primarily to an ethical or moral understanding. When they are talking about Buddhism, for which the standard or rule is the Dharma, the usual connotation is strongly scientific or philosophical in nature as opposed to ethical.

Zen Master Dōgen made a famous utterance regarding his study in China:

> I had not visited many Chinese training halls, and I was most fortunate in encountering my late master Ju-ching. It enabled me to verify that my eyes are horizontal and my nose is up and down, so now no one can deceive me. I returned to Japan empty-handed, without so much as a trace of the Buddha's Dharma. I pass the time effortlessly. The sun rises each morning in the east, the moon disappears each evening in the west. . . . The intercalary year arrives in three years. The rooster crows at the fifth watch.

Dōgen states that while he doesn't remember a great deal about the years he spent studying Zen in China, what he does remember is that while he was there, he came to see with complete certainty that his eyes are horizontal and his nose is vertical so that no one, no matter what they say, will ever be able to deceive him. The sun rises every morning in the east, the moon sinks every night in the west, roosters crow to announce the dawn, there is an intercalary year every fourth year. Beyond these primary rules or truths of nature unfolding under our very eyes, there is nothing fixed in the Buddha Dharma.

Moral theories vary among ethnic groups and the world's religions and change at different periods of history. However, scientific truth, which is to say, the law or Dharma, is something that everyone must accept whoever they are and wherever and whenever they live. Among the unalterable laws Shakyamuni discovered and went on to promulgate is one that he formulated as "All beings (all phenomena) are impermanent." This articulates the truth that all worldly existence is in constant movement or flux and that all things that come into existence must perish. It is true at all times regardless of religion or ethnic filiation; it must be observed. Because it was Shakyamuni who discovered it, we call it Buddhism, but as a truth or law, as Dharma, it would exist unchanged and undiminished even if Shakyamuni had not been born and discovered it.

The Buddha's Dharma is thus like a mathematical axiom that everyone is obliged to believe and obey. As Zen Master Lin-chi points out, however, "Dharma means the Dharma of mind"— it differs from natural science in being not a law of objects but a law of the mind. In other words, it is a psychological truth. Buddhism already possessed a psychology or science of mind at the time of Shakyamuni, one that compares favorably with those of the modern day. It breaks down the mental function into eight divisions or consciousnesses. The first five are consciousnesses of perception, the sixth is thought consciousness, the seventh is *manas* consciousness, and the eighth is alaya consciousness. The first five are visual, auditory, olfactory, gustatory, and tactile consciousnesses, the functions of the five senses. The sixth consciousness is a mental function that discriminates and makes continual judgments based on its knowledge and experience. The eighth, or alaya consciousness, at times referred to as the "storehouse consciousness," is, briefly stated, the mind itself. It is sometimes referred to as *shinnō*, or "mind master."

The seventh, or manas consciousness, sometimes described as the "transmitting consciousness," has the role of a king's chamberlain. It receives and considers messages from the first five consciousnesses and reports them to the mind master, and it also relays the mind master's orders to the sixth consciousness and the first five consciousnesses. Yet in transmitting the chamberlain's messages, errors often occur, so that impulses from the top downward and from the bottom up are not transmitted properly. When this happens, an impure self-consciousness, selfishness, and partiality easily insinuate themselves into the mental activity. The seventh consciousness is apparently the culprit, fundamentally responsible for leading us astray from correct thought, action, and life in general.

When an ordinary, unenlightened person's eight consciousnesses are disciplined through zazen practice and purified through the light of kenshō, they become the Four Buddha Wisdoms. The first five consciousness become the Wisdom of Perfect Practice (*jōshosa-chi*); the sixth, the Wisdom of Wondrous

Insight (*myōkan-zatchi*); the seventh, the Wisdom of Nondiscrimination (*byōdo-shōchi*); and the eighth, the Great and Perfect Mirror Wisdom (*daien-kyōchi*) manifesting its inherent and radiant brightness. This is Hakuin's *How boundless the cloudless sky of samadhi! / How radiant and full the four wisdoms' moon!*

The ordinary unenlightened person's eighth consciousness, thus purified and becoming identical with the Three Buddha Bodies and Four Buddha Wisdoms, blossoms into a pure and marvelous flower. This does not mean that the ordinary person's mind suddenly undergoes a change and becomes the four wisdoms. It simply means that through the incomprehensible power of zazen practice, the clouds and mists of delusory thought and afflicting passions are swept away and the pure and original shape of human nature manifests itself. *All beings are from the first buddhas.*

An old verse, which has been attributed to both Musō Kokushi and Musō's teacher Bukkoku Kokushi, alludes to this.

MY MIND IS LIKE THE AUTUMN MOON

Do not assume the light appears when the clouds lift,
The pale moon was there in the morning sky all along.

It is this state of mind the Zen poet Han-shan (Kanzan, "Cold
Mountain") writes of in his well-known verse:

My mind is like the autumn moon,
Immaculately bright in a blue pool.
Not a single thing to compare it to;
Can you tell me how to describe it?

We see in this verse by the Pure Land teacher Hōnen Shōnin,

While there's not a single village
    Moonlight does not reach,
It exists most clearly in the mind
    Of the person who is viewing it,

that the believing mind of the *tariki*, or other-power tradition,
is, in the end, nothing other than the mind that can savor, at its
ground, this fundamental clarity.

74

"A SINGLE *TCHK!* AND I FORGOT ALL I EVER KNEW"

H SIANG-YEN Chih-hsien was a Chinese priest who lived during the T'ang dynasty. When his teacher Zen Master Huang-po passed away, he went to study under Huang-po's student Kuei-shan. Kuei-shan asked him, "I've heard you're a very clever monk and a good scholar. But I don't want to hear about what you've read in books or stories you've heard from others. Tell me about yourself before you left your mother's womb, when you couldn't even tell east from west."

Hsiang-yen was indeed a very considerable scholar, so he carried a great many fine words and famous sayings around with him, which he would cite in his talks. But that of course cut no ice with Kuei-shan. Whenever Hsiang-yen tried to say something, Kuei-shan would reply, "What book did you get that from? Whose words are those?" and demand, "Say something of your own!!" Hsiang-yen would comb through the notes he had written down looking for something he could use for a response, but he couldn't come up with a single word that would satisfy Kuei-shan.

Finally Hsiang-yen admitted defeat. "I've run out of things to say," he confessed. "Please teach me." "It would be easy to teach you something," Kuei-shan said, pressing the attack, "but anything I told you would be mine. I want *you* to say something!" Hsiang-yen, unwilled tears filling his eyes, thought, "I'm finished. I studied hard. I believed the practice I had performed was sufficient as well. To be raked over the coals on such a minor matter, unable to spit out a single word, makes me ashamed to show my face as a Buddhist monk. I'll try to find some mountain temple where no one ever goes and spend the rest of my life there unknown to others—cleaning gardens will be the best kind of life for me." He left Kuei-shan's temple and proceeded to Mount Pai-yai in Nan-yang, a famous mountain where National Master Hui-chung had gone for a retreat many years before and stayed on for forty years practicing zazen, later to be invited to the capital and honored with the title National Master.

Hsiang-yen spent many years living at the mountain temple cleaning the gardens, but Kuei-shan's question about the self before it leaves its mother's womb and can't tell east from west remained in his mind as a challenge, as a demand: *"Who are you?"* I believe as he continued to focus unceasingly on getting to the bottom of this, he was, without realizing it, entering into a state of deeper and deeper samadhi.

One day Hsiang-yen went into a bamboo grove to dump some garden sweepings that included a few tile fragments. One of the fragments struck against a bamboo trunk. When Hsiang-yen heard the sound—*tchk!*—he glanced up with a start, his face beaming in an uncontrollable grin: "Ah, that was it! That was it!" He had heard the self that was prior to his birth, prior to knowing what was east and west. The sound when the tile struck the bamboo was not learned from books. It was not learned from others. Hearing it, Hsiang-yen understood the self as it exists in its true suchness, prior to birth and experience. It was the voice of a new world unfolding.

Hsiang-yen responded with profound emotion to the utterly new world the sound had revealed to him. Beside himself with joy, he purified himself by dousing a bucket of water over his body; he faced in the direction of Kuei-shan's temple, lit some incense, and performed countless prostrations to express his thanks to his former teacher. "Great Priest Kuei-shan, I owe you a debt greater than that I owe my own parents. They gave me my physical body, but you gave me my spirit and soul. If you had not treated me the way you did at that time, or if you had tried to give me a teaching of some kind, how could I ever have experienced the great joy I feel today?" Hsiang-yen had left Kuei-shan's temple in tears. He now wept once again, this time tears of thankfulness.

Hsiang-yen returned to Kuei-shan's temple to tell him about his satori, presenting him with an enlightenment verse he had composed, and Kuei-shan confirmed his attainment. One line from that verse read, *A single* tchk! *and I forgot all I ever knew. And it was not the result of any practice.* When Hsiang-yen heard the sound of the tile striking the bamboo and all his experience and learning fell away, he self-awakened to a fresh new life, indeed to life itself. And the self that heard the sound did not hear it as a result of learning or religious training. Hsiang-yen's verse conveys his realization that the mind he had received at birth, which knows neither east nor west, had heard the sound with the utmost clarity and without any effort at all.

Grasping this inborn mind—the pure, unalloyed nature of your being—is Zen enlightenment. No, since what you inherit from your parents is acquired at birth, it is better to say that what you must grasp is the self prior to your birth and your parents' births as well. Grasping this so-called original face that is prior to birth is enlightenment. This pristine self, the very nature of human being, uniform in all people, is called the buddha-nature, also the pure mind of the self-nature. It is exemplified in the Great and Perfect Mirror Wisdom.

The buddha wisdom that we call the Great and Perfect Mirror Wisdom and the unenlightened mind that we call the alaya consciousness are essentially not two different things. *Alaya* means "storehouse" (alaya consciousness is normally translated "storehouse consciousness"), and this truly describes our mind, which stores away all our experiences and knowledge as memory. It stores not only the experience and knowledge we have acquired since our birth but experience and knowledge prior to that as well—the experience of our human ancestors, even the creatures who existed long in the past prior to the emergence of the human species. Even though this occurs unconsciously, tremendous amounts of subconscious experience are also stored there. Although modern psychology and physiology are apparently pretty much in the dark about where the mind stores such a tremendous volume of memory, we nevertheless, with a bit of thought, can bring those memories forth. It can only be described as an inexplicable mystery.

Far from being unnecessary, this experience and knowledge is extremely important to us. Without it we would be unable to carry on with our lives. But if we attach to it as though it were something absolute, we fall into a very grave error. Assuming a different shape in each and every person, experience and knowledge are by their nature limited and restricted; they are certainly not absolute. What we must do is realize that deep within that experience and knowledge, perhaps at their very foundation, there is a pure and universal, vast and radiant realm that transcends all the experience and knowledge—this transcendental ground is the world of the buddha-nature.

75

A PURE POVERTY

THE JAPANESE WORD *seihin* may be translated "pure poverty," or perhaps "honorable poverty." I can think of no poverty purer or more honorable than that of Kanzan Egen (1277—1360), the founder of our Myōshin-ji. As the highly respected founder and head abbot of an important Zen temple and a teacher of the emperor, you might suppose that Kanzan lived in luxurious surroundings. Such was not at all the case. Kanzan's entire life was spent in the manner of an ordinary unsui, or monk in training. It is true that Emperor Hanazono donated one of his villas to be turned into a temple for Kanzan, but the buildings in question were apparently not richly appointed. I have heard that the villa itself was originally intended as temporary quarters for the emperor but was actually used for only a few days. Kanzan was in any case averse to the idea of becoming the head priest of a great temple, and he made himself scarce, obliging the emperor to send him a letter urging him to return. This famous letter, written during the emperor's final illness, came to be known as *Onen no go-shinkan*. It contained his promise to construct the Myōshin-ji for Kanzan and his urgent request that Kanzan reconsider his objections to serving as abbot and accept that he was the only priest in the entire country capable of returning the Zen school to its former prosperity. In any event, evidence seems to show that in these early days, and certainly during Kanzan's incumbency, Myōshin-ji was largely a temple in name only, not even equipped with a single proper temple hall.

It is said that when an important guest arrived and Kanzan was informed there was no firewood to heat the water for his bath, he told the monks to make some kindling from the eaves and flooring of the building. In the temple buildings in a state of such dilapidation, with even his own chambers in grievous disrepair, Master Kanzan lived out the remaining years of his life as abbot of Myōshin-ji.

When water started pouring from the ceiling during a heavy rain, Kanzan barked, "Get me something for this!" One of the monks ran off and brought back a bamboo sieve. Extremely pleased, Kanzan announced, "Just what I wanted!" He reviled another monk as a hopeless fool when he returned carrying a bucket. Kanzan was no doubt delighted at the state of *mushin* (no-mind) the first monk displayed in bringing a sieve to catch the leaking water. As for the second monk's solution, the roof was apparently so porous it would have been pointless even to set out multiple buckets.

A member of the Takanashi clan from Kanzan's native Shinano Province was appalled at the ruinous neglect he saw on a visit to the temple. He whispered to Kanzan's attendant, "If you would accept it, we would be glad to donate a new abbot's quarters." Kanzan got wind of the offer and immediately drove the man away. "You've had your interview," he said. "Your visit is over. Country bumpkin, coming here to the capital and meddling in our affairs!"

Kanzan was a close friend of Musō Soseki (1275–1351), his illustrious contemporary who served as abbot of the nearby Tenryū-ji. The two men would often visit each other. There is even a legend that Kanzan lived for a time in the Saihō-ji, which Musō had rebuilt at Matsuo to the south of Tenryū-ji. When Kanzan visited Tenryū-ji, he would stop before the Yukake Jizō, a stone image of the Bodhisattva Jizō that can still be seen in the Sagano district of Kyoto where Tenryū-ji is located, to wash his feet in a rivulet before putting on wooden geta and proceeding to the temple. He did not feel it proper to enter such a magnificent temple with soiled feet.

Tenryū-ji monks later moved the stone where Kanzan sat to wash his feet to Tenryū-ji, where it came to be cherished as "Kanzan's Foot-Washing Stone." In the first year of the Genji era (1864–1865), when marauding soldiers put Tenryū-ji to the torch, the stone was moved to Myōshin-ji where it is preserved today in the garden of the Dairyū-in subtemple.

Another legend tells of a visit Musō made to Myōshin-ji. Kanzan, having nothing to offer his guest, produced a cup of coarse homemade tea and dispatched a disciple to buy a few *ya-kimochi* (toasted rice cakes) at a shop outside the temple gate. As they had nothing to serve the rice cakes on, Kanzan set the cakes before Musō on a sheet of paper folded over his inkstone case. It is said that when Musō left Myōshin-ji to return to Ten-ryū-ji, he glanced to his right and left and sighed, "Kanzan is going to carry off all my descendants."

Indeed today, not only are many famous temples Musō founded—such as Erin-ji, Kochōzen-ji, and Tōkō-ji in Kai Province, and Daichū-ji in Numazu—affiliated to Kanzan's Myōshin-ji line, even great training temples such as Tenryū-ji and Shōkoku-ji in Kyoto and Kokei-zan Eihō-ji in Gifu, also founded by Musō, are now headed by descendants of National Master Kanzan.

Every morning in the Tenryū-ji training hall the names of the patriarchs in the Zen transmission beginning with Bodhidharma are read out. Kanzan's name is among them, but Musō's is not. I remember Gaō Rōshi (1853–1900), a former teacher of mine at Tenryū-ji, recalling with deep feeling, "It would be too unbearably sad for the priests in Kanzan's line to read out Musō's name for worship in the very training hall he himself had established."

Nonetheless, it must also be admitted that with its profound origins and enduring vitality, the Dharma lamp Kanzan lit continues to burn sternly and resolutely even today as a result of his singleminded pursuit of the Way, his life of contented poverty of the purest kind, and his total lack of concern with lifeless carcasses of any kind.

The free, unfettered manner of Kanzan's life that sought no support or help from others is seen even in the ring he attached to his *kesa*, or surplice, which he fashioned himself from a wisteria vine. A pure and simple poverty informed not only his practice and teaching but also his living quarters, which were utterly devoid of furniture or other objects, the sole exceptions being two pieces of calligraphy written by his students Emperor Hanazono and Emperor Kōmei. All distractions were banished, including the collection and enjoyment of paintings and calligraphy. He kept no sutras or Zen records and apparently possessed not a single volume of a non-Buddhist nature either. He did not follow the custom prevalent among Zen priests to engage in calligraphy or ink painting, or to write poems in Chinese or Japanese. As a result, no verses by his hand extolling the moon or cherry blossoms exist. He never became absorbed in the pleasures of tea or sake drinking. It appears that he did not give formal Zen lectures (*teishō*) or Dharma talks, and no Zen records attributed to him—not a single page—are known to have been transmitted.

Kanzan evinced not the slightest interest in creating a large monastery, and he gave markedly short shrift to the observance of monastic rules and regulations. Sutra chanting consisted of a single brief text, the *Dharani of Great Compassion* (*Daihi Dharani*). Spurning worldly fame, unmindful of others' approval or praise, he forbade any *chinsō* portrait or statue of him to be made after his death, leaving his disciples only an ensō circle inscribed on a sheet of paper in black ink to serve as an object to which they could pay their respects. Kanzan had truly penetrated to the vital ground of absolutely pristine poverty not only in a material sense but on a formless or spiritual level as well.

Kanzan dedicated his life solely to the Way. Monks from around the country who came to study under him were subjected to the most rigorous treatment. He is said to have driven away one monk who said, "I have come to achieve emancipation from birth-and-death," with the retort, "You won't find any birth-and-death around here!" He had only a single Dharma heir, Zen Master Juō Sōhitsu (1296–1389). Aside from that Dharma transmission, Kanzan left behind not so much as a particle of dust at his death, having lived his eighty-four years embodying the true spirit of pure and noble poverty. In the fifth year of the Enbun era (1360), on the twelfth day of the twelfth month, beside the Fūsui Well within the temple precincts, he entrusted his final instructions to his Dharma heir Juō, and his life without birth-and-death quietly came to an end.

Six hundred years have passed since that day, and next year we at Myōshin-ji will hold a great ceremony to commemorate the anniversary of Master Kanzan's death. It is with the deepest respect and unbounded veneration that I avail myself of this opportunity to pay tribute to his life of poverty.

76

"NO BIRTH-AND-DEATH AROUND HERE!"

THESE ARE MY words to celebrate the New Year.

Once Zen Master Kuei-tsung paid a visit to the temple kitchen. Finding the monks busily at work, he asked, "What are you doing today?" "Milling," they replied. They were probably hulling rice or milling flour, or perhaps grinding soybeans to make tofu. Whatever it was, they were diligently engaged in turning a stone mill to grind something. "It's all right to turn the mill," Kuei-tsung said, "but don't grind the core." He then abruptly returned to his quarters.

"It's all right to turn the mill but don't grind the core"—an intriguing utterance. Everything in the world exists in a state of flux, and we too must move along with it. But this movement must have a central and unmoving core, otherwise it will simply go blindly and meaninglessly on.

Ordinary citizens often ask me, "How can we spend our time

in this busy world just sitting in zazen, doing nothing? It seems utterly meaningless. At least if I spent the same time reading a book, I might get some knowledge out of it. If I was working, I might make some money. I can't see what I can gain by just sitting silently. On the contrary, I would feel I was wasting precious time that could be used to do something productive and useful."

In one sense, they have a point. But no matter how much you work, work that has no clear purpose is merely blind exertion; it is pointless. It is equally pointless to go rushing about aimlessly imitating what others do.

Meaningless activity of this kind has become quite common in recent years. As long as people continue to blindly follow others, pressed on by the crowd, I can see little difference between the new democracy and our old feudal society. Modern entanglements become particularly doubtful when the political activism we see in today's students turns into a kind of blinkered, unthinking militancy.

In the Meiji period, when the Battle of Ueno between imperial forces and the Shōgitai (the former Tokugawa retainers who opposed the new Meiji government) was at its peak, Professor Fukuzawa Yūkichi remained at the new Keiō Gijuku (the precursor of Keiō University), continuing to lecture to his students, completely detached from the tumultuous conflict unfolding around them. To maintain such a presence of mind under those circumstances is surely worthy of our praise. Before moving forward, it is necessary for you to first stop and examine things—to the front and to the back, to the right and to the left—and seriously consider how you should act and what your purpose is.

Kawakami Tetsuharu, the star baseball player for the Yomiuri Giants, was recently written up in the newspaper for having practiced zazen at Shōgen-ji in Ibuka in Mino Province. Kawakami gained great fame in his chosen profession, but I think his greatest "hit" was his prompt realization that his career had reached a turning point and his decision to throw everything else aside to devote himself singlemindedly to a rigorous regimen of Zen training.

People always speak of progress, of forging ahead, but if you move one of your legs forward, the other leg must be firmly planted on the ground. If you start moving both legs forward at the same time, you are not forging ahead; you are hopping. I think the anxiety people suffer nowadays comes from a habit of making these precarious little hops instead of adopting a method of steady progress. What I want to say is, I do not think your lifestyle will ever have true stability unless there is within it something that is unmoving and immovable.

The icebreaker *Sōya* belonging to the Japanese Antarctic Research Expedition has now completed three missions to the Antarctic region. Built before the war, the ship was recently renovated so as to minimize pitching and yawing. This was, of course, very much appreciated by everyone on board. It is desirable for a ship to move as swiftly as possible through the water, but at the same time it should maintain stable equilibrium. It was likewise necessary for the new high-speed train between

Kobe and Tokyo, which now makes the trip in six and a half hours, to move as fast as possible yet keep passengers from experiencing too much vibration.

To my mind, religion means maintaining a mental state that is unwavering under any circumstance, no matter what you may be confronted with as you live in this impermanent world, with all its endless shifts and changes. This is what I meant before in the story of Kuei-tsung, when I said that it is proper for the stone mill to move a great deal, turning and grinding, but it must, just as the changing conditions of the times should, retain a central core that does not move. Pure Land Buddhists call this unwavering mind that remains unaffected by events shinjin, the "believing mind."

Surely Shinran Shōnin's famous declaration, "I really do not know whether the Nembutsu is the cause for my birth into the Pure Land or an act that will send me to hell, but I regret nothing, even if my teacher Hōnen Shōnin deceived me and I fall into hell by saying the Nembutsu," occupies the ultimate reaches of the believing mind. Zen Master Lin-chi always had this rebuke for students: "The trouble with you is you don't have faith in yourselves!"

The notations jotted down by the philosopher Nishida Kitarō (1870–1945) in a youthful diary give a truly moving account of his commitment to Zen practice: "Today I did zazen for two hours, at night, zazen for three hours. Beginning tomorrow, three hours of zazen every morning." I have quoted before a verse he wrote at around this time:

I believe my mind
    Has depths no joy
Or waves of sorrow
    Can ever reach.

This suggests that although on its surface our mind—our life
of emotions—is always in a state of flux like waves on the water,
moving with the will of the wind, sometimes happy, sometimes
sad, there is a place deep, deep within that is as still and unmoving as the depths of a bottomless abyss, a place where the spirit
remains utterly firm and stable. A Zen phrase says, "The wind
blows but the moon at the margins of the sky does not move."
The mind at its inmost depths does not waver no matter what
circumstances or eventualities arise, whether you are praised or
reviled, whether you win or lose, whether you live or die.

The *Dhammapada* says,

Once you have broken free of winning and losing, if you
win, you do not cause resentment in others; and if you
lose, it does not keep you awake at night—your mind is
at peace whether sleeping or waking.

The real winner is the person who breaks free of the opposition
of winning and losing, in the same way that true longevity is attained by the person who breaks free of birth-and-death. The
Dhammapada also says, "Someone who lives without ever knowing the state of no-death may live a hundred years, but their life

still cannot equal that of someone who lives a single day knowing the state of no-death."

Master Kanzan's Zen activity must have been truly intim-
idating. He was merciless in his treatment of the monks who
came to him from all over the country. He thought nothing of
throwing a monk out on his ears. When he asked one of them,
"Why have you come here?" and received the reply, "To escape birth-and-death," he drove him away, barking, "There's no
birth-and-death around here!" Is not our Myōshin-ji, the temple of no birth-and-death, favored with unparalleled good fortune?

77

WHEREVER THERE IS SEEKING, ALL IS SUFFERING

AFTER A TALK I gave last summer at a research institute in Shimane prefecture, during the discussion period, a young man asked me this question:

Which takes priority for human beings, living or believing—day-to-day pursuits or religion? One of my older friends was isolated on an island in the South Pacific during the war. He told me that when food ran out, he tried praying and reciting the Nembutsu, but it did nothing to appease his hunger. He stayed alive by combing the jungle for food, eating snakes and wild yams. He said—and I have to agree with him—that for a human being, staying alive must take precedence over belief. Once your livelihood is secured, it is commendable for you to engage in religion if you have the time to spare. How would you respond to what he said?

The young man posed a legitimate question. What he said is true, as far as it goes. Essentially, however, I do not think religion and daily life should be treated as though they were separate activities. His question issues from a belief that religion is somehow meant to supply us with a means to live. But religion is not only connected with life at a material level; it is not merely a matter of getting something, of earning money or curing illness. I won't say that such a connection does not exist, but I don't think religion should be explained in those terms alone. For me, religion is something that reveals to us the meaning of human life, the fundamental way we should live.

My response was as follows:

In your question you focus a great deal on living, but to what degree are we able to live under our own power? To live we must first of all have air to breathe. Did we create the air? We need water, the sun's warmth, light, and so on, but we did not produce any of those necessities either. As soon as we are born, we receive milk, and that too came from another. Although we can live for ten or twenty days without consuming any food at all, we need water and air every day. We partake of these fundamental necessities free, at no cost, just as we do any of the other natural resources we make use of. You may say that farmers produce their own food, but do they grow rice and vegetables by means of their own power? Everything they produce is dependent on the earth's natural bounty. The farmers merely help this along. That is why at the autumn harvest they take the first ears of rice and offer them in thanksgiving to the Shintō kami.

In this sense, I think, when a feeling of thankfulness rises within you as you realize you do not keep yourself alive but are kept alive by others, that is the self-awakening of the religious mind. Being able to live owing to the labor performed by other members of society, feeling a prayerful gratitude for the blessings of the world and nature and toward our ancestors from the beginning of human history—is that not the proper way of life for human beings? I believe that if my questioner's friend, isolated on that island subsisting on snakes and wild yams, uttered a prayer of thanks—"This too is a blessing"—then his activity would be inspired by religion. Not merely a matter of surviving but living every day in joyful thanks, is that not the best, the most joyful way for human beings to live?

My answer apparently satisfied the young man.

Shinran has a well-known saying: "Deeply pondering Amida's vow, which he made after five kalpas of deepest thought, I now realize it was all for me, Shinran, alone." Now, Amida did not make his original vow (*hongan*) for Shinran alone. It was beyond question made for all living beings. Yet despite that, I think that in Shinran's understanding of it being for him alone we can discern the true depths of his profound religious insight.

Following this train of thought, I press my palms together in thanks to the sun that shines for me alone, in thanks to the moon sending its light for me alone, to the birds singing for me, the flowers blossoming for me, the weavers working into the night at their looms for me, the farmers weeding their gardens on my behalf, indeed to nature as a whole and to all other human beings for working solely to enable me to live. The very moment the thought that makes you press your hands together in gratitude flashes into your mind, boundless love and compassion for the world and humanity will surge up within you and with it a manifest desire to serve them both with deep humility. The world exists for me; I exist for the world. Will an existence so welcome as to comprise such a grand conception of human life come again? Hakuin's lines *How radiant and full the four wisdoms' moon! / Now that you have nothing further to seek* sing of this state of mind that is inspirited by such profound gratitude. I believe Goethe's "Human character is the greatest good fortune for the children of this earth" alludes to this happy state as well.

I have written before about the appalling circumstances in which Zen Master Kanzan lived—the sodden wooden floors, rotting in the passageways of his temple, its cracked and broken roof beams and leaky ceilings. If he had gone to members of the imperial court, his daimyo acquaintances, or his lay followers, these conditions would no doubt have immediately improved. The fact that Kanzan did not make the least effort in that regard bears out, I think, the thoroughgoing character of his religious life. When a member of the Takanashi clan visiting from Kanzan's native province saw the appalling living conditions at the temple and offered to rebuild the abbot's quarters, Kanzan drove him away, reviling him as a "country bumpkin" for "com-ing here to the capital and meddling in our affairs!"

This way of life exemplifies what Bodhidharma called "the practice of nonseeking." It is what the sutras teach: "Where there is seeking, all is suffering. Where there is no seeking, there is pleasure and contentment." This profound instruction grasps the true inner workings of human life. I think it is also linked to the state of mind Zen Master Lin-chi speaks of when he says, "If you want to engage in practice and seek Buddha, Buddha will become a sure sign that you remain within the confines of birth-and-death."

Once you establish a religious life in which you are armed internally with this great spiritual wealth and nobility long ex-tolled as the jewel beyond price, and you devote yourself out-wardly to serving the world and humanity with boundless love, performing gasshō in gratitude to them, at that point *you have nothing further to seek.* As you reach this state of mind in which you have nothing more to seek, materially or spiritually, you be-come a truly religious person, the kind the Zen school calls "the truly noble person who has nothing left to do" (*buji kore kijin*).

78

IF THE MIND IS *MU*

THE THEME of the imperial poetry contest this spring was "window." Not the ordinary sense of the word alone but as an opening that enables us to have access to the outside world. Because houses have windows, sunlight and moonlight can enter; falling cherry petals and maple leaves can flutter in; cool breezes and, at times, rain, snow, and sleet can intrude as well. Windows are gates or entrances to everything in the outside world. Lao Tzu said, "Clay is fired to make a vessel; the vessel's usefulness depends on its emptiness. Windows and doors are pierced in walls to make houses; the usefulness of a house depends on these empty spaces." Windows are open to all things in the outer world because they are *Mu*, "empty." Most people delight in the fact that things exist while remaining ignorant of the importance of their emptiness.

The eyes, it is said, are the windows of the soul. The pupils of the eyes, as small as soybeans, are capable of taking in all things from the outer world because they are empty. The ears hear the myriad sounds because they are empty. The nose senses smells, the tongue tastes, the body feels the outer world it comes in contact with—all because of their emptiness. If the mind is empty as well, it is able to embrace all the things of the external world just as they are. The Buddhist term *rokkon-shōjō*, "purification of the six sense organs," conveys this meaning. For the six sense organs—eyes, ears, nose, tongue, body, and mental processes—to be empty and pure is the proper and healthy state of the human mind. Master Hakuin alludes to both body and mind in a state of emptiness when he writes *The peace of nirvana reigns far and wide.*

The priest Ryōkan wrote, "When calamity comes, it is fitting to suffer calamity; when death arrives, it is fitting to suffer death." What he means, I think, is that if your mind is pure, if the mind is *Mu*, you should be able to accept without reservation—matter-of-factly, just as they are—all of human life's many difficult problems and adversities as they come, affirming even the great, intolerable calamities, painful illness, and even death, the greatest event of all. Hakuin says, *The peace of nirvana reigns far and wide, / Where you are is the Land of Lotus Flowers.* If your own mind is empty and utterly pure, everything you see is pure, and you realize that the world itself is the Pure Land paradise. As the *Vimalakirti Sutra* frames it, "Because the mind is pure, the buddha-land is pure as well."

A Zen monk visited Master Chao-chou and asked him,

"What is the meaning of the First Patriarch's coming from the West?" What was going on in the mind of a great, perfectly enlightened priest like Bodhidharma when he decided to make the long trip from India to China? Chao-chou's answer: "The cypress tree in the garden." He pointed to a cypress tree growing in the temple garden and said, "That is the clear purpose of the great master Bodhidharma." For someone of Chao-chou's unclouded state of mind, not only the cypress tree but everything else appears pure as well—the clear, unmitigated purpose of Bodhidharma's mind.

In order for us to understand Bodhidharma's mind or Chao-chou's mind, to understand the cypress tree, our own minds must be pure. Kanzan Egen commented on this koan: "Chao-chou's answer, 'The cypress tree in the garden,' has a truly terrifying power that yanks all evil passions and deluded thoughts up by the roots, leaving the mind with no recourse than to become utterly pure." This is the burden of Kanzan's celebrated statement, "The cypress tree in the garden has a Zen function that works like a bandit!" The words have the audacity of a ruthless villain who takes with brute force everything you have. Three hundred years after Kanzan's time, when the seventeenth-century Chinese Zen master Yin-yuan came to Japan and visited Myōshin-ji, he was told that the temple founder, Kanzan Egen, had left no Zen writings or records. But when he was told of Kanzan's comment, "The cypress tree in the garden has a Zen function that works like a bandit!" he expressed the most intense admiration. "That single utterance," he said, "is better than a thousand volumes of Zen records!"

I heard the following story from Tanaka Fumio, the former chief of patients at the Aisei-en Sanatorium on Nagashima, an island in the Inland Sea off the coast of Okayama prefecture. The Aisei-en facility was founded in 1930 for the treatment of leprosy.

People who come to this island often comment on what a fine place it is, its splendid location in the Inland Sea, its good climate and wonderful scenery. "A veritable paradise on earth," they say, concluding that everyone being treated here must be truly happy. But they are only here for brief visits. The inmates themselves are in the very depths of despair when they are brought here, feeling just as though they have been thrown into a pitch-black abyss. Do you imagine they see the scenery here? After three years, five years, seven years, when they have read more about the disease and listened to what others have told them, they are finally able to accept their fate and come to realize that contracting the disease was a matter of bad luck. They learn to be resentful of others or they curse the world in general.

But there is more to the story. The doctors persist in devoting their lives to the patients. How can we be worthy of such selfless dedication? All those young nurses came here against their parents' wishes because in the purity of their hearts they felt pity for the afflicted men and women here. My heart bleeds for them. The national government guarantees the inmates food, housing, and clothing, so they can live here without any material lack. Ordinary people from the outside world come here to visit all the time, bringing us entertainment—standup comedians, *naniwabushi*,* movies. What a delight it is for us! Moreover, Empress Teimei, the wife of Emperor Taishō, took a particular interest in us and initiated a project, funded with a very large endowment, to help us. Isn't it a tremendous honor for us?

So the world may have abandoned us, but amazingly the gods and buddhas have not! How wonderful! How undeserving we are! When the feeling arose in my mind to press my palms together in thanks, when gratitude welled up within me, my inner eye opened for the first time, and I realized that this is indeed a beautiful island. I gazed out over the beautiful sea, across the fine beaches and the lovely pine trees. It is not a large island, so as I make my way back and forth along the same familiar course every day I recognize each and every tree and rock. One day it comforts me to see the plum trees blossoming across the bay; on another day, the violets. I am now convinced that this island is indeed a genuine paradise. I live here thinking with deep gratitude that it is the Pure Land of Bliss.

Mr. Tanaka's words made a deep impression on me. I knew when I heard them that they came from direct personal expe-

---

* A genre of Japanese narrative song accompanied by a samisen.

rience. It is only when discontent and grumbling and troubling thoughts vanish and the mind becomes pure that you can know this world is indeed the Pure Land.

79

SWELLING WITH
DEEP EMOTION

IT WAS AN American or European author who wrote, "To understand all things is to love all things." An all-embracing mind that accepts and understands all things just as they are is also a mind that feels deep compassion for all things. Shakyamuni expresses this in the *Lotus Sutra:* "Now this threefold world is all my domain, and the living beings in it are all my children." A buddha's mind, being perfectly selfless, takes in all beings throughout the world just as they are and loves them as a parent cherishes their children. The wisdom that can see the world as its own world and the compassion that cannot help but feel love and sympathy can be said to be the chief characteristics of what we call "Buddha." No, they are not characteristics of Buddha alone but rather of humanity as a whole in its purest form. All human beings, in the purity of their essential character, are buddhas.

Thus when Shakyamuni attained enlightenment he cried out, "Extraordinary! Extraordinary! Living beings all possess the virtues of the Tathagata's wisdom!" "Virtues" refers, I believe, to Buddha's compassion. Pristine human nature and the Buddha's mind are essentially no different; they exist in a state of nondualistic sameness. Master Kanzan Egen shed many bitter tears in constantly teaching us: "Why do you people who are all originally fully enlightened buddhas turn into deluded beings? Aren't you all buddhas? Aren't you buddhas? Don't you understand? Don't you understand?"

The only reason we don't understand, Shakyamuni said, is "because of delusions and attachments," because the mind is not in a state of emptiness or "no-mind," because it is not pure. But when the virtuous power inherent in zazen practice finally attains maturity and you are able to understand *your own self-nature being no-nature*, and you achieve a mental state in which *your every thought is a thought of no-thought* so that *the four wisdoms' moon* shines *radiant and full*—at that time, *you have nothing further to seek.*

Not a single delusive thought or a single thought attachment arises. They all vanish, dissipating like clouds or mist, and *the peace of nirvana*—free of the passions and birth-and-death—is then immediately present before you. *Where you are is the Land of Lotus Flowers.* The myriad phenomena shine resplendently in their radiance, as you realize *Your body is the same as Buddha himself.* The Buddha's light, emanating from his original nature fully realized, gleams brightly out. What greater or deeper joy could there be than this? The you who is a Buddha, who is also an ordinary, unenlightened person, is reveling joyfully in a Pure Land that is, as such, the present world of defilements. The purpose of all that is born into the world, the ultimate goal of human existence, here reaches fulfillment in your realization. The truth of human nature is not mere nothingness or pristine purity but boundless love and tolerance, the self-awakening of a free and creative subjectivity.

Moreover, this truth of human nature is not attained as a result of religious practice. It is bestowed in equal measure on all people at birth. All are buddhas when they come into this world. Every man and woman is born a person of great dignity and character. We must for this reason accord equal respect to the human nature of our fellow human beings, and we must worship one another as well.

Never Disparaging is the name of a bodhisattva who appears in the *Lotus Sutra*. He did not spend his life doing zazen or chanting sutras or even preaching. He went into town every day and bowed in obeisance to everyone he met. Bowing was the religious practice of this bodhisattva-monk. As he bowed to people he would say, "I would never dare treat you with disparagement or arrogance. Why? Because you are all practicing the Bodhisattva Way and are certain to attain buddhahood."

This provoked anger in some of those to whom he bowed in worship. They would pelt him with stones and strike him with sticks, saying, "Who is this ignorant monk, presuming to declare that he does not disparage us and delivering meaningless predictions that we will attain buddhahood!?" But even as the bodhisattva ran off, keeping his distance from them, he would continue calling out in a loud voice, "I would never disparage you, for you are certain to attain buddhahood." Continuing this practice throughout his life, he came to be called the Bodhisattva Never Disparaging. According to the *Lotus Sutra*, he was in a previous existence incarnated as Shakyamuni Buddha.

I believe this story has great significance for society today— what we refer to as the democratic way of life. To begin with, is not the greatest, most genuine religion one of self-awakening to gratitude and joy, knowing one possesses a perfect human character and then endeavoring to have everyone else achieve that joy as well? Is not a religion in which we realize god or Buddha in ourselves, then proceed to respect and worship one another and work to establish a heaven on earth, a religion of the most scientific, up-to-date kind? Zen, I believe, is just such a religion. It is based on the self-awakening of Shakyamuni Buddha, a self-awakening that illuminates the world of today and the world of the future as well. What is more, when I recall that Kanzan Egen's lineage alone has preserved the transmission of the Zen lamp to the present day, I am made keenly aware of the magnitude of the responsibility we of Myōshin-ji bear as descendants of that great master.

It is springtime, the fourth month. We approach the six hundredth anniversary of the founder Kanzan Egen's death. The Founder's Hall, Bishō-an, and other buildings have been renovated. The priests and lay followers belonging to his Myōshin-ji school are streaming in from all parts of the country. Grand ceremonies are being carried out, a splendid new Hanazono Hall has been constructed, and we hear of gratifying improvements to educational facilities at Hanazono University. These are all extremely welcome and highly commendable. Nonetheless, I believe that our greatest debt to Master Kanzan lies in the unquestionable fact that it was he who kept the true Dharma from disappearing from the world. If the true Dharma that has been transmitted for the past six hundred years from one enlightened mind to another had by some chance died out, how could any of us as Rinzai priests stand before the Founder's Hall and face the master?

To feel the deepest gratitude for one's indebtedness to others and to desire to requite that debt in full—this is the very lifeblood of Master Kanzan's spiritual legacy. To raise high the Dharma lamp of Mahayana Zen, responding to the demands of the world while striving to fulfill the compassionate vow to save one's fellow beings—I believe this is the greatest way for us to repay our debt to him.

It was my great good fortune to be born a human being, to have encountered the incomparable Buddha Dharma, and, what is more, to have become part of the Dharma lineage of the great master Kanzan, whose six-hundredth death anniversary we are now celebrating. All of this affects me deeply. It moves me beyond words. With a heart swelling with emotion, I quietly put down my unworthy pen and offer you my thanks.

AFTERWORD

WHEN *ZAZEN WASAN KŌWA* was first published in 1962, well over a half century ago, Zen masters wrote their books in a distinctive style that strongly reflected their careers and the character of their religious teaching. They expressed their ideas and presented their subject matter in a way that demanded specialized understanding, so it was no easy matter for general readers to grasp their meaning and gain understanding from them. Mumon Rōshi's book, consisting of a series of essays he had contributed to *Hanazono*, a monthly periodical Myōshin-ji published for distribution to temples and the lay community, was written in a modern perspective that addressed a postwar audience, dealing with matters that they would all be familiar with and instructed by. Unexpectedly, as it turned out, the book became a primer of sorts, one that served to introduce people not only to Zen but Buddhism as a whole.

AFTERWORD

Since first being introduced to Western audiences through the English writings of Suzuki Daisetz, Zen has continued to evoke keen interest in the Western intellectual community and has inspired many Westerners to undertake the practice of Zen. It is my hope and indeed expectation that this translation of Mumon Rōshi's essays will further deepen the understanding of Zen Buddhism throughout the world and stimulate students in even greater numbers to undertake the practice of Zen as well.

Yūgen-kutsu Taitsū,
abbot of Myōshin-ji Zen Monastery

ABOUT THE AUTHOR

NORMAN WADDELL, born in Washington, D.C. in 1940, was attracted to Japan by the works of the legendary D. T. Suzuki and his friend and follower R. H. Blyth. Waddell taught at Otani University for over thirty years and was editor of the *Eastern Buddhist Journal* for several decades. He has published more than a dozen books on Japanese Zen Buddhism and is considered one of the finest translators of sacred texts of our time. He is the authoritative English translator of works by and about Hakuin.